D1316292

GERONTOLOGY SERIES
Sheldon R. Roen, Ph.D., Series Editor

ON DYING AND DENYING / AVERY D. WEISMAN, M.D.

MY GRANDPA DIED TODAY / JOAN FASSLER, Ph.D. (Children's Book)

RESEARCH, PLANNING, AND ACTION FOR THE ELDERLY / DONALD P. KENT, Ph.D., ROBERT KASTENBAUM, Ph.D., and SYLVIA SHERWOOD, Ph.D., Editors

RETIREMENT / FRANCES M. CARP, Ph.D.

THE GERONTOLOGICAL APPERCEPTION TEST / ROBERT L. WOLK, Ph.D. and ROCHELLE B. WOLK, Ph.D.

THE PSYCHOLOGICAL AUTOPSY / AVERY D. WEISMAN, M.D. and ROBERT KASTENBAUM, Ph.D.

Retirement

Edited by **Frances M. Carp, Ph.D.**

Research Psychologist,
Institute for Urban and Regional Development
University of California, Berkeley

for The National Institute of Child Health
and Human Development

Behavioral Publications, Inc.   New York

HQ
1064
.U5R39

Library of Congress Catalog Card Number 70-157318
Standard Book Number 87705-050-3
Copyright © 1972 by Behavioral Publications

All rights reserved. No part of this work may be reproduced
or utilized in any form or by any means, electronic or mechanical,
including photocopying, microfilm and recording,
or by any information storage and retrieval system
without permission in writing from the publisher

Behavioral Publications, 2852 Broadway–Morningside Heights,
New York, New York 10025

Printed in the United States of America

Edward L. Bortz, M.D.
Chairman, American Medical Association
Committee on Aging

1896 — 1970

_____

409649

CONTENTS

PREFACE

Since its establishment in 1963, the National Institute for Child Health and Human Development (NICHD) has emphasized the life-span orientation of its mandate to increase understanding of development, and has made special efforts to stimulate research on the relatively neglected years of adult life and aging. Similarly the NICHD has consistently made explicit its intention to support behavioral and social as well as biological approaches in the study of development. To further both of these goals, in late 1966 the NICHD proposed the topic of retirement as one major focus of its Adult Development and Aging Branch.

In December of 1966, a group of investigators was called together to review the state of research in the field by exchanging results of their own studies which had not yet been published and, in light of that review, to advise the NICHD regarding tactics and strategy for implementing its goal of stimulating systematic investigation of that transitional stage in human development which presently is roughly coincident with retirement from work. The proceedings of this conference were reported in *The Retirement Process* (Carp, 1968).

Conference participants agreed that the retirement transition is an important and neglected phase of human development, and that its investigation merits the highest priority. In their judgment the most serious limitation on systematic investigation of retirement was the absence of theories which provide frameworks within which individual studies can be developed and coordinated and which supply constantly updated, organized views of knowledge in the field as they are corrected and extended by the results of empirical studies.

Additional conferences were not likely to meet this need. However, discussions could stimulate productive thinking and lead individual participants to make systematic statements of their own viewpoints. These might become conceptual models and, eventually, theories of the retirement process as a phase of human development. In the hope that properly oriented discussion would initiate theory building, a second conference was called for the spring of 1967. Prepared papers were barred; the informal agenda emphasized free discussion and data were used only in exemplary fashion. Veteran conferees often complain that their best ideas come to mind on the way home from the meeting or two weeks later—therefore, the conference was held in two sessions with an interval of about six weeks.

By the end of the second meeting several participants had taken tentative steps toward building models of the retirement process. Understandably, these initial thrusts were fragmentary and poorly organized. In the most optimistic view, they were in germinal stages. Each needed intensive re-thinking and extensive explication and revision before it could springboard empirical studies or profit from their execution. The busy people in whom ideas were germinating were not likely to bring their tentative thoughts to useful formulation and clear statement without funds to free the necessary time and deadlines to structure it.

The NICHD maintained momentum by providing organization and support. Under Contract # PH-43-68-974 several of the ideas were brought to fuller and more systematic statement. They are published here in the hope that each "model" will stimulate and guide investigations which will, in turn, influence its evolution so that it becomes increasingly capable of performing the vital functions of a theory.

Frances M. Carp
316 Wurster Hall, University of California
Berkeley
August, 1971

ACKNOWLEDGEMENTS

The authors

The task undertaken by the authors of chapters in this book was a heroic one. The need was urgent: Absence of theories had been identified as the most critical impediment to research in an important but undeveloped domain. From the outset it was obvious that meeting the need would be an extremely difficult undertaking. Had theory development been an easy accomplishment, theories would have been available. The writers of these chapters accepted a grueling task, which they found to be quite unlike their accustomed research activities of planning, performing, and reporting studies involving data.

Indeed, these are the survivors of a larger group of starters. Several persons who were invited to contribute to the volume declined on grounds that the task would be too difficult. Three eminent investigators, after several months of effort, found that they could not accomplish the goal. Those who completed the assignment deserve congratulations for perseverance in an intractable and sometimes painful undertaking. If, as is hoped, the products of their efforts attract investigators in many disciplines to retirement studies and organize research in the field so that each study adds maximally to the fund of knowledge, the research community will owe these persons an immeasurable debt. Reciprocally, each author will feel repaid in full if his efforts at systematization serve the purposes for which they were intended.

The nicest compliment a reader can pay to any of them will be an investigation designed to test his embryonic theory.

The reviewers

Each author wished to express his appreciation of the anonymous reviewers who read the first draft of his chapter and provided comments, criticisms, and suggestions for his use in making revisions. In order to preserve at least the fiction of anonymity, this general acknowledgement is made in the name of all the authors for the thoughtful and useful critiques by:

Nancy Bayley, Ph.D.
Research Psychologist
Institute of Human Development
University of California, Berkeley

Lenore Epstein Bixby
Director, Division of Retirement
  and Survivors Studies
Office of Research and Statistics
Social Security Administration

Jack Block, Ph.D.
Professor of Psychology
University of California, Berkeley

Ewald W. Busse, M.D.
Professor and Chairman
Department of Psychiatry
Duke University Medical Center

Betty E. Cogswell, Ph.D.
Director, Program for Family
  Dynamics
Carolina Population Center
University of North Carolina

Elaine Cumming, Ph.D.
Director, Mental Health Research
  Unit
State of New York
Department of Mental Hygiene

Leon J. Epstein, M.D.
Professor of Psychiatry
University of California
San Francisco Medical Center

Robert Glaser, Ph.D.
Professor of Psychology and
  Education
Director, Learning Research and
  Development Center
University of Pittsburgh

Margaret K. Harlow, Ph.D.
Primate Laboratory and
  Department of Educational
  Psychology
University of Wisconsin

Acknowledgements

Harry F. Harlow, Ph.D.
Director, Primate Laboratory
University of Wisconsin

Marie R. Haug, Ph.D.
Assistant Professor of Sociology
Case Western Reserve University

Robert J. Havighurst, Ph.D.
Professor of Education and
   Human Development
University of Chicago

William E. Henry, Ph.D.
Professor of Psychology and
   Human Development
Chairman, Committee on Human
   Development
University of Chicago

Wayne H. Holtzman, Ph.D.
Dean, College of Education
University of Texas

Donald P. Kent, Ph.D.
Chairman, Department of
   Sociology
Pennsylvania State University

Alfred H. Lawton, M.D., Ph.D.
Dean of the College of Medicine
Associate Dean of Academic
   Affairs
University of South Florida

Arthur A. Lumsdaine, Ph.D.
Professor of Psychology
University of Washington

Adrian M. Ostfeld, M.D.
Professor and Chairman
Department of Epidemiology
   and Public Health
Yale University

James H. Schulz, Ph.D.
Associate Professor of
   Economics
University of New Hampshire

Bernard J. Siegel, Ph.D.
Professor of Anthropology
Stanford University

Norman Sprague
Director, National Institute of
   Industrial Gerontology
National Council on the Aging

Gordon F. Streib, Ph.D.
Professor of Sociology
Cornell University

Clark Tibbitts
Director, Training Grant
   Program
Administration on Aging

Richard H. Williams, Ph.D.
Assistant to the Director for
   Special Projects
National Institute for Mental
   Health

The National Institute of Child Health and Human Development

This project was supported by the National Institute for Child Health and Human Development. Institute funds freed time for the authors to prepare initial drafts, for two reviewers to consider ways in which each could be improved, and for the authors to revise their statements in view of the critiques. Without this financial assistance, it is most unlikely that these steps toward development theory systems would have been taken.

1: RETIREMENT AS A TRANSITIONAL LIFE STAGE

FRANCES M. CARP

A LIFELONG VIEW OF DEVELOPMENT

There is a growing trend toward taking a life-span view of development. For example, the relatively new National Institute of Child Health and Human Development (established in 1963) is concerned with "the biological and psychological processes that transform the individual as he passes *from conception to old age* and with the interactions of the changing individual and society" (Duncan, 1968, p. ix) [italics added]. However, most information on development relates to early periods. In order that human life become understood in its entire sweep, there is need to expand knowledge of the later years (Carp, 1968a).

Judging from the number of investigators involved, the amount of research money granted, and the volume of research publications, adolescence is the last life stage of major interest. Behavioral scientists, especially, have tended to act as if, once the issues of adolescence are resolved, the person is to all intents and purposes "finished."

No one seriously holds this view about himself or the people he knows. Obviously the human individual undergoes many changes from the onset of adulthood until death. However, stages past the attainment of maturity have received relatively little attention. How many transitions does the normal person undergo, and through how many relatively stable periods does he pass between adolescence and senescence? These later phases of life have yet to be discerned, separated, and described, let alone understood. The fragmentary knowledge about them makes impossible a balanced and comprehensive understanding of the course of human life.

The long-range goal, then, is to extend knowledge of development through to the end of life. To many people, such a statement is a contradiction in terms; such a goal, incongruous. The adult years often are perceived as separate from development. For example, in the structure of the American Psychological Association, the membership of the Division of Developmental Psychology is primarily concerned with infants, children, and youth. Investigators interested in older organisms established a separate Division on Maturity and Old Age.

Development often is paired with "growth" and considered applicable only to periods of life during which increase is clearly discernible and dominant in observations of the normal individual. The term tends to be withheld from phases subsequent to youth because increments are considered unlikely and retrogression is observed. This may be a naive and superficial view of development. Whether increment or decrement seems to predominate at any point depends upon the selection of variables to observe and upon the way they are measured. Important increases or losses may occur unnoticed. There is a tendency to study what is easily measured rather than to devise techniques to investigate what is important. Some widely accepted decrements of adult years may be artifacts of research design (Birren, 1967).

The conclusion that growth and development characterize early life while decrement and deterioration are characteristic of later periods may oversimplify. Early in life, normal development requires deceleration as well as acceleration, loss as well as gain, retrogression as well as progression. The same may hold true throughout the life course. Even at very early stages of life, some organs and organ systems must complete their roles and decline if the individual is to survive and develop normally (Cowdry, 1942). Throughout life, cell death is intrinsically related to the continued normal function of organs (Korenchevsky, 1961; Strehler, 1962).

Psychological development, like biological, rests on processes of decline and dissolution as well as on those of expansion and addition. Learning theorists recognize that decay or destruction of old habits facilitates the acquisition of new and more appropriate ones (Guthrie, 1935, 1952) for human beings as well as for rats and for adults as well as for immature organisms. Child psychologists, clinicians, and personality theorists know that "fixation" at any "infantile" level is faulty development. Earlier modes of perceiving, reacting, and enjoying are supplanted by those appropriate to the current developmental level in normal children and adolescents (Erikson, 1963; Freud, 1955; Piaget, 1952, 1954). Optimal early development requires giving up as well as getting. The importance of food must decline if the infant is to become a child; the need for immediate gratification must be tempered by tension binding if the child is to be tolerated; and self-interest must decline relative to the satisfaction of serving others if the individual is to achieve maturity. Growth, maturation, retrogression, and deterioration may be inextricably involved in normal progress *throughout* the life history.

Those who work with children and youth accept this as fact. The changing set of standards for judging the individual as he moves from one developmental stage to another incorporates the concept of loss into that of development. An infant is expected to be engrossed in food, but a sixteen-year-old who regards eating as the most important thing in life is a candidate for therapy. Screaming until he is fed or diapered is accepted as normal for a six-month-old; a six-year-old is punished unless he gives up such behavior. A parent is judged inadequate if he cannot, at least part of the time, forego his own pleasures to meet the needs of his child, while no such sacrifice is expected of the young child.

From birth through the achievement of adult status, the psychosocial stages have been mapped and the development tasks and appropriate behaviors for each are fairly well established. The infant is not judged against the standards for the two-year-old, nor the teenager against those for the young adult. The notion of progress as well as that of change is involved. The necessity to apply to an individual's acts the standard of an earlier life stage implies maldevelopment. The youth who acts like a child is retarded. The one who sacrifices earlier gratifications and loses earlier behaviors is making developmental progress.

From conception through adolescence, the blueprint is rather clear. Consistently it points to the future and at every stage it requires discard or subordination of old ways and acceptance of new. For stages of life beyond early adulthood, there has been little conceptualization of life stages and little research into developmental tasks and appropriate behaviors (Cavan, Burgess, Havighurst, & Goldhamer, 1949; Burgess, 1950; Orbach and Shaw, 1957; Donahue, Orbach, & Pollak, 1960; Rosow, 1963; Carp, 1968a). Older people do not know what they "ought to" do and feel, and others are not sure what standards to use in judging their behavior, except that the general expectation is for decrement and deterioration (Ginzburg, 1952; Tuckman & Lorge, 1953; Neugarten & Garron, 1959; Kogan, 1961; Zola, 1962; Rosow, 1968).

To some extent this negative expectation may derive from the absence of age-appropriate standards and from the tendency to use those for younger people when judging the behaviors and satisfactions of older adults. Advertisements suggest that youth is popularly regarded as the golden period of life. People over the age of 50 tend to look back on the early years of marriage and child-rearing as the best of their lives (Carp, 1966). Rosow perceives the early or middle fifties as the high-water mark for individual adjustment because "a person has raised, and discharged the bulk of responsibility to, his children" (1963, p. 215). Rosow recommends that investigators accept the early or middle fifties as the "criterion period" and assume that "the best life is the life that changes least" in subsequent years (ibid., p. 216).

Imposition of the standards of any previous stage, whether youth or early adult life or the fifties, may be inappropriate. The developmental tasks, behaviors, and satisfactions of the period selected would be established not only as the goals of prior phases but also as the criteria for performance and experience throughout the remainder of life. All subsequent periods would be predefined, and individual experience and reaction prejudged adaptive or maladaptive, in terms of their similarity to the arbitrarily determined criterion stage.

Such a decision on the part of the research community would simplify investigation by providing a common and relatively well-defined criterion. It would settle, once and for all, the question of the relative merits of two theories of aging, disengagement (Cumming & Henry, 1961) and activity theory (Havighurst & Albrecht, 1953). However, such an *a priori* decision seems to beg the issue and to prohibit rather than facilitate understanding. The resultant research stance would predetermine results. Group trends must be decremental or deteriorative, and older persons must be failures, insofar as they deviate from the typical behavior of persons in an earlier life stage. By definition, "optimal" adjustment during maturity would be at best "fixated," and change of any sort must be "regressive." Research would be limited to decrement and deterioration. The possibility of discovering novel or emergent issues, motivations, and resolutions would be foreclosed.

It is interesting to speculate about the results if a similar decision had been made in regard to adolescence, when that life stage came into the research domain. How well would adolescence be understood and managed if the developmental tasks and suitable behaviors of some earlier phase of life had been extended as criteria to the new stage? In terms of what is known about adolescence today, its developmental utility lies exactly in the fact that it differs from infancy and childhood. The youth becomes an adult through this metamorphosis. Old goals, old behaviors, and old gratifications must give way to new in order that adult status be attained.

Should subsequent life stages, then, be investigated on the basis of a prejudgment that youth or young adult life or middle age is the summit of human development? This would be a radical departure from the philosophy underlying exploration of other periods of life. An obvious alternative is to treat later life periods like any others and to study each in its own terms. What are its basic issues and the possible resolutions? What criteria are appropriate for assessing outcomes?

Because life is continuous and ongoing, standards for periods so far mapped have derived largely from consideration of the requirements of future life stages. To be consistent, the question must be asked about each phase of later maturity: to what does it lead? Because the life course is cohesive, an effective effort to deal with any stage must be predicated upon all that have gone before. Later years must be studied in knowledge of all their predecessors. Equally true, the results of that study may cast different light upon earlier phases. Better understanding of later maturity may have implications for optimal development earlier in life and may cause reinterpretation of the goals of those preparatory stages. Because of the continuity of individual experience and behavior, it seems unlikely that any part of life can be adequately comprehended outside the context of knowledge concerning the entire span. Lack of information about the final portions prohibits this comprehensive view.

THE RETIREMENT PROCESS

In an effort to extend understanding of development into the relatively uncharted years of later life, one strategy is to attend first to a clearly discernible stage. Transitional periods seem to generate research more readily than do those of relative stability (Carp, 1968a). Adolescence, for example, has excited extensive study. This transitional period emerged to importance as the result of social changes which extended the period of juvenile dependency. Experience with adolescence may be of some assistance in dealing with the phases of later maturity which are being created by the efficiency of production and medical systems.

A new transition is rapidly becoming part of the normal life history. It occurs when the person or the spouse leaves the job held during the major working years and enters retirement. A post-work phase of life for most people is a novelty in human history (Donahue, Orbach, & Pollak, 1960). As more people live to be old and their life expectancy increases (Brotman, 1968), the amount of time they are tolerated in the labor force declines (Kreps & Spengler, 1966). Both the number of persons in retirement and the number of years between cessation of work and end of life are increasing.

Yet to be seen is whether these post-work years will enable mankind to realize new levels of creative development or whether they will be a degrading period of obsolescence for the retired person, during which he is a burden on society and a disruptive influence on the development of younger persons. The manner in which individuals make the transition—the process of retiring— merits careful attention. Systematic investigation of the determinants and consequences of this transition should reveal the developmental tasks of the period and assist definition of subsequent life stages in terms of normal and optimal development as well as in those of personal and social problems. This information is necessary to a life-span view of normal and abnormal human development. It is also of crucial practical importance to rapidly increasing numbers of people (Brotman, 1968).

Research on adolescence indicates that the needs of society and those of the individual may conflict to produce serious problems for both. Furthermore, investigations into the nature of adolescence and the optimal resolution of this transition reinforce the notion that each phase of life has its own parameters, though they are intimately related to those of the periods preceding and following. It is regressive to judge the adolescent against the norms of childhood, and futile or damaging to assess his behavior in terms of adult performance. If adolescence is to be traversed successfully, the individual must accomplish the developmental tasks appropriate to that period of life. In describing the ongoing course of development, when adolescence is reached new concepts are requisite. So, perhaps, with retirement. This later transition must come to be understood in its own terms, and in the context of the whole span of the human life course.

What, then, can be done to stimulate systematic investigation of the retirement transition? The absence of relevant theory systems, conceptual models, or systematic formulations has been identified as the most serious lack (Carp, 1968a). The history of research indicates that coordinate progress of theory and observation is the sound and economical path to knowledge. Theoretical frameworks organize information to maximize its meaning and point the way to design of decisive experiments. Systematic statements reveal gaps in knowledge and warn against useless repetition. They juxtapose finding in ways which facilitate creative insights regarding the possible relationships of parameters and suggest research designs which shortcut to clarification. Reciprocally, the empirical results of studies designed in terms of theoretical formulations require amendment of these statements and indicate which are most promising as guides for further investigations. Without data, theory is speculation. Without theory, data collection is incoordinate, repetitive, and incomplete, and data tend to be inscrutable.

This basic tenet of scientific procedure is well known to investigators, funding agencies, and editors. The result is considerable pressure to present a study in terms of some theory. While adoption or adaptation of an established theoretical position may seem to insure respectability, it can mislead or stultify exploration of a new domain. The relevance of the framework may be more apparent than real. Its acceptance may lead to careful exploration of variables which are tangential or irrelevant. The fact that the investigator is following the guidance of theory may blind him to the necessity of determining the parameters of his problem.

Even if the dimensions of a theory are relevant, its adoption may be inappropriate because the relative weights of the variables are different or the central issues dissimilar. Verbal resemblance can be misleading. For example, "dependence" is a problem in adolescence and in old age. However, neither the determinants, the options available, nor their consequences bear much resemblance at the two points in life. Any attempt to state the dependency conflict of later life in terms of a theory developed about the adolescent crisis should be made only after each problem has been carefully analyzed in its own right. A likely place to look for prefabricated theories when studying retirement is the developmental repertory. However, the importance of various physiological, psychological, and cultural factors waxes and wanes from one life stage to the next. New components appear from time to time. One set of central issues supplants another. Because the life history is cumulative, a particular danger is that a conceptual formulation will be too simple for any subsequent life stage.

THE FRAMEWORKS

There is urgent need, then, to provide the research community with theoretical frameworks which accommodate the phenomena of retirement and which can guide research along systematic and efficient lines. This book was prepared as a first step toward filling that need. Each of the chapters which follow was written from a different point of view. All attempt to organize existing information in such a way as to stimulate and systematize research. Hopefully, future investigations will test hypotheses derived from these statements, and results of the empirical studies will be used to review the statements. As a consequence, they will be extended, redirected, and refined. Each revision will be a step in theory building and will sharpen the design of the next cycle of studies. In this way, each hypothesis-generating statement will become an increasingly sophisticated conceptual model or it will be discarded. Understanding retirement must be an interdisciplinary undertaking because the transition involves interactive processes at all levels—biological, psychological, social, and cultural. Ultimately the learning theorist's model of the process must be concordant with that of his fellow psychologist trained in development or in social psychology as well as with that of the sociologist, the economist, and the anthropologist. At present, efforts to build one general theory, or even one per discipline, seem premature. The base of knowledge is not yet sufficiently broad or secure. Disciplines and subspecialties have begun investigation in different parts of the domain. Therefore consideration of a general theory which accounts for all processes on all levels and is accepted by all branches of all disciplines was postponed. Rather, an effort was made to initiate as many models as necessary to accommodate available information and provide systematic direction for new studies, in terms most convenient for a wide variety of potential investigators in many fields.

The volume makes no pretense to cover all possibilities. Chapter assignments were not based on an analysis of the subject-matter domain into its component parts or on some plan for fair representation of the relevant disciplines. Rather, contributors were chosen because they were competent in research, had something worthwhile to say about the process of retirement, and were willing to invest the considerable time and effort necessary to make a systematic presentation. Within the limits imposed by this general strategy, model builders were selected to provide maximum diversity of discipline and viewpoint. The eleven persons who contributed chapters represent several disciplines: anthropology, economics, medicine, psychiatry, psychology, and sociology.

There was no attempt or desire to create a set of similar or parallel theoretical models in the various disciplines. The goal was a variety of preliminary but systematic statements, each of which would intrigue some investigators and give direction to their data collection and analysis so that the results of their studies would validate and correct the hypothetical model. All contributors were asked to deal with retirement as a process rather than as a momentary event or a status lasting the remainder of life (Carp, 1968a). Aside from that, each was encouraged to develop a chapter in his own way. Even within disciplines, authors took highly individual stances.

A theory of retirement prepared by these authors in conference would have powerful impact on research in the field. However, subsequent knowledge might resemble the proverbial committee-produced animal. No matter how many compromises had been involved in its preparation or how unsatisfactory it might be to each committee member, a joint statement would have the appearance of unanimity as well as of authority and prestige, mitigating toward relatively uncritical adoption. The dangers of premature statement of a comprehensive theory or acceptance of a majority report as the research model are similar to those of unwarranted application to retirement of a theory which has proved useful in dealing with some other phenomenon. At the present stage of knowledge, the wisest course seems to be free competition among a diversity of theoretical frameworks to account for existing facts and stimulate the discovery of additional knowledge.

Nevertheless, the essentially interdisciplinary nature of the task must not be forgotten. An investigator working within one discipline or theoretical framework should be aware of what is going on in others so that he can capitalize on progress within them. The conferences which lead to the preparation of this volume demonstrated the excitement of multidisciplinary interaction and its capacity to erode preconceptions and stimulate creative reintegrations of old information. Therefore the eleven statements are bound together within this volume.

Multidisciplinary publication has the added advantage of imposing the use of everyday language in everyday ways or explanation of terms in plain English. As definitions are made more explicit, the communication obstacle is reduced. There are some amazing transformations when everyone speaks the same language: A contributing physician pleads for and designs behavioral-science research, a psychiatrist proposes new legislation, and a sociologist is preoccupied with the experiencing individual.

The order in which the chapters naturally seemed to fall had nothing to do with the disciplinary identifications of their authors. Chapter order was determined on the basis of approach to the task of model-building. Some authors presented overviews of the retirement process and analyzed it into elements. Others selected for attention certain aspects of the transition and developed systems to account for relevant research findings and to predict the results of manipulating certain variables. Still others dealt with retirement in terms of, or as a special case of, some broader theory. Chapters are organized according to the author's approach. As a consequence, the disciplines are rather thoroughly distributed.

Comprehensive Frameworks

Each of the first three chapters takes an inclusive view of the retirement process and points toward a comprehensive research strategy and theory. A sociologist analyzes the transition into its elements and diagrams their interactions; a psychologist reduces an exhaustive review of the literature on development to a set of major principles applicable to retirement; and an anthropologist divides the phenomenological domain into its components.

An option-maintenance model

The central variable in the retirement process, in Marvin Sussman's view, is the number of options an individual can exercise. The practical problems in regard to improvement of life in retirement are to develop alternative courses of action and make them truly available to more people. The individual's tasks are to be aware of the widest range of choices open to him and to decide which course to pursue. The theoretical problem is to identify all determinants of option availability and use, so that they can be investigated.

Dr. Sussman points out that only very recently has society become sufficiently affluent to offer many of its members a variety of "careers" at the end of the work life. He believes that negative stereotyping of retirement is largely the result of an outmoded perception of this range of choices, and he warns researchers against building theories or research designs which reflect this bias and preclude positive outcomes.

Self-respect and social reponsibility are identified by Dr. Sussman as criteria of success for the retirement process. The fulfillment of these needs is critical in order to counteract the social stereotype, but opportunities to satisfy them are diminished by retirement. The central task is to resist this narrowing of options. The most successful retiree has the most choices, is most aware of their range, is best able to match them with his needs and capabilities, and is most capable of taking effective action to exercise his options.

Dr. Sussman identifies the elements related to maintenance and exercise of options and organizes them into a diagram of the retirement process, which begins well before the cessation of work and continues until death. A series of "careers" may be carried out after leaving the major job of the working years. The "outer boundaries" of his system are variables which set limits upon options but do not necessarily determine the course of the retirement process: biological and physiographic statuses, public and private benefits, and society's value system.

Within the constraints imposed by these factors, others operate to determine the maintenance or foreclosure of options: character-istics of the person and of his situation prior to retirement, the circumstances in which he retired, and his perception of his situation. Because he is a social creature, the individual's options are strongly influenced by his use of "linking systems": friendship groups, the kinship network, the marital, inheritance, and work systems, and voluntary organizations. There are additional "within boundary" constraints such as the state of the economy and intergenerational conflict.

The options open to the individual at retirement and his ability to make use of these options are determined by the interplay of the variables in all of these categories. Dr. Sussman's organized presentation of them will allow testing of his central hypothesis that option maintenance is directly related to self-esteem and social responsibility in retirement, and it provides a framework for establishing the relative weights of the various elements and their interactions in maintaining options and facilitating their exercise.

A systems-analysis approach

Charles Taylor's chapter provides an extensive review and a

valuable bibliography of the developmental literature. Dr. Taylor focuses the information in this literature upon problems and issues germane to statement of a theory of the retirement process. He reviews current definitions of development and the range of theoretical postures toward developmental processes, and he considers the uses to which resulting concepts have been put in research. His chapter organizes developmental theories into "families." It summarizes the concepts of each which seem relevant to the study of retirement and evaluates their strengths and limitations for application to retirement. Dr. Taylor concludes that none shows much promise for understanding the retirement process.

A systems-analysis approach to retirement phenomena is suggested as more fruitful. Accordingly Dr. Taylor derives, from the literature review he has presented, a series of eight propositions about retirement. He then draws on published research findings to demonstrate the relevance of these concepts to the study of the retirement process and suggests how they might expedite and systematize investigation. These eight statements reveal a wealth of important research issues and generate a plethora of hypotheses to be tested. Feedback from their investigation can transform the list of conceptual statements into a developmental psychological theory of the retirement transition.

The dimensions of cultural reality

Margaret Clark reviews what anthropology has said and proposes what it should be able to say about the retirement transition. Anthropologists can and should look at retirement in two different ways: as an institution (social anthropologists) and as a set of personal meanings (psychological anthropologists). Dr. Clark brings together relevant findings from social anthropology and suggests additional areas of research which should be undertaken with the concepts and tools of the social anthropologist.

Her major concern is with the potential in psychological

anthropology. According to Dr. Clark, in present-day Western society, retirement may affect every aspect of the relationship between an individual and his culture: self-concept, social relationships, orientation in time and space, motivations and values. Therefore categorization of culturally defined reality provides a useful outline for cross-cultural studies which will clarify the role of retirement in urban-industrial societies and lead to a pancultural theory.

Against the background of the phenomenological categories, Dr. Clark reviews the scant literature and proposes an almost overwhelming list of research questions. Among them are: What are the roles of work and retirement in personal identity and in personality integration and disintegration? Are relationships with supernatural entities tightened by loss of work? How does retirement affect territoriality and the use of space? How does it affect orientation in time? Does the work-retirement discontinuity contribute to memory loss?

Dr. Clark points out that, in addition to the insights crosscultural studies give into general principles of human behavior, they can provide useful information about our current situation. For example, the value system in American society is undergoing changes which may alter the meaning and impact of retirement. Comparative studies which involve cultures with value systems different from our own may be useful in making predictions regarding our future.

Models Focused on Selected Variables

The next three chapters deal with variables selected from the total domain on the basis of their importance. Each predicts the effects of manipulating these variables. Criteria as well as independent variables vary from chapter to chapter. A psychiatrist proposes a number of changes in social policy and predicts their consequences for retired people. A psychologist holds that new learning of any kind is the critical factor in improving retirement and predicts the results of strategies to insure continued learning of new material. A retired Commissioner of the Social Security Administration counters with the proposal that direct training for retirement is most effective, and he recommends implementation of retirement-preparation programs and their systematic evaluation as the means to improve and to understand retirement.

Manipulation of social policies

In Robert Butler's view, certain social policies are the major determinants of the retirement phase of the life cycle. They affect the retiring and retired person directly, and through him have important impact on the rest of society. Therefore Dr. Butler proposes to solve some of the problems of retirement, to improve its quality for retirees, and to increase its benefits to the rest of society by restructuring these public policies.

Dr. Butler stresses the need to take a life-cycle perspective, and he uses research findings to provide a picture of the typical person in the retirement phase of life. He relates the attributes and characteristics of individuals at this stage of the life cycle with public policies which affect them, and he proposes to facilitate the retirement process and reduce the problems of retirees by manipulating these social policies to make them more congruent with the life-stage characteristics.

His model predicts the effects upon retirees and upon all of society if these public policies are changed in specific ways. In order to test it, investigators will need to use the natural laboratory of our common political life in which such factors as legislation, regulation, and funding are the independent variables. Dr. Butler's concern with social policy is immediate and practical as well as systematic and theoretical. For example, he was an

Elected Delegate to the 1968 Democratic Party National Convention. His chapter may tempt other members of the research community to follow him into the political arena in order to arrange for experiments which will test his model.

The critical variable: new learning

Continuing to learn is the major determinant of success in retirement, according to Meredith Belbin. Any sort of material will do; the only requirement is that it be new to the learner. Dr. Belbin's criteria of success are maintenance of capabilities and promotion of personal satisfaction. These two are central because they are primary needs among retirees in all economic, social, and cultural conditions.

Dr. Belbin describes two "archetypes" of retirement. One is characterized by low level of activity and dependence upon previous learning. This archetype allows for either satisfaction or dissatisfaction, but probably leads inevitably to ability losses and perhaps to physiological deterioration of neuronic control mechanisms due to disuse. The second archetype of retirement, which involves high activity level and new learning, promotes both preservation of abilities and personal satisfaction.

Dr. Belbin considers existing evidence regarding the means by which capabilities can be maintained and satisfactions promoted during retirement, and from this review he derives a strategy for accomplishing his type-two retirement. He specifies the personal and situational factors which determine the success of attempts to use this strategy, and he suggests specific and practical ways to implement it.

Tests of the efficacy of Dr. Belbin's strategy will consist of studies which relate the recommended means for carrying out type-two retirement, in interaction with the conditioning factors, to the criteria of capability maintenance and personal satisfaction.

The model also allows testing his assumption regarding the superiority of archetype-two retirement, for various sorts of persons, in a variety of circumstances. In addition it suggests and enables investigation of the relationship between his criterion components, personal satisfaction and capability maintenance, as persons and situations vary.

The key: direct training

William Mitchell experienced retirement and then its reversal when he undertook to study retirement-preparation programs. He gives an experiential account of the retirement process from its origin long before the last day of work through various phases subsequent to that date. Of particular interest is his account of benefit policies and practices, and of preretirement counselling, as they are experienced by the employee. Though obviously he is familiar with research in the field, Mr. Mitchell chooses to write as a sensitive layman who has undergone retirement and observed it in others.

While Dr. Belbin holds that new learning of any sort has beneficial effects, Mr. Mitchell believes that direct instruction on the essentials of retirement is the crucial variable. He bases this position on the assumption that the typical retiree is capable of learning and that the necessary knowledge and skills can be identified and taught.

Mr. Mitchell insists that the average person, by the time he reaches retirement age, is richly experienced in adjusting to change and can reasonably be expected to adapt successfully to this latest dislocation. The retirement process must be perceived as an individual responsibility rather than a social problem. Adaptation at this, as at any other life stage, will be consistent with the person's previous life style. Success will depend upon the extent to which he can provide for himself the *sine qua non* of retirement: health, income, and friends, in that order of importance. Life style is durable, and age at retirement is given for any individual. Recognition of the need for the three essentials and ability to obtain them can be varied by training.

Mr. Mitchell proposes implementation of a wide variety of retirement preparation programs, and their systematic evaluation, as the most effective way to improve satisfaction in retirement and to explore the deteminants of this satisfaction. Mr. Mitchell sees little evidence that existing programs deal systematically with them. Many programs are destructive of the individual's ability to meet the challenge of retirement, because they confuse retirement with aging and illness and thereby exaggerate the negative aspects of the adjustment task.

In Mr. Mitchell's experience, unsuccessful retirement adaptation is rare. He suggests that the incidence of poor adjustment is overestimated because physicians tend to see the ill and other service personnel to deal with "bad risk" retirees. This exaggerated view of the casualties is an additional hazard for the person undergoing retirement. On the contrary, Mr. Mitchell believes that the large majority of people adapt successfully, and that a significant minority find greater personal satisfaction than ever before. Society can increase this number by presenting a more balanced view of the process.

Adaptations of Existing Theories

Four authors deal with the retirement process in terms of theories which were developed in other contexts. A sociologist demonstrates that two alternative explanations of the mechanism of adjustment to retirement have been tacitly accepted by investigators and so have structured and strongly influenced research, though neither is considered to be a theory of retirement. She considers the implications of bringing these theories from underground. A psychiatrist-psychologist, an ego psychologist, and a social psychologist suggest ways in which various theories developed in other contexts have been and may be applied to retirement.

Covert theories: Substitution and accommodation

Lack of theory systems may be more apparent than real in the field of retirement, according to Ethel Shanas, and covertly functioning theoretical orientations may be as hazardous to research progress as is the absence of guiding principles. In her search for an appropriate theoretical model, Dr. Shanas reviews the literature for evidences of research stances which reveal preconceptions casually or unconsciously accepted by investigators. She demonstrates that two alternative assumptions have strongly influenced research on adjustment to retirement though neither is recognized or explicitly used as a theory.

Though she is by training and identification a sociologist, Dr. Shanas's concern here is with the experiencing person as he meets the adjustment problems posed by the end of his work life. Two ways have been suggested by means of which this process takes place. One possibility is that the individual re-establishes internal equilibrium by finding satisfactions to substitute for those previously provided through his job. Alternatively, the process may be a more complex one which involves adaptation to a variety of life changes related to retirement. In a process of "accommodation" rather than one of "substitution," the self may redistribute its energies and reorganize its system of gratifications.

Investigators tend to favor one of these explanatory principles over the other. This preference serves to organize and give direction to their research so that, in a sense, these comprise two theories of retirement. Because they are informally accepted and not explicitly built into research designs, their effects may be more confusing than systematizing. Using existing research results, Dr. Shanas demonstrates the negative consequences of the covert status of these two basic orientations. Her chapter explores the consequences of bringing substitution and accommodation to overt status as theories of adjustment to retirement. She states the presuppositions which are inevitably involved and the essential research issues which are naturally defined by each, and she outlines the types of research to which substitution theory and accommodation theory lead.

Dr. Shanas concludes that the weight of evidence is in favor of accommodation as the mechanism more relevant to the process of retirement as it occurs in present-day American life, and she suggests some ways to test this tentative conclusion. Dr. Shanas sketches an accommodation model which emphasizes the distinction between variables which influence exit from the world of work and variables which are influenced by cessation of paid labor.

Crisis, reinforcement, and motivational-style models

Carl Eisdorfer adapts to the study of retirement phenomena three psychological theory systems which have stimulated and been clarified by extensive research in other contexts. Each of the three models points to particular forms of intervention to facilitate the process of retiring and improve the quality of life in retirement. Implementation of these remedial programs and evaluation of their impact will also provide tests of theories as applied by Dr. Eisdorfer to retirement.

For investigations of immediate reactions to termination of the work life, Dr. Eisdorfer suggests a "crisis model." It follows the tradition of homeostasis and related concepts as they were extended from the biological sciences to psychology. In this model, retirement is a stressor which disturbs the equilibrium between the person and his environment. His established modes of coping are no longer appropriate, and he experiences discomfort. Depending upon the traits of the retiree and characteristics of his situation, the resolution may lie anywhere between personality disorganization and increased adaptive capacity.

As a framework for studying the long-range effects of retirement, Dr. Eisdorfer suggests a reinforcement model derived from learning theory. Retirement behavior and experience reflect the congruence between personal motives and the reinforcers available in the post-work situation. The quality of the long-range adaptation of the individual following retirement depends upon the balance between positive and negative reinforcers at present, in relation to that balance at other stages of life.

Still another model for research into the transition from work to post-work life is suggested by Dr. Eisdorfer. His "motivational-style model" is an application of dissonance theory to a domain often subsumed under disengagement. Again Dr. Eisdorfer focuses on the "fit" between person and situation as a source of predicting retirement outcomes. When fear of failure and conservation of energy are predominant motives, retirement will reduce dissonance and be welcome. If need achievement is high, retirement will produce or increase dissonance and lead to depression and other negative consequences for the individual.

A male mastery-style model

David Gutmann incorporates his view of the retirement process into a more general developmental theory of crisis and crisis resolution in men. He describes the retirement process by contrasting it with a crisis which seems to occur spontaneously among men in later maturity, even within cultures which do not practice retirement in the style of Western industrial society. His conceptual model provides predictions regarding both. As background Dr. Gutmann presents two ego-psychological models applicable to crisis. In one, the conflict is internal, between functions of the personality. In the other, it is waged between the ego and the external world. Dr. Gutmann suggests that the latter model is appropriate to retirement, while the former is exemplified in the mid-life male crisis.

In predicting the resolution of either type of conflict, the salient personality characteristic is "mastery style." Dr. Gutmann presents a typology of mastery styles which provides the basis for explaining both the retirement process and the middle-age crisis in men. He exemplifies the reactions of each type and subtype with thematic apperception story data from men in several societies.

Dr. Gutmann contrasts the internal ego crisis precipitated by the seemingly universal conflict of middle age with the crisis imposed upon the ego by the social institution of withdrawal from work. He speculates regarding the meanings of work and retirement for men in the various categories of his typology and in various types of social setting, and he derives hypotheses regarding the consequences of retirement for individuals in each of the ego-situation cells of his formulation of the problem.

Consequences occur both in ego processes and behavior. They are influenced by mastery style and by the social setting. Furthermore, the success of a resolution of the retirement crisis depends upon the mastery type and upon the setting, so that no one criterion will suffice. In case of failure, ameliorative measures must also be individually tailored to ego orientation and social setting. Dr. Gutmann discusses successful and unsuccessful resolutions and remedial procedures for each subgroup. These remedial suggestions provide additional hypotheses for studies to test his conceptual model.

A normative-transition model

Marjorie Lowenthal presents a life-cycle model in which retirement is treated as one instance of adaptation to a normal stage of the life cycle. Like Dr. Gutmann, she relates retirement to a mid-life crisis which at the present time in this society precedes and strongly conditions adaptation to retirement. Understanding of the transition precipitated by retirement and prediction of individual adaptations to it are best made on the basis of reactions in the mid-life crisis.

Mrs. Lowenthal stresses the ongoing nature of adaptation, the fact that reactions at any transitional stage depend upon patterns of adaptation established earlier in life. Adaptation is a function of the person and of his social setting, *as they are perceived by the individual.* Of particular importance is the congruence of self and situation. Change is precipitated by alterations in the self or in the social situation which alter the degree of fit between the two.

The central categories in Mrs. Lowenthal's conceptual model are the individual's goals and his life style. At any point in the life cycle, an individual's adaptation is a function of what he wants out of life and how he is living it. Again the concept of congruence is central. Consistency between purposes and behavior, and among elements within each of the two categories, is of utmost importance. Stress is experienced when there is a perception of a discrepancy between goals and behavior, or of conflict among goals, or of inconsistency within the life style. The consequent adaptation may involve change in goals, in behavior, or in both.

Using the two central variables, purposes and behavior, Mrs. Lowenthal generates a typology of adaptation styles. Its nine categories are intended to accommodate data on any life stage and provide the base for predictions regarding any transitional adaptation. Out of the nine general types generated by her purposive-behavioral dimensions, Mrs. Lowenthal selects five for discussion in regard to the crises of middle-age and retirement. Her chapter provides a number of predictions regarding the impact of retirement on people who, at mid-life, were in each of the five categories of her typology. Studies based on hypotheses drawn from her model will not only clarify the nature of the retirement process but will also test her general theory of life-cycle adaptation.

An evolutionary view

The final chapter returns to a broad look at retirement. In it Edward Bortz, a retired physician, considers the potential role of retirement for the individual and for humankind. He reviews many of the points made in previous chapters and presents a comprehensive research framework which includes variables at the biological, psychological, social, and spiritual levels. Dr. Bortz advocates a coordinate effort by anthropology, psychology, and sociology, along with medicine, to study and to promote the unfolding of human potential.

His basic philosophy is that the post-retirement period not only can but should be a creative one. Persons beyond the labor force are useful to maintain continuity and therefore security for all generations, and to advance human development in the contemplative areas. Dr. Bortz believes that man's normal life span of one hundred years soon will be realized. He considers the "hazards of medicated survival" but concludes that the third trimester of life can be its zenith. Retirement should provide a creative life stage for individuals and should make possible the next step upward of evolving mankind.

Dr. Bortz conceptualizes the retirement process in terms of its relationship to the biological timetable, physical and mental conditioning, a variety of environmental variables (both social and chemical) which may be manipulated, and existing and potential variations in the form and timing of the retirement event. He enumerates the necessary precursors and accompaniments of what he considers the optimal retirement style: creative use of leisure which includes new experience, growth, and enrichment. He also specifies the essential traits of the successfully retired. Therefore his model permits the derivation of hypotheses regarding the relationships of biological, personality, and circumstantial determinants with specific retirement outcomes.

THE AUTHORS AND THEIR CHAPTERS

In the following chapters these eleven frameworks for research are presented in greater detail. A brief biographical sketch of each author precedes the presentation of his research model. The reader may approach the volume as it is assembled, or start with chapters written by persons in his own discipline. He is urged not to limit himself to familiar authors because cross-fertilization seems likely. The psychiatrist may gain insights for the formulation of knowledge in his own field by reading of the way in which a systems analyst would approach the problem. The anthropologist, psychologist, or sociologist may discover that the conceptual models in the other two disciplines are equally applicable to his data. In this important sense, the book is interdisciplinary.

MARVIN B. SUSSMAN, PH.D.

Dr. Sussman is Director of the Institute on the Family and the Bureaucratic Society at Case Western Reserve University and Selah Chamberlain Professor of Sociology. He serves as a consultant at the Carolina Population Center, University of North Carolina at Chapel Hill. His area of special interest is the family, but his research extends to comparative, occupational, and medical sociology.

Currently Dr. Sussman is President of the Groves Conference on Marriage and the Family, a member of the Sociological Research Association, a former Chairman of the Family Section of the American Sociological Association, and past-Editor of the *Journal of Marriage and the Family*. He served as chairman of Forum 14 of the White House Conference on Children, 1970, and is on the technical committee for training of the 1971 White House Conference on Aging. He is a former member of the Behavioral Sciences Training Committee of the National Institute of Mental Health.

Dr. Sussman edited *Sourcebook in Marriage and the Family* (third edition, 1968) and *Sociology and Rehabilitation* (1966), and wrote *Community Structure and Analysis* (1959). He is co-author of several other volumes, including *The Family and Inheritance* (1970), and has published extensively in professional journals.

2: AN ANALYTIC MODEL FOR THE SOCIOLOGICAL STUDY OF RETIREMENT

MARVIN B. SUSSMAN

Retirement is a phenomenon with multiple meanings. It may be studied as a status or as a process, and it has many components. Retirement is a status which carries the connotation that the individual is still active in some life sectors, less so or not at all in others. The expression, "He is retired," implies that the individual has a selected number of remaining roles and that those in the work sector of society are omitted.

Status is a position an individual holds in a particular group or organization. In each group—occupational, family, religious, and so on—he has a status. These statuses are linked to each other, to those of other individuals, and to roles. They are also linked to the values, ideologies, and goals of society. Behavioral expectations govern the interaction of status incumbents with other members of a group or organization. Each individual in the status knows, for the most part, how a person in another position will respond in a given situation.

Reaching the status of retirement has an effect upon all other positions held by the individual and upon all relationships with others. Retirement is a demotion in the work system. For most individuals it means a sharp reduction in income. Less income may result in inability to meet behavioral expectations in a group or organization. The consequence is a change in status.

Change in status requires socialization into new roles. They should be societally acceptable, congruent with the interests and aspirations of the retiree, and attainable within the constraints imposed by institutional systems. Socialization involves learning new skills and competencies to handle the demands placed on the individual because of his newly acquired status. It also requires the development of identification with the roles associated with this status.

The process of retirement suggests a change over time. A person begins, sustains, and finishes activity in a career; he is in continuous movement toward the final act which removes him from the field. In modern societies, retirement from a work career usually occurs before death. For the most part, occupational systems determine the age of retirement from gainful employment. Disability of self or a family member, individual choice, and group norms are other determinants of the time to retire from the job.

In relation to the process of retirement, we attempt to identify uniformity in the patterns of behavior from the beginning to the end of a sequence. Marked changes in ongoing behavior which are noted by the observer are often labeled as steps in the sequence. They may or may not be formally recognized as *rites de passage* such as graduation from secondary school.

A work career may consist of several steps: learner, apprentice, novice worker, skilled worker, highly skilled worker, and retired worker. Unfortunately, the example may promote the notion that all career lines consist of lineal progression to elevated work capabilities before retirement. Obviously there are various patterns, and different numbers of steps, for individual careers. Downward movement or no skill development is possible. The sequence has an impact on the lifeways of the individual and those closely associated with him. Each step requires new forms of socialization, new roles and their mastery, and new status rewards. Each step involves estimation of options and decisions regarding their use. Each demands acquisition of knowledge and skills, changes in interaction styles, and internalization of new values.

Development of the concept of retirement and specification of its components involve analysis of the historical antecedents. How, why, and under what circumstances did retirement come into existence? The temporal component of retirement suggests the relevance of a life-cycle view. For each individual this cycle begins at birth and ends at death. It has relatively fixed intervals of learning, work, and leisure. There is a continuous flow of socialization over the life cycle.

Modern societies like our own, as well as traditional ones, require formal systems for handling work, leisure, and retirement. Retirement has become an institutionalized status as a consequence of complex industrialization, a basic requirement of which is the orderly replacement of old with new workers. The presumptions are that new generations must succeed the old, that chronological age is correlated with diminished capabilities to perform work tasks, and more recently that retirement to a non-work career, or leisure, is a reward.

Other contextual elements are the systems developed by societies to effect retirement at a given age, support the retiree, evolve new non-gainful careers, make available to retirees options for entering these new career sequences, and create socialization systems for reorganization of old roles or learning of new ones. Societal values, philosophical postures, and ideological and religious positions regarding work, leisure, generational conflict, service, responsibility for others and self, independence, and familial obligations are additional elements. This chapter examines those components of the retirement concept which, when linked into an analytic model, seem to provide the greatest explanatory power in regard to the retirement process.

THEORETICAL FOCUS

The central theme is that retirement need not be a negative event. The perpetuation of a negatively loaded image of retirement is questioned. This posture may be ameliorated if one can show that for some retirees options are available, recognized, and used. An important hypothesis for sociological research is that there is available for retirees a range of options in all life sectors. Exposure to, knowledge of, and use of options are related to a variety of societal, institutional, social-psychological, and personality variables. One task is to explain the relationships of these variables to option awareness and use. A second and more practical undertaking is to make options available to the retiree and facilitate their use.

It is probably fair to say that the societal image of retirement has a negative connotation. Retirement counters the norms of youth and health, gainful employment, productivity, and active contribution to society. This societal view of retirement places limitations on the adjustment of retirees. However, it does not necessarily have negative consequences for all individuals.

Social-psychological analysis of retiree behavior would probably reveal many techniques used in face-to-face interaction to create a positive personal and social identity. (Personal identity is the individual's image of self; social identity is the image others hold of the individual.) Also by his exercise of options, the retiree may structure for himself a very pleasant and worthwhile life. Thus, while analysis of retirement from a societal perspective may indicate negative consequences, analysis from a social-psychological perspective may reveal that a certain proportion of retirees reap positive consequences. Societal analysis defines the social structure within which the retiree operates; social-psychological analysis should reveal the ways in which individuals, given these societal definitions, achieve optimum outcomes.

Social researchers in the field of retirement have tended to approach this period of life as one in which the retiree is allocated a degraded status. As scientists, we should leave the question open for substantiation. Instruments should test for positive as well as negative elements in retirement. The conceptual model presented in this chapter permits the emergence of positive elements. At the same time it permits the researcher to note the step or steps in the retirement process that caused the individual to falter or to take a route leading to negative consequences. It is a process model, and so provides an understanding of retirement which goes beyond determining the success or failure of a retirement career or program for retirees. It delineates the sequential steps, and therefore makes possible recommendations regarding interventions to increase the probability of success in a retirement career or retirement program.

POLEMICS

A sanguine posture that retirement need not be the end of all things good, worthwhile, and individually important requires all the optimism one can generate. By definition, retirement implies withdrawal, leaving the scene of action. There is the notion that being "out of things" makes the individual less valued. In the marketplace, withdrawing means giving up one's usual line of work. The individual is said to have retired when he no longer performs the role he once did in the economic sector. Since withdrawal implies little or no contribution to the group's welfare, the quitter loses power. Those who remain in control institutionalize this change to retirement by giving it a devalued status. This assignment provides a rationale for claiming a superior status and insuring their own domination in the group.

I recognize the importance of this posture and wish to describe it more fully, not because I share the sweeping conclusions derived from it, but because this notion is held by many lay members of society as well as by a group of gerontological researchers.* Understanding more fully the nuances of this intellectual position sensitizes the model builder to the constraints, both real and ideological, within which he can construct a conceptual model and suggest associated research procedures. By means of these he hopes realistically to relate beliefs about retirement to practices in the empirical world. What non-retirees think and believe about the retiree, and what the retiree thinks and believes about himself, are relevant.

It is believed that withdrawal from usual roles and activities creates a behavior syndrome similar to the one associated with major long-term illness. Reaching retirement age, like the event of illness, produces trauma, crisis, and concomitant stress for a large number of individuals. The anguish centers around the transfer from an active to a nonactive status.

The crisis-stress phenomenon is believed to occur from loss of work, even when the individual knew in advance that he would be retired at a specified age and had some preparation for this transfer of status (anticipatory socialization). The 45-year-old man who has had a mild cardiac infarction and who, upon recovery, must change his occupation is in a crisis requiring reallocation of roles within the family and modification of family interactional patterns with outside social organizations. The university professor at age 65, after a long career teaching and doing research, is given praise and hosannas and is viewed by his colleagues to be in an "unstructured" situation. He does not have students to train, supportive personnel to help him in his research and scholarship,

---

*Explanations of this position are found in Irving Rosow (1962) and Ernest Burgess (1960). Goffman has indicated that patterned status loss is not unique with the aged. His notion of devalued status and stigma has been aptly applied to the retirement status. See Erving Goffman (1963).

professional colleagues, an office at the university, or in some instances even library privileges.

Societal imagery reinforces the view that retirement is the end of an ordered period of life for the individual, and that the destruction of this stability—whether it has existed for one, five, or fifty years—produces a crisis for the individual and the consequent need to be resocialized into new roles. This crisis orientation is pervasive. Even if individuals choose to withdraw from work, many observers believe that a crisis must be produced. If the individual convinced others that he was happy about his voluntary retirement, his actions might be considered neurotic or responsible for inducing crisis in persons close to him, such as members of his immediate family.

Events of the past can, in part, provide an explanation for this notion that retirement is tantamount to crisis. Societies high on the scale of modernism have only in recent times provided a significant proportion of their citizens with means for affluent living. Consequently, modern man has a larger number of options than did traditional man. One option is withdrawal from a career in one life sector to take advantage of opportunities for a different kind of career. Before this era of relative affluence, people had few options at the end of the ordered work period of life. Because of the increasing number of options, it is now possible to view retirement as a period in which the individual can explore pathways which might satisfy his own needs and achieve his personal goals.

Even if one accepts the contention that retirement is a crisis, it is reasonable to hypothesize that it is differentially experienced by individuals in modern societies according to their socioeconomic levels. At all levels, psychological restoration may be required of many individuals who move into a status requiring new role learning for which there is little or no preparation (anticipatory socialization). Some class-related differences in retirement experience many be consequences of differential loss of income in relation to prior life style. Loss of income may be a crisis. Currently, retirement has greater impact on lower socioeconomic groups. Some amelioration will result from the development of society-wide systems of income maintenance, health, welfare, medical care, and leisure-time programs. Yet, despite increasing societal affluence and government programs which raise the probabilities for survival, comfortable maintenance, and participation in the society after retirement, individuals will experience the dilemma of retirement differently according to their positions in the social structure.

In an analytic sense, retirement is withdrawal from accustomed roles. People can withdraw from participation in any life sector at any age. Retirement customarily is described as a process of abandoning middle-age roles and taking on a smaller complement of retirement roles. Retirement has been associated with aging, and therein lies the "hangup" in meaning. Retirement should be separated from aging, because of the latter's negative connotations of dissolution and decay. Even with respect to gainful employment, to which retirement is most often related, one can leave a career at any time one chooses. Of course, in most cases of retirement from work, the decision has been made for the individual by institutional policies and norms reinforced by societal expectations.

This analysis deals with retirement from economic activity. Sixty or 65 is the age at which individuals are expected to retire and often do. There are different needs, problems of socialization, types of institutional support, and family involvements for different age cohorts after the age of 60. The retired group is not one homogeneous mass in terms of needs for interaction, housing, emotional support, or new careers.

PHILOSOPHICAL BASES

Taking a view that retirement is a process which has a beginning and an end, one might utilize the biological model with its built-in time clock. The biological cycle is one of growth, development, and maturation to a peak of physical capabilities in early maturity, a plateau-like period of stability, and finally decline and death. This is the pattern of all living species—the rise, peak, and decline—with variations in the smoothness of the curve according to the species. For *Homo sapiens* there has probably been an extension of the period of plateau during the past 75 years. Diminished manual dexterity and stamina and changes in metabolism probably occur later in the life span.

Institutions such as retirement are social inventions related to man's biological makeup but also to many other factors. The question is whether the institution of retirement coincides with the biological cycle. Man arranges the context within which he functions, accounting for biological constraints by developing social institutions, value systems, and ideologies of high complexity. It does not follow necessarily that retirement and the biological cycle are completely synchronized.

Two observations should be made about man's biological and social development over the life cycle. First, there is no point in denying the association of age with increasing physical deficits and probability of death, or the constraints upon the individual's behavior as a consequence of declining physical prowess. The important notion is that the mix of biological and social factors provides a series of contexts within which retirement occurs. Often overlooked is the synergistic effect of this mixture upon perceptions of the retirement status, use of options by retirees, institutional policies and societal values regarding retirement, and the retirement process itself.

Physical decrement and increasing prospects of death with age are universally held premises. From a societal viewpoint, retirement is a necessary process of worker replacement in order to minimize disruption as a consequence of death or disability. Most individuals are aware of their declining physical abilities and tailor their choice of options and level of activity to these limitations. The boss views the aging worker from a perspective of contribution to the productive process. The cost factor is most important: insurance and health cost, retirement contributions, and the expense of potential accidents. The family perceives decline in the physical and mental ability of one of its members largely within an affective context. What does it mean to the individual and his interactions with others of his family and kin group? What kind of supportive behavior will now be required by members of the retiree's family? These few examples illustrate that retirement can be viewed in a variety of ways, in which a combination of biological and social-environmental factors provide the context for a particular posture.

The second observation is that our culture is more likely than others to arrange events in sequence, a chronological order suggesting a causal relationship between happenings. Moreover, this arrangement of events is climactic. There is an ascending line of reality, a building up of significance, meaning, and achievement.* The implication of this notion is that any activity evolves and builds to a crescendo. A work career may be viewed as a line of progress and achievement with concomitant rewards; retirement may be seen as an anticlimax.

A related issue is that different occupations may have different climactic peaks. The myth, or at least the rhetoric, is that mathematicians, metallurgists, and physicists peak in their early

---

*An excellent discussion of the codification and of a line of reality is to be found in D. Lee (1959).

twenties; musicians and composers, in their late twenties; architects, academic physicians, and behavioral scientists, in their late forties. Regardless of whether differential peaking of creative talent occurs, or whether its etiology is to be found in biological-genetic or socio-environmental factors, the fact remains that we have a lineally ascending perspective of reality. In relation to work, man is seen as becoming increasingly competent with experience over time. He reaches a peak of expertise well along in his career. This peaking occurs before retirement, which thus becomes anticlimactic.

Is there any reason to believe that the desires to be useful, constructive, appreciated, and innovative necessarily decline with age, much as dexterity, stamina, and energy are lost? If creative talents peak in the middle years of life, can this level of functioning be maintained in the post-retirement period? Evidence is inconclusive as to whether man has an intellectual and spiritual pattern of development with peaking and decline similar to that of the biological cycle. One hypothesis is that, as man achieves greater influence over the biological forces which control his life, he will be able to sustain for a longer period of time the level of physical fitness and mental functioning achieved during the pinnacle years.

American society, like all modern ones which share the Western tradition, is work-oriented. Ideology and religious precepts espouse values which favor productive contribution. Characteristics such as independence, individual effort, and high motivation are considered virtues. What is the impact upon the retiree of this set of values which provides a rationale for the organization and workings of our social institutions? How does the new retiree harmonize such values with the requirements and expectations of his new status?

There is a strong effort to get people out of things when they reach retirement age. The purpose is to allow the younger generation to take over quickly and efficiently without discontinuity—much like the transfer of political power. Yet, while power and status are shifted from the old to the young, there is an overriding concern with keeping people busy. Eager professionals of client-centered organizations have even suggested ways for persons to continue to contribute to the gross national product through voluntary work activity.

The consequences of these confusing and contradictory philosophical positions to "get off the world" or to "keep busy" have led me to take the following tack: Life has meaning only when one contributes to it in his own way, and such a contribution need not be measured in economic terms alone. One of the main tasks during retirement is for the individual to discover meaningful ways of relating to society, which in turn provides him with positive personal and social identities. Consequently, there is a necessity for a number of different options for post-retirement careers.

ISSUES BASIC TO SOCIOLOGICAL ANALYSIS OF RETIREMENT

In analyzing retirement, it is advantageous to consider the basic needs of individuals. The essential question is: What is important to flesh-and-blood beings, to people? What are the social and psychological essentials of life in addition to the biological ones? Estimating the needs of societal members is done within the context of the culture in which they were reared. Postulating the patterns of human needs which are found in our society, one can speculate about their importance to individuals who have retired. The need to maintain self-respect and the need to be socially responsible are selected as the two most critical, because they are most germane to countermanding the effects of the negative status assigned to retirement by society. Fixed lineal ascendency in work roles leads to perception of retirement as anticlimactic, and consequently to reduction of the capability to be socially responsible. Structured procedures for effecting retirement according to chronological age without regard to mental or physical competence, in order to make way for younger generations, assault self-esteem. The task of the retiree is to maintain the level of self-respect achieved during his work life. The level varies with individuals. Whatever may be this level, the need to feel worthy, important, highly regarded, and necessary persists at all stages of the life cycle. It remains a basic need during the period of retirement.

Self-respect is derived from man's activity in human groups. Man, as a social being, has a need to interact with others. Few people can live apart from others and take up the lives of hermits. From conception until death, one is in great need of emotional support, bodily contact, love, and affection. Receiving these nonmaterial things is as important as nutritional intake if one is to survive. The form and intensity of an individual's interaction differ in relation to his membership in groups in various life sectors, his class identification, and his cultural experience; but the need to interact with others is rooted in primordial origins and is almost instinctual.

The need for interaction is accompanied by the desire to communicate to others a body of knowledge and experience accumulated over a lifetime. In all societies there persists a pattern of generational linkage in which the older generation takes principal responsibility for the socialization of the younger one so that the latter will eventually assume power in the society. Retirement does not delimit the process or reduce the importance of this type of transmission. The giving of one's knowledge and experience to others, that is, giving part of oneself to others, is basic to fulfillment of the potentials of human personality.

The active life which characterizes man as a social animal implies a desire to engage in those endeavors which are personally satisfying and exciting, and in which the level of boredom is reduced to a minimum. The pathways to interesting activities are many. Each person establishes for himself one or more activities which he considers to be important and intriguing. They may or may not involve large numbers of people. The need to be involved in satisfying activities is not modified by old age. In fact, there may be even greater need to reduce the level of boredom among those who have retired.

Is there any reason to disbelieve that the individual's need to achieve self-respect and, more generally, to "do his own thing" continues throughout the life cycle? Activity of some kind—the enterprise itself or benefits derived from it, such as income—is the best undertaking to satisfy the need for self-respect. After retirement, with the loss of the primary occupational role, these needs must be met by *new* careers, either in the labor sector or in other life sectors such as family, leisure, and community service. Relatively few retirees can enter new careers as gainfully employed individuals. The task for the majority is to expand or take on roles in nonemployment sectors. Expansion of roles in the leisure sector is the solution for the majority of retirees.

Social responsibility is also derived from group experience. The individual develops ingroup feelings, interest in others, and sentiments of care and protection. The beginnings of social responsibility occur in the family or peer group. It extends to encompass neighbors, community members, and fellow citizens. Social responsibility is rooted deeply in the fabric of all cultures because survival requires mutual aid and expectations of reciprocity. The individual who cannot accept social responsibility is often given deviant status. He may function as a change agent, but he has little control over existing institutions.

Retirement as Status or as Process

Research on retirement as a process has different objectives, conceptualizations, and research designs than research on retirement as a condition or status. Studies of the retirement process require a conceptualization which is not constricted by observations at a given point in time, but which encompasses change over time and provides a descriptive analysis of interaction. The conceptualization embodies the sequence of events for the individual experiencing retirement. A panel of retirees may be followed over time. Alternatively, one may use a cross-sectional sample, age-graded so as to effect a sequential analysis. Techniques vary, but they involve collection of data in a time series, such as the keeping of diaries and repeated interviewing. Analysis focuses on patterned behavior in different settings and life sectors. The major objective is to understand the process of the retirement career. Such knowledge can suggest more effective strategies for meeting the needs of the retired person.

The model presented in this chapter focuses on the social-psychological process as experienced by retiring individuals. It is set within a context of societal, biological, and physiographical factors. These contextual factors limit but do not necessarily determine the course of the retirement career of the individual.

Options Available to the Retiree*

Modern society is so structured that its members have increased opportunities and alternatives in areas other than work. There are

---

* This notion of option usage was initially discussed by the research team of Cross-National Research Studies on the Family. Betty E. Cogswell, David Kallen, and Erwin K. Scheuch were particularly helpful in the development of this concept in relation to my efforts to make it fit the retirement process.

options regarding participation in political and social activities, and selection of memberships, relationships, and reference groups. The number of options is limited by the person's societal position and by his social-psychological and personality attributes. "Option" is conceptualized at two levels of abstraction: societal or structural, as a concomitant of modernity; and social-psychological, as an individual process requiring the acquisition of skills in order to become aware of, articulate, and choose among alternatives.

Differentiation is a characteristic condition of modern societies. Mass production, occupational specialization, diversification in functions, and separation of home and work are some of the conditions which increase the number of sectors available to man and the number of roles for which he can opt within each sector. Life sectors such as work, recreation, religion, welfare, education, and medicine can be subdivided into subsectors according to function and organizational structure. For example, the medical sector can be split into functions regarding prevention or care of the ill or disabled. Further divisions can be made in reference to types of prevention and care. The delivery system of medicine, from training facilities to custodial institutions for the disabled aged, is another basis for separating this life sector into its component parts. Theoretically, this differentiation increases the number of options for worker and consumer. In the medical sector, the worker can fix upon one of an ever increasing number of organizational systems and occupations in which to make a livelihood. The consumer can match his ailment or disability, or be linked by those in control, with the appropriate health care or rehabilitation institution. The fitting together in a variety of ways the need for medical services with available delivery systems provides combinations for the choice of users.

Universal availability of options does not exist. Societal sub-groups have different patterns of using options. Ethnic and racial minorities within a society, for instance, may find that options become available increasingly when disciminatory constraints on the minority group diminish with general societal modernization. On the other hand, the pattern for these groups may follow some erratic configuration, as formal and informal constraints upon different minority groups fluctuate with gross political changes within the society. In fact, any ascriptive term such as "aged" or "retired" which defines a subgroup of a given society may effect major differences in the option-availability pattern of the group.

Within the constraints imposed by societal and institutional structures, the individual makes choices of roles and careers within each life sector. This freedom to opt for a particular role or career is in line with the dominant value system of this society. The rights and needs of the individual are considered as important as those of the group. The availability and use of options go hand in hand with individualism. This freedom to act independently is constrained by the needs of the group. There is a delicate balance between individual freedom and group responsibility. One indicator of modernity is the ability of a society to harmonize these two conditions without diminishing the expression of either.

The possibility of opting for something and making a decision about it by oneself suggests the presence of privacy. Privacy may be conceptualized as a component or attribute of independence. On a pragmatic level, modern man has more options for relationships outside the primary group, the family. He can be more independent of family members and the services they perform; he can be secretive about outside relationships. The individual develops a private sector in his life. Presumably, with the greater differentiation and specialization in an urbanized society, he becomes less visible when he leaves the house. He has more options to develop private role relationships.

Opting for roles and careers with fewer group controls and less need for approval by others occurs within a framework of organizational surveillance. In modern societies all individuals are part of a record system. From the time of conception until death, each person accumulates a performance record in almost every sector of the society. The educational system keeps a growing inventory of his intellectual accomplishments, which accompanies the person throughout life and in some instances even in death. His employment history is recorded and checked. It becomes part of "who he is," and determines his mobility in society. His union, professional association, social club and service-organization memberships and activities are irrevocably noted. In effect, the history is a constraining force.

In summary, in modern societies the individual and the family may have greater privacy in space, yet less privacy in time. The identity of an individual through time is controlled through the record he has established—the record as a worker, member of the armed forces, pupil in school, buyer on credit in the economy, and so forth. The individual's use of options is controlled by his performance record. He closes the number of options available by his mistakes, and retribution and rehabilitation are of limited value in restoring options.

For the retiree, the task is to maintain options and counteract the tendency to revert to a central social identity such as that which characterizes childhood. The posture assumed in this paper is that the number of options and the amount of privacy need not be correlated with age. Other factors such as personality, physical condition, and structural variables other than age constrict opportunities. Taking into account diminished physical capabilities and desire to use options, I would hypothesize a curve of option availability and use other than the bell-shaped one (see Fig. 1). The latter represents the view that loss occurs rapidly after retirement and soon approximates the level of childhood.

Physical loss plays havoc with the option sequence. The individual, as he moves across the life span, is faced with the continuous need to make choices because of physical delimita-

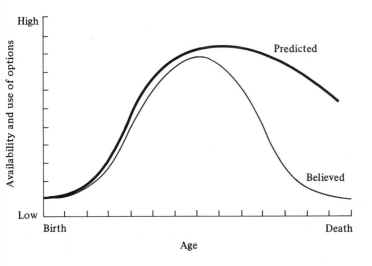

FIGURE 1.

tions. He may be using up his options by the failure to make a decision because of physical incapacity. Such choices, by decision or non-decision, are usually irreversible. There is an inevitable reduction in the number of options as one reaches old age.

A central concept of this model is the option sequence; another is career. The career is a line of activity an individual pursues in one of the life sectors He may be gainfully employed or work as a volunteer. The career is a sequence which has a beginning and an end and, therefore, is time-limited. It is patterned activity which has a series of limited events. Norms govern the tasks to be undertaken by the individual. The career has it own socialization structure, processes, and outcomes. In most instances the activity which embodies a career is sanctioned and legitimatized. It may be perceived as necessary or useful to society, personally satisfying to the individual, or simply as "a way to make a living" or to "keep busy."

The concepts of option sequence and of career are intricately linked. They can be viewed as polar points of a continuum which describes what happens to the individual after he reaches retirement from the traditional work sector and until his demise. The point of entry into another career comes about at the time of retirement, when the individual evaluates his options and makes a choice. The predominant career pattern he assumes is influenced by his previous experiences, his perception of the situation, and the options available to him. Figure 2 presents a diagram of the model.

COMPONENT PARTS OF A SOCIOLOGIC ANALYTIC MODEL

Outer Boundaries

The outer boundaries of the model circumscribe the limits within which options are exercised in relation to careers in various life sectors. They provide the context within which the retirement process occurs, but do not necessarily determine the use of options or the course of retirement. A discussion of these boundary constraints and their relationship to the option sequence and retirement process follows.

One outer boundary of the model is the biologic cycle. The organism undergoes physiologic and chemical changes from conception until death. Nutritional needs vary with age. There is a very definite but not yet clearly described linkage between biologic status and behavior. The biologic status of the individual, whether it is conceived in terms of nutritional standing or neurosensory capabilities, imposes constraints upon the behavior of individuals. Specifically, it imposes restraints upon his options in given life sectors. A classic example of such constricting effects of the biologic forces is the professional football player who is forced into retirement between the ages of 30 and 35. He no longer has the stamina, agility, or speed to compete with younger and more vigorous aspirants who are bucking for his job. The airplane pilot's visual acuity may diminish ever so slightly, so that he does not meet the exacting physical requirements for pilot's status, though he still has adequate vision to take on a variety of roles. He will lose his captain's status, pay, and perquisites, and be grounded into another position within the transportation-work sector.

With increasing age, especially after 60, constraints are imposed by faltering biological systems upon the individual's desire to function in specific roles. Sheer physical incapability forces the individual—even against his will—to limit the number of career options in order to continue a particular career in a given life sector.

A second outer boundary is the physiographic. It consists of the retiree's geographical location: the climate in his living area, and the availability of stores and of medical, religious, recreational, social, welfare, and educational facilities. These environmental factors determine the availability and use of options, and the particular course of the retirement process for the individual.

A third outer boundary of the model is the government and private maintenance systems. With increasing modernity there is greater participation of government in maintenance and welfare programs, parelleling development of privately financed programs, whose aims are to care for individuals who cannot make it on their own within the economic system because of physical, psychological, social, or cultural deficits. There is some correlation between increasing modernization and the number and scope of "cradle-to-the-grave" benefits. There still exist inequities in the distribution of supportive services and financial aid among segments of the population but, overall, there is an increase in

BIOLOGICAL CYC
PHYSIOGRAPHI

PRE-RETIREMENT FACTORS

SITUATIONAL AND STRUC-
TURAL VARIABLES
1. Circumstances of retirement
2. Social class position
3. Retirement income
4. Marital and kinship status
5. Pre-retirement preparation
6. Incentives and constraints to
   availability of optimal systems

UTILIZATION OF LINKING
SYSTEMS
1. Friendship groups
2. Kinship networks
3. Marital system
4. Inheritance system
5. Work systems
6. Voluntary organizations

ENTRY PERIOD TO
RETIREMENT CAREER

PERCEPTION OF SITUATION

1. Choice of options, evaluation of
   alternatives
2. Anticipating outcomes, probabilities that a particular alternative produces a particular outcome
3. Use of previous experiences
4. Social context of interactions
5. Time-use patterns

CHOICE
OF
SECTORS

INDIVIDUAL VARIABLES

1. Life styles: obsessive instrumental; instrumental other-
   directed; receptive-nurturant;
   autonomous; self-protective
2. Motives, needs, goals
3. Problem solving, discrimination
   ability, competence, information level
4. Generalized habits and attitudes
5. Value orientations

WITHIN BOUNDARY CON-
STRAINTS
1. Societal definitions
2. Economic-generational cycle
3. Professional-bureaucratic
   organizational postures
4. Generational power conflicts

GOVERNMENT AND PRIVAT

SOCIETA

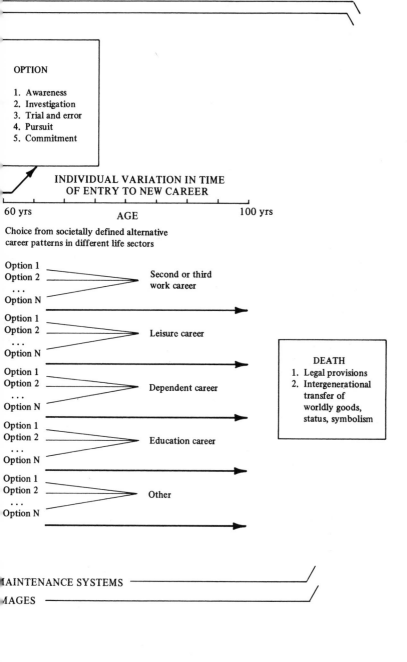

OPTION

1. Awareness
2. Investigation
3. Trial and error
4. Pursuit
5. Commitment

INDIVIDUAL VARIATION IN TIME
OF ENTRY TO NEW CAREER

60 yrs

AGE

100 yrs

Choice from societally defined alternative
career patterns in different life sectors

Option 1
Option 2
. . .
Option N

Second or third
work career

Option 1
Option 2
. . .
Option N

Leisure career

Option 1
Option 2
. . .
Option N

Dependent career

Option 1
Option 2
. . .
Option N

Education career

Option 1
Option 2
. . .
Option N

Other

DEATH
1. Legal provisions
2. Intergenerational
transfer of
worldly goods,
status, symbolism

MAINTENANCE SYSTEMS

IMAGES

expenditures for these services and aids in societies of high social complexity.

Such society-wide supports and economic transfers have been largely functions of the political superstructures of modern societies, and have overshadowed individual efforts to provide for economic maintenance. Increasingly, individuals who are between the ages of 18 and 55, those in gainful productive employment, provide the economic support for the retired and the very young. In the United States this has been a major development. Life and work-life expectancy at birth in years 1900-1960 increased markedly; life expectancy increased from 48.2 years in 1900 to 66.6 in 1960, and work-life expectancy from 32.1 in 1900 to 41.4 in 1960. At the same time, however, the percentage of individuals outside the labor force increased from 16.1 in 1900 to 25.2 in 1960, indicating that the very young and old are being supported by a smaller percentage of the population in gainful employment (Wolfbein, 1963). This pattern persists because of automation in industry and the consequent ability to create goods and services over and above those which are needed for societal survival.

How well an individual uses options and linking systems at the time of departure from the work force depends upon his income: savings, property, Social Security payments, pension, gifts, and other economic support. The level of support available to him is a very critical factor in deciding which life sectors he will enter or enlarge, and which options he will choose within each of these sectors.

Undergirding government and private maintenance systems is societal imagery. In the broadest sense, societal images are what people believe to be predominant values and expectations of behavior in relation to these values. Values are the underpinnings of social behavior and change. They provide the rationale for action. Williams (1965) has enumerated a set of basic values which

are held by the majority of people in American society and
buttress the normative patterns which are basic to the functioning
of all social systems.

Values have to do with feelings and perceptions of what are
desirable qualities in behavior. As a consequence of interaction
with others and in consonance with perceptions of what is correct
and right, individuals act in various ways in relation to the norms
of groups, social organizations, and institutions. The value orientations which make up one component of societal imagery have a
diffuse influence over the individual. He is guided and constrained
by them, and in specific situations he may evaluate their
influences in relation to contemplated behavior. Where the
individual is accepting of the value orientation, he seeks to
harmonize his actions in reference to the value. His perception of
the value determines his response.

In addition to general societal values, there is in each life sector a
subset, usually ordered in terms of importance, which probably has
far greater influence over the individual's behavior than the more
general array. Consider for the moment the individual approaching
retirement. This individual is probably more affected by the values
concerned with the consumption of goods and services than is an
individual in mid-career. On the one hand, in a production-oriented
society, the worth of a man is estimated by his economic
contribution to the good of the group. Yet, in the pre-retirement
period, there emerges another value which emphasizes consumption
of goods and services. Consequently, the individual is expected to
relinquish his value which espouses a balance between producing and
consuming. Societal expectations are that the individual near
retirement should not "fight" giving up his productive role. He is
expected to become consumer-oriented, even though he may not
have the means to consume extensively.

The value of productive activity, economic or otherwise, is

somewhat contradicted by another value which favors disengagement. A continuous bombardment of messages through the mass media say that retirees ought to get out of their patterned activities and "do their own thing" independently of families friends, reference groups, and other organizations.

It is difficult to determine the rationale which underlies this urgency. The push to become independent and uninvolved probably comes more from the friends, relatives, and institutional functionaries than from the retiree. One bit of evidence to support this notion is the location of community organizations such as hospitals and homes for the aged. In recent years there has been an effort to integrate medical and custodial-care services of aged persons into general hospitals. This location change is a consequence of a new philosophy regarding medical care and of the desire to reduce the inconvenience for medical and service personnel.

Another indicator that independence of the retiree is desired as much by the children and other kin as by the aged person is the distribution of inheritance under testate (where there is a will) or intestate conditions (where there is no will) (Sussman, Cates, & Smith, 1970). If the testator is survived by a spouse and lineal kin the spouse is named in the will as the sole heir in an overwhelming majority of cases. This is identified as the spouse-all pattern of inheritance. When the individual is intestate, the inheritance law provides for property disposition on a fair-share basis between surviving spouse and issue.

The majority of these intestate cases deviate from the fair-share principle because children sign over their shares of the estate to the surviving parent. This voluntary transfer occurs because of filial responsibility, a sense of justice, and a realistic appraisal of the surviving parent's financial situation. In the bulk of cases in this study, if the testator did not invoke a spouse-all pattern or is children took their share under intestate distribution, then the surviving spouse, usually the wife, became economically dependent upon family members and societal systems such as welfare. Children prefer to defer this economic responsibility, which might incur change in living arrangements and interaction patterns among family members.

Generational shifts in power occur in due course. The young take power from the old in a continuous cycle. The expectations are that such shifts should occur with a minimum of conflict, and that the newly retired should substitute respect and deference for power. Ceremonial events at retirement symbolize the shift from power to respect. Plaques, watches, luggage, and titles such as "elder statesman" are used to indicate this change.

Another societal image is that retirement confers a deviant status on the individual (Rosow, 1962). Burgess (1952) has written about the roleless role. Essentially it is one devalued and associated with chronic illness, senility, disability, ugliness, and "dirty work." The physical needs of some aged persons are similar to those of infants, with one major difference. The expectation is that the child will bloom into a mature and useful person. For the aged, the prospect is not growth but death. Efforts to satisfy their physical and psychological needs are perceived as dirty work. Those who provide it have, themselves, a devalued status.

These societal images undergird the actions of all people and impose constraints upon the individual's behavior. The retired person is constrained in his use of options because of his perception of these values. Limitations are imposed by others, whether members of primary groups such as families, or functionaries of the organizations of society. Effects of these values vary according to class, level of modernity in the society, and individual lifetime experiences. These values have pervasive effects upon the career line of the retiree in the various life sectors.

Pre-Retirement Factors

Any consideration of what a person does when he is retired from a work career is related to the life style of the individual in the past, accumulated experiences, and ways of perceiving and feeling the world around him. The sociologist, psychologist, and gerontologist have isolated these pre-retirement postures and experiences into a number of descriptive categories and have used them separately or together to anticipate the consequences of retirement for the individual. For convenience, these pre-retirement factors have been arranged in two groups: (a) situational and structural variables, and (b) individual variables.

Situational and structural variables

The perception of the about-to-be-retired individual regarding options, choice of sectors, and use of linking systems is affected by situational and structural variables. One major factor is the circumstance under which retirement occurs. Retirement may be voluntary or involuntary. Voluntary retirement occurs under one's own timetable. In most instances the individual has economic resources or decides to "leave the system" at a relatively early age and pursue a nonwork career. There are two types of involuntary retirement. One is institutionalized by work systems which specify the age of retirement. The second occurs when there is illness or disability, and the person is unable to work in gainful employment.

If the individual is among the very few who retire from their steady work career on their own volition, it is likely that he will have a greater number of options in moving into other life sectors in order to pursue other careers, and he is apt to be better prepared to take on new roles in these life sectors. If, on the other hand, the individual is forcibly retired because of regulations which set the age of retirement or because of disability, one would expect the range of options to be limited. This individual would be more reliant on primary groups such as the family, and on health, rehabilitation, and welfare organizations for resocialization into retirement roles.

In some occupational fields such as flying, sports, and entertainment, forcible retirement at an early age is anticipated, and programs of informal resocialization into new careers take place well before the person retires. Today, when amateur football and basketball players of outstanding ability sign an initial professional contract, they are guaranteed a second career when their playing days are over. Pilots may use their seniority to obtain a desired flight schedule, such as two days a week coast-to-coast flying, and on other work days operate a business such as insurance or real estate.

A related structural variable is the individual's social class position. Social class implies distinctive life styles, perceptions, ideological postures, and patterns of behavior. In each social class there are values regarding retirement. There is probably a relationship between social class and the option sequence, especially in relation to the individual's independence of or dependence on social organizations in the selection of options and pursuit of the option sequence.

The level of income available upon retirement from gainful employment is the most constraining factor upon the individual's perception of available options, their choice and implementation, and the use of linking systems. There are class differences in the availability of income upon retirement. While expenditures for the retired couple or single person are severely reduced from what they may have been during the child-bearing and child-rearing periods, retirement income is relatively low for a large majority of American citizens. The consequences are restraints in relation to the availability and use of options.

Whether the individual is married and living with a spouse, children, or other relatives, and whether he is active in a kinship network are additional variables which affect his choice of life sectors and careers. It should be emphasized that the quality of husband-wife interaction and the purpose and meaning of the exchanges between nuclear families in a kin network, rather than the interaction *per se,* are major determinants in the selection of career patterns and pursuit of activities in the several life sectors.

The degree of pre-retirement preparation affects selection of options and rate of movement from pre- to post-retirement roles. Retirement, like other phenomena, cannot be experienced until it occurs, but preparation takes the form of anticipatory socialization. It is likely that the development of new interests, skills, and expectations during the middle years of life facilitates a smooth shift from pre-retirement to post-retirement roles.

These situational and structural variables provide incentives and constraints in relation both to the availability and to the choice of options for new careers in available life sectors.

Individual variables

Another group of factors which influence retirement is the set focusing around the individual: his personality, motives, needs, problem-solving capabilities, habits, and attitudes. Such factors affect selection of options and their use. The individual's ability to solve problems; whether he is a risk-taker; his cognitive style; his ability to sift information and tease out the essentials in a situation; his linguistic competence, especially his language congruity with those individuals who direct the maintenance systems; his taste and esthetic appreciation; and his command of information about available resources are elements which affect his status and behavior as a retired person.

Before retirement the individual has established habits which enable him to handle most interactions, and an attitudinal posture which may be conservative or liberal in its expression. Essentially these habits and attitudes are *what the individual is*. They impose self-constraints upon the choice of options and the use of primary groups and linking associations. It is a rare situation when an individual, conservative in attitudes and behavior, takes on the role of innovator. The probabilities are that he will select a new career that enables him to function effectively according to well-established and comfortable habits and attitudes.

Other pre-retirement factors which affect retirement outcomes are the individual's value orientations. These orientations are part of the person's psychological makeup, the way he perceives himself and others according to a set of values he has selected as guides to his behavior. Anthropologists (Kluckhohn & Strodtbeck, 1961) have suggested a large number of personal value orientations including three of particular relevance here. The first is *self versus other* orientation. Does the individual's behavior reflect self-interest or does he have the interest of others in mind? A second value orientation is *fatalistic versus manipulative*. Does the individual feel that outcomes depend largely upon the behavior of others rather than himself? In most instances, the fatalistic person believes that a force greater than himself, such as God, is fixing the outcome. At the opposite position is the individual who feels that he is able to manipulate conditions under all circumstances in order to effect an outcome. In this sense he has control over his own destiny.

The individual may be future-, or present-, or past-oriented. The person who is future-oriented anticipates the consequences of present-day events for the next day, the next year, or the next decade. Individuals who are present- and past-oriented use historical explanations for current conditions and are more concerned about things here and now than in the future. These orientations affect the selection of options and the pursuit of new careers after retirement.

Perception of the situation

At the point of entry into the retirement career, the individual perceives what his options are in relation to pre-retirement conditions, the circumstances under which retirement has occurred, and the availability of resources. There are a number of routes to the use of options. One involves a rational approach to the problem, in which the individual evaluates alternatives and, in a logical manner, estimates the possibilities that a particular alternative would provide him with the greatest payoff. In making such evaluations he uses his previous experience and examines carefully the resources of each situation. At the same time, members of organizational systems influence him and in some cases try to steer him into the selection of options which they judge to be "good" for him. If the individual has been subordinate in most of his relationships, it is likely that he will be pressed into a post-retirement career in which the organization has a dominant role.

The time-orientedness of the individual is another factor which enters into his perception of retirement. If his past life has been run by a clock, he may move quickly into decision and select a career line which is time-oriented. On the other hand, if the individual worked under the restraint of the clock and has been unhappy about being constrained by time, he will perceive his options in quite a different light and probably will select a retirement in which the exactness of time is relatively unimportant.

Maladjustment is usually experienced by individuals during the transition from old into new roles, when they must select options and careers, and develop fresh relationships. The individual on the verge of retirement is especially vulnerable to intensive self-searching: "Who am I?" He is probably more prone at this time of life than at any other to make extreme judgments of self. He may assume himself useless and prefer a vegetable-like existence or feel euphoric that life is beginning anew.

Linking Systems

Individuals do not operate as isolates, but as members of primary and reference groups, of social organizations, and even of intellectual disciplines, ideological postures, and social movements. This truism takes on new meaning in relation to the retirement process. The individual does not face retirement alone. It is an experience shared with his compatriots and with functionaries of societal organizations. Linking systems may aid or constrain the individual in the selection of options. In one sense, linking systems themselves are optional. The individual can choose to use or not use these systems.

Friendship groups

A friendship group is a primary structure in which there is intimate interaction of members and in which the individual develops an identity and takes on standards and norms which guide his behavior within the group and outside it (Sherif, Harvey, White, Hood, & Sherif, 1961). Such primary group experiences may be the result of neighboring, of membership in professional associations, unions, voluntary organizations, or of retirement housing.

Kinship network

The kinship network is a voluntary association of families in which members perform instrumental, affective, and expressive tasks. The network is based upon exchanges of unequal value, in which bargaining is one of the principal techniques, and the pattern of mutual aid between the generations takes the form of serial reciprocity. The network usually has a service orientation without exploitation (Sussman, 1968a).

A retiree who participates in a kinship network or friendship group may have little need for the services of organizations created to help the aged person. The two types of linking system will greatly influence the choice of a particular career pattern as well as the life sector in which such a career will evolve (Rosow, 1967).

Marital system

The marital system is another influence on the use of options and career selection. There are great differences in use of options between married and unmarried individuals at the time of retirement. It appears that when the married man retires there is a great "press" on the spouse. She may experience stress greater than that which occurred when the children left home for schools, jobs, marriage, or war. In addition to having "a man under foot," she has to explain the retired status of her husband, change her living and work habits both within and outside the home, and face the task of restructuring friendship and reference groups. In addition there is a need to reallocate tasks within the home and to achieve a new goal consensus which accounts for the sharing of responsibilities and activities.

Inheritance system

The inheritance system is introduced as a linking system, even though it is not an indentifiable structure composed of living persons in interaction with one another. It can, under many circumstances, affect the position of the retired person in the family network. The fact that the individual holds property and has the right to give it to deserving kin means that he has some bargaining power to maintain his status in the family system. In giving to those who show interest and concern about his welfare, the testator is stating his right to have a meaningful life and to receive affection and deference from his potential heirs and legatees. In the study of inheritance previously discussed, it was clearly demonstrated that the patterns of testation were so developed that the retired person maintained his independence and reduced to a minimum the responsibility for his care by his children. Also, receiving inheritance may increase the economic base after retirement, and permit a wider selection of options and career lines.

Work systems

From the beginning of an individual's adult career he works in gainful employment. Sometimes he is a volunteer in different work systems. A factory worker may be a scout leader and, in the most technical sense, have a service career which parallels his line of work in the economic system. The individual may change from one career to the second. In the example, the person may become competent as a scout leader. With some additional training he may become a professional scouter, leaving his factory job and moving into what has been identified as second career (Haug & Sussman, 1967). Upon retirement, the individual is influenced by his previous experiences in a number of work systems, and he has options to move into a second or third career for which he may be paid or volunteer. His past exposure to different types of work systems influences his choice of life sectors and of available career patterns within them.

Voluntary organizations

Voluntary organizations for the retired person are plentiful. They serve as socialization systems in which the individual shifts from instrumental roles in the economic sector to non-instrumental roles in other life sectors. It is questionable whether these voluntary organizations help the individual find meaning in life after retirement. These organizations are activity-oriented. There may be extensive pressure on retired persons to engage in programs in order to contribute to society on a non-remunerative basis. Is this pressure desirable or is it exploitation? If one examines the sources of the pressure for volunteering, one finds that a major one is the professional in an organization which has as part of its rhetoric the notion that "busy people are happy people."

Within-Boundary Constraints

In the discussion of pre-retirement factors, a variety of constraints were mentioned which influence the individual's perception of retirement status and his choice of options. These constraints are expressed through sometimes contradictory societal values which recommend that at retirement one should disengage, give up power, accept isolation if necessary, keep busy to be healthy and happy, accept the devalued role, and become a consumer in a society where honor is heaped on the producer. Until the time of retirement, societal constraints operate as guidelines for appropriate behavior following the day when retirement occurs. This is a form of anticipatory socialization, but without formal training for retirement roles. These constraints establish the boundaries within which option use and career selection occur. The individual also learns by observing the effects of these societal constraints upon those who have retired. Constraints provide the person with a perspective of the array of retirement roles. He may, by the time of retirement, attain an intellectual acceptance of the probable effects of these societal constraints upon his behavior. Emotional acceptance will occur afterward, if at all.

The actual retirement is the moment of reality when constraints become less diffuse and more specific in their impact. No longer is the notion that productive employment is for the young and middle-aged a mouthing; it becomes a reality. The machinery of social organizations becomes alive, and computer-like retirements are effected. What has been believed now becomes an actuality. The individual experiences the effects of societal constraints and handles them according to his position in the social structure, his previous life experiences, his personality characteristics, and his perception of the societal definition of retirement.

Societal definitions

The societal definition of the retirement condition is ambiguous to the retiree and to the social scientist, who find contradictory norms being advocated. The producer is a valued person, while the consumer—particularly the individual who does not contribute to the gross national product—has a devalued status. The position is further buttressed by the notion that members of this society have the responsibility to be productive and to maintain their independence as long as possible. Productivity, independence, and self-help are cherished values and expectations.

Economic

Few highly modern societies with entrepreneurial-capitalistic economic systems can absorb in their work forces all those who desire gainful employment. Unemployment is a common phenomenon, and the aged are a target population for forced withdrawal from the labor market. The constant press for the older worker to move from an economic to a non-economic producing role as a volunteer worker, or to become a consumer, can constrain the retiree in his desire or effort for a second career involving gainful employment in the labor force.

Professional-bureaucratic

The individual facing retirement is guided into the use of available options by the norms of the work and organizational systems in which he has held membership over the years. If the work system is inflexible regarding the age of retirement, and if his union or professional association supports this position, then it is unlikely that the individual will receive from this system appropriate anticipatory socialization for a second career. If the work system is flexible regarding age of retirement and receives support in this posture from secondary associations, then the retiree's orientation is likely to be towards engaging in voluntary or paid work, possibly another career, after leaving his usual employment.

Generational power conflicts

The experience the individual has in intergenerational relationships as a member of a kinship network restricts his choice and use of options and mitigates the influence of other linking systems in options selection and use. If generational power conflicts were the most salient feature of relationships, the retiree might opt for a second work or leisure career which would maximize independent living. He would avoid, if at all possible, the dependent career involving family support, and use institutional care systems if he should suffer illness or disability.

A ,possible effect of generational power conflicts is retreatism and withdrawal. Being in the midst of power, fighting to obtain and keep it over one's lifetime, leads to the adoption of game rules that one should leave the field with some degree of grace and dignity. Then the battle between generations is over and the transfer of power from the old to the young has occurred. The consequence of these experiences may be to pick a "safe" career line in the post-retirement period in order to avoid the psychological hazards of another transfer of power.

Option

Option is viewed as a sequence involving steps from awareness of all possible choices to commitment to a particular career. Knowledge of available alternatives is a combination of pre-retirement experiences, perception of the situation, utilization of linking systems, and within-boundary constraints. Availability of options is related to the retiree's state of health, motivation, self-image, interests, and desires; to organizational and familial support programs; and to the activities of individuals in linking systems.

A logical step, after investigating options, is to narrow them to a few for serious consideration, and to try them out. Trial and error is one major process of socialization before adopting a new career. The airplane pilot described previously enters the option sequence prior to his retirement and is already "taking a crack at" another occupation. The pursuit of the option starts when the decision is reached: "This is it." The form and intensity of the quest depend upon the outer and within-boundary constraints, and upon the accumulated cultural experience and current perception of the retiree. Commitment to a career depends on satisfaction with activity, payoff, physical condition, and the behavior of others in linking systems.

The option sequence implies a high degree of freedom to choose a role or career in each life sector. Implied also is a funnel-shaped process in which options are selected out, with the remaining one being the most desirable to pursue. Many individuals who begin the option sequence with a high degree of awareness of what is available in a particular life sector discover that, at any step of the process, choices are forced by institutional functionaries and others, and logical evaluation of options and decisions regarding one's choice becomes impossible.

Predominant Career Patterns

This chapter departs from the usual definition of career as gainful employment in an occupation. The use of "career" in this model is much broader. It includes any line of activity the individual undertakes. The individual is influenced in the choice of a retirement career by pre-retirement factors, his perception of the retirement situation, the level of constraints he experiences in selecting his options, participation in linking systems, and the degree of support or negative evaluation given to his choice of options.

In the various life sectors open to the individual, he can select one or more career patterns. He can, upon retirement, enter a completely new line of work. The retired businessman may choose to enter the church; the college professor may take up a career in administration or consultation; and the factory worker may be retrained for work with the mentally retarded or the blind.* In all these cases the individuals reorganize their accumulated experiences and skills to meet a new work situation and subsequently can be gainfully employed beyond the time of normally expected retirement.

---

*See Sussman and Haug (1967) for suggestion of new roles for retirees in service occupations.

The retiree can opt for a leisure career in which most of his time is spent as a consumer. If the means are available, the individual can work seriously at those activities which at one time were occasional pursuits or avocations. He can opt for a new leisure role, one with which he has had no previous experience, and the choice of which is influenced by linking systems. Social class, obviously, is an important factor which influences the choice of a leisure option and subsequent learning of the leisure role.

The individual can choose a dependent career, in which he becomes part of an organization or family and receives from them physical and psychological care. The individual may be forced into this choice because of chronic illness or disability. If the choice was deliberate on his part, there may be some opposition to his selecting the "vegetable" role. He will have to make some effort to maintain independence, at least in activities of daily living. However, society expects increasing dependency with age, and the person who chooses a dependent role need not make a very great effort to become independent.

The field of education offers the retiree a new career as a student. The pursuit of knowledge is a widely held value in this society, and being a student all through life is becoming an accepted role. Consequently, returning to school, taking postgraduate courses, or engaging in living-room learning programs with no particular objective except enjoyment and "bettering oneself for living" is another role the individual can assume.

Other lines of activity can be described. The major point is that, at the time of retirement from the work force, the individual has a variety of options to pursue a career pattern. Retirement need not be a hopeless condition of disengagement from all life sectors.

Variation in Time of Entry to New Career

The model includes a time scale called "variations in time of entry into new career." The reason for introducing this notion is that the individual may assume different careers between retirement and death. The change in career line may be a consequence of increasing disability or change in interest. For example, the individual who enters a second career and is gainfully employed from the age of 65 through 70 may find that he has accumulated sufficient assets to pursue seriously an avocation such as deep-sea fishing. He may decide, at the age of 70, to purchase a boat and equipment, and begin to live with this leisure career. Another individual who opted for a leisure career finds that increasing disability necessitates giving up deep-sea fishing. He may retire to land and take on a dependent career. There is a constant shift in careers during the retirement period. Modifications in interest and physical condition are the most important factors in such changes.

Death

The end of the model coincides with the demise of the individual. Societies develop structures and processes for legitimizing the exit of the individual from the world. Death certification, probate processes, and burial procedures are a few of the means devised to tidy up the disposition of the mortal remains of man. In addition to these third-party transactions carried out by the state in the interest of the common good, death involves a transfer of property and status. Often such transfers are more important in their symbolic meaning to the recipients than in the cash value of the transferred property. The inheritance signifies the continuity of family and the affectional and love links of family members. They express the change in responsibility, power, and status within family systems over generations.

SUMMARY

This is one investigator's perception of the important components of retirement. In developing this analytic model, the major questions were: What is vitally important to a person who is retiring from a lifetime work career? What does he feel, want, and aspire to? What options are available to him? A secondary and less specific question was: Which concepts of social change should be used in the study of retirement because of their high explanatory power?

The problem was conceptualized and defined on two levels. The first is specific and concrete. It defines the problem in terms of specific needs and desires of the retired person in the process of moving into the retired status. The second level is more abstract and general. It considers the social structure of modern society: the institutional relationships, the social organizations, and the mix of social systems, groups, and man.

Modern man has an increasing number of options in various life sectors such as work, leisure, politics, and religion. The option sequence is used by individuals to obtain societally approved goals. Supportive linking systems facilitate the choice of options and perpetuate freedom to choose careers in various life sectors. If options are available at the point of retirement and individuals enter new careers in various life sectors, the stigma of retirement may be reduced. Furthermore, the stereotype that retired persons are one homogeneous group, with similar needs and expectations, may be eliminated. Most important, the option sequence provides an analytic tool for examining the assumption of new career patterns in various life sectors by retired persons.

Retirement precipitates consequences which may or may not be markedly different from other types of intervention experienced by individuals in the pre-retirement period. The consequences of retirement for the individual are not fully understood, but retirement status is characterized as stark deprivation, physical and psychological loss, and isolation. The pathological condition of retirement has been exaggerated, in part through lack of understanding of the option sequence as it operates in the pre-retirement period and continues after the individual leaves the work force.

The number of programs and social organizations to serve aged persons has increased markedly in the last two decades. One need of the retiree is to develop knowledge, skills, and techniques for the selection of social organizations which can provide the services he requires. His best chance for a comfortable level of living is to match his needs with the interests of organizations.

Consequently, one major objective is to develop a high order of retiree competence in selecting options and handling interactions with such bureaucracies as rehabilitation hospitals, golden age centers, welfare organizations, and housing developments. Today's client-centered organizations have established objectives which involve perception of what is good for the individual. The task is to socialize the retired individual into a "handling" role which incorporates the best means to use the organization's services without destroying his self-image or impeding his attainment of personal gratification. Ideally, this socialization should begin in the middle years of life before the individual retires from the work sector. Anticipatory socialization during pre-retirement should focus on providing the individual, upon retirement, a large array of options: opportunities to develop one or more careers in life sectors still open to him.

An increasing number of options are available to modern man, and a variety of linking systems relate him to social organizations and facilitate his exercise of options. Constraints exist because of societal norms, previous experience, cognitive styles, and perceptions of self and others. These constraints structure the problems of retirement.

CHARLES TAYLOR, PH.D.

Syracuse University awarded Charles Taylor two baccalaureate degrees, one in psychology and one in music. Following a period of study at the University of Paris during which he earned a License in psychology, he returned to Syracuse to complete the doctorate in psychology.

For ten years he taught psychology at Brigham Young University. In 1964 he joined the faculty of Pennsylvania State University, where he holds the rank of Professor with joint appointments in the Departments of Psychology and Human Development. Dr. Taylor was the first President of the Rocky Mountain Gerontological Association. From 1961 to 1963 he was the Director of the Utah Council on Aging.

Dr. Taylor's lifelong interests in music and in psychology join in one of his leisure-time activities. He has a large collection of tapes of performances of famous pianists, arranged to show developmental change. Dr. Taylor also is the lay leader of a church congregation of 350 people.

3: DEVELOPMENTAL CONCEPTIONS AND THE RETIREMENT PROCESS

CHARLES TAYLOR

Retirement can be considered as an *event* precipitating significant changes in behavior or as a *process* paralleling other ongoing processes. If it is regarded in the first light, emphasis will probably be placed on defining and delineating the event, especially in terms of its intensity and personal meaning; on individual differences in reactivity to the event; and on the prediction and modification of the subsequent behavior and adjustment of the individual. The event must, for best comprehension, be related to previous events and to the behavioral components manifested in response to them.

If, on the other hand, the major emphasis is upon an orderly process of anticipation, severance, and return to relative stability, the chain of antecedent and subsequent elements becomes more important than a description of the nature of the event itself. An implication follows that this process must share some important abstract elements of change and equilibrium with other processes at other periods of life. While descriptions of events, of the social matrix in which they occur, and of the personal and social disruptions which occur supposedly because of them are subject matter at the very core of many disciplines in behavioral science, process elements are of particular interest to the developmental orientation.

The purpose of this paper is to explore a range of conceptions about development in the adult years and to consider their implications for retirement. Before we can assess the usefulness of developmental concepts for retirement, it will be necessary to review the various meanings of the concept of development and differing theoretical positions about the developmental process.

DEFINITIONS OF DEVELOPMENT

Developmental conceptions are not uniformly used by students of change during the life span. Spiker (1966), in considering relevant and irrelevant issues in child development, has stated that the problem of the meaning of the term "development" is the most basic issue in developmental thinking. He strongly suggested that that term be restricted to changes in behavior which normally occur with increases in chronological age, directly equating "developmental" with "ontogenetic." Many researchers use this simplistic concept and much of the literature in human development can be comprehended with such a definition.

Kessen (1960) has pointed out that such a definition does not provide much meaning and can be simply expressed as the equation: $R = f(A)$. For him a characteristic can be said to be developmental only if it can be related to age in an orderly or lawful way. He points out that two other equations must be used to take into account possible differences between populations $R = f(A,P)$ and influences from various situational factors $R = f(A,S \ldots S_n)$. Schaie (1965) has noted that a fourth equation would be needed to account for cultural differences in the history of each age cohort.

Many would reserve the term "developmental" for those aspects of change which are close to the genetic potentiality of the organism, unfolding in programmed sequence biological or morphological steps (Harris, 1957). The concept of maturation, not now so much of an issue as in the prime days of the nature-nurture controversies, is close to such a use. An unfolding of structural qualities does not give a picture of development of special interest to the behavioral scientist, no matter how disposed he is to a reductionistic viewpoint, unless the facts derived therefrom have some high degree of relationship to emergent behavioral functions.

Indeed, one developmentalist (Neugarten, 1966) has explicitly denied the crucial importance of processes biologically inherent in the organism, or inevitable. For her the use of the term should be reserved for processes

> by which the organism, by interacting with the environment, is changed or transformed; so that, as the result of the life history with its accumulating fund of adaption to both biological and social events, there is a continually changing basis within the individual for perceiving and responding to new events in the outer world—processes which follow an orderly progression with the passage of time [p. 63].

Here the emphasis is on transition from state to state, giving maximum attention to intrapsychic factors but not ignoring situational ones. Provocative as such a definition is, it is difficult to see how this might differ from conceptions of learning, except that sequences occur over larger reaches of time. Psychology has long since paid little attention to Wheeler (1932), whose organismic theory of learning used a single set of principles to account for both development and learning. In addition, as Kessen (1962) has argued, descriptions of states of being, concerns over the uniqueness of the processes of change in an individual, and statements of rules of transition are difficult to combine in a single research orientation.

Still others (Buhler, 1961; D. B. Gardner, 1964) tend to look on development as an orderly sequential progression toward end states. Contributions towards achievement of those end states may come from biological growth, from psychological adaptions, and from social and cultural pressures. Detours, regressions, and stoppages may be seen as clinical rather than developmental in such a context.

For still another group a process can be seen as developmental if it enhances the ability of the organism to adjust to its environment and proceeds in an orderly, harmonious way (Werner, 1957; Watson, 1959; Strehler, 1960). Neither chaotic growth nor decline can be seen as developmental processes in such a context.

Some developmentalists would move from the organism and give to abstractions the burden of illuminating the nature of development. Kastenbaum (1964), for example, suggests that the developmental approach is a mode of thinking which is concerned with the principles and processes by which one event unfolds from another. The organism is thus a part of explanation but not the focus of it.

Developmental ideas are most useful when they attempt to bring order to a large number of variables in interaction. The study of human development differs from other disciplines because of the aim of the theorist to combine many streams of thought into an interrelated pattern (Kuo, 1967). Murray (1959), discussing the thought processes which lead to his theory of personality, noted that he had to learn to account for progressive transformations, eliminations, and reconstructions, learnings, extinctions, and relearnings, regressions and deteriorations, and for the determinants of such changes. Whether any student of human development can keep so many balls in the air at once is problematical. Our insistence on the multivariate quality of human development has slowed the development of theory and has often led to the feeling that *any* perceptible movement within the system through time has considerable explanatory value for the whole system (Zigler, 1963).

Students of human development typically fall into three classes:

I. Those who trace a number of variables through some segment of the life span, with maximal effort given to showing relationships between one event in time and other related events elsewhere in time. Rules of transition are of paramount importance.

II. Those who emphasize the widest and most complete picture of the organism at any certain period of life. Any and all descriptive data are assembled, and relationships to other periods of life minimized.

III. Those who concentrate on some psychological or social variable. Change over time is important only as one dimension of the variable in question. Special relationships to other variables are presumed to exist at various points in time but are not emphasized.

DEVELOPMENT AND AGING

The period of life in which retirement usually occurs raises some particular problems fundamental to an understanding of human development. Whether development is a conception applicable to the whole life span or not has been frequently discussed (Birren, 1964a; Neugarten, 1966; Bromley, 1966; Kastenbaum, 1967). Svancara (1966) suggests that early and late life are simply different phases of a single life cycle with common conceptualizations and generalizations, among them concepts of psychological deprivation, changes in schedules of activity and use of vital energy. Anderson (1964) proposes that development and aging alike show irreversible, continuous, cumulative changes, more obvious as the observation periods are lengthened. Kuo (1967) has stated that development is a continuous process of growing, changing, and declining, without any perceptible point at which a certain function or behavior can be said to have reached maturity. For him, development at any age is restrictive as well as expansive, since only a small number of the original indeterminate and extensive range of potential behavior patterns are actualized during the process of development; all other potentials are prevented from realization due to the gradual reduction of plasticity. An opposing view is taken by Donahue (1968), who feels that more is contributed to an understanding of age-associated changes if development and age are differentiated.

There are three principal conceptual discriminations between development and aging.

I. Development is the building up of an organismic structure with a repertoire of adaptive functions; when the structure deteriorates, dysfunctional concommitants can be called aging. Strehler (1960), for example, uses the terms "universal," "progressive," and "intrinsic" for changes occurring both in development and aging, but adds for aging the term "deleterious." There is nothing in this point of view to contradict the fact that in some functions development may be occurring while in others aging may be seen.

II. Aging is a phenomenon which affects biological functions only. Growth in structural components ceases and deterioration occurs in ever-increasing amounts; but, on the other hand, there is no necessary deterioration in psychological functioning. Peck (1956) has suggested in this vein that only when new, different, uniquely human powers grow to their fullest extent may aspects of the years beyond 35 be called developmental.

III. The third suggests that the term "aging" itself may not be very useful, particularly as a contrast to the term development. Kastenbaum (1967) has questioned whether the term "aging" is not a disguise for our ignorance of the complex processes which go on at all levels during much of the life span, especially ignoring historical, ideographic, and cultural variables. Especially critical is the considerable ignorance of developmental trends during the periods of early and middle adulthood.

Each of the points of view has its own logic. It is important, however, to note that all of the terms used in the general systemic model proposed by Anderson (1957), with the exception of *growth*, may be used equally as well for aging as for development. Terms like "maturation" and "aging" may imply direction away from and towards events (such as birth and death) rather than expressing particular systems of change and behavior, even though they lose much of their meaning by such use.

THEORIES OF DEVELOPMENT

Probably because of the complexity of the problems involved in developmental thinking, developmental theories are not common in behavioral science. Zigler (1963) contends that most developmental theories tend to be of two sorts: those which are little more than short-hand, often esoteric, redesignations of descriptive data and those which are highly conjectural, often far from any empirical operations. Constructs which are in the middle range, which move from raw data to higher abstractions, are rare.

The situation is further complicated by the fact that theories which are designated as belonging to other areas of the social sciences, such as personality, learning, and role or family theory must contain strong elements of developmental change if they are to be at all useful, particularly for prediction. In this respect, such theories tend to be unsatisfactory in explaining change over time, either ignoring much of the life span or using conceptualizations which are as diffuse or inadequate as those more specifically labeled developmental. When change is dominant, every theory must be developmental; when change is minimal, almost any other theory may well be more heuristic.

Theories which have as a central focus the course of change over the life span may be divided into three general classes: (1) those which propose stages in development, with special attention to antecedent, process, and outcome variables; (2) those which have a teleological character and speculate upon end-states; and, (3) those which concern themselves with general principles of development, focusing more on dynamic elements than upon any particular period or condition.

Theories of Stage and/or End Products

Some theoretical statements point out special characteristics of certain stages of the life span, often delineating major problems and characteristic modal resolutions which occur at various stages.

Every student of human development is familiar with Freud's psychosexual stages. Although the full course of development was seen by Freud to take place in the years before maturity, with an almost total disregard for the adult except as he retraced his epigenetic development, there are theoretical elements which fit a life span perspective. Since development is reversible through the principle of regression, later stages in life could be seen as returns, through lack of ego maintenance, to earlier stages of development (Zetzel, 1965).

Jung (1958) gave prominence in his theory of personality development to adult stages but they are not detailed in a fashion which makes derivations from the theory easy or productive. Movement through adulthood has two main themes, to some degree antithetical: turning (1) from meeting social role demands to more complete involvement in the self and its potential, and (2) from natural (or biological) involvement to "cultural" involvement, with an understanding of society as a major goal.

Erikson (1959) has provided a widely accepted framework for a life-span developmental theory with stages oriented to nuclear crises in ego identity, emergent in a fixed developmental order. With functional maturation the signal for the crisis, the outcomes for each stage can be expressed in bipolar outcomes which have a relatively permanent influence on later crises.

Since Erikson subsumes perhaps half the life span under a single crisis, Peck (1956) has reworked the Erikson formula to make more discernible the problems of middle and old age. They involve: (1) valuing wisdom vs. valuing physical powers; (2) socializing vs. sexualizing in human relationships; (3) cathectic flexibility vs. cathectic impoverishment; (4) mental flexibility vs. mental rigidity; (5) ego differentiation vs. work-role preoccupation; (6) body transcendence vs. body preoccupation; and (7) ego transcendence vs. ego preoccupation.

In a number of publications (1959, 1961, 1968), Charlotte Buhler has presented a developmental theory oriented towards changes in the distribution of four basic drives; (I) need satisfaction, (II) adaptive self-limitation, (III) creative expansion, and (IV) upholding of the internal order. This dynamic theory has the psychological advantage of providing profiles of development, rather than either-or categorizations. The interplay between the drives is explicitly stated for the years up to age 70: the years past 70 are seen as a "ripening period." The scheme for development can be expressed in the rubric in Table 1.

TABLE 1
Drives at various stages of development

Stage	Dominant Need	Other Needs	Time Perspective
Young child	I	Incipient	Present
Older child	II	Restrains I, III, and incipient IV	Vague future
Adolescent	III	Restrains I, II, incipient IV	Specific future
40's to 60's	IV	Orderly unification	Past-in-present

Linden and Courtney (1953), operating from a psychoanalytic point of view, have posited two opposing dynamic principles, evolescence and senescence. The course of life is from early egocentricity and pleasure, with little group involvement, to eventual unselfishness and social participation for society's betterment; life stages are marked by successive social tasks.

Banham (1951), whose early work on the genesis of emotions had been provocative (Bridges, 1930), subsequently extended her theorizing to the later years of life. In infancy, responses to emotion-producing experience are seen as undifferentiated and random; by maturity, emotions are differentiated into the palette of pleasant and unpleasant emotions, with much sensitivity to a wide range of cues and suitable control of emotive responses. By old age the range of responses has shrunk and the adaptability to cues is minimal. Thus, childhood and senescence are the poles of a continuum leading from generalized excitement in infancy to generalized apathy and passivity in old age.

A theory of behavior developed by Allport (1960), not often specified as developmental, has a sequential nature which is not unlike that of Buhler. Allport turns to ancient Hindu thinking for his developmental periods. The first stage is dominated by a desire for pleasure, characterized in psychology by such terms as tension reduction, reinforcement, libido, and needs. The second stage emphasizes desire for power and success. In the third stage, coming in late adulthood, the desire is for doing one's duty and discharging responsibility. Finally, people seek a philosophical or religious understanding which will liberate them from the earlier three periods.

Certain existential formulations concern themselves with life purposes and goal-striving without specific age delineations (Rogers, 1963; Fromm, 1941; Maslow, 1962; Snygg & Combs, 1959). Goldstein (1967) in the final months of life said it well:

> Adequacy is achieved by man's creative power; it is, so
> to say, a secret activity of life by which our self-
> realization becomes possible. That procedure demands
> that we take the risk of insecurity; only when
> confronted by some insecurity are we able to realize
> ourselves, which means to exist [p. 155].

The list of theories cited range in the precision of their
postulates. They share to greater or lesser degree a common fault
of attempting to explain an event or behavioral stage in terms of
its results without describing interval mechanisms. They lack
"critical tests" of theory; research generated by them is inclined to
be more concerned with furnishing contemporary facts from which
the theory might have been more confidently derived than in
testing hypotheses drawn from them. They remain, however,
required reading for persons who wish to make meaningful
statements about the conditions of adult life.

Theories of Developmental Process

Another variety of theory attempts to describe the processes
through which change occurs. Though such theories have stressed
change during childhood, the mechanisms seem to have some
heuristic value for research with adults (Kastenbaum, 1964).

A most influential theory for development in childhood is that
of Piaget (1960). Indeed, this theory at present dominates research
in child development (Bronfenbrenner, 1963). Although explica-
tions of Piaget's theory have been confined almost exclusively to
stages of childhood and to cognitive functions, he believes that the
principles are broad and general enough to apply to a large variety
of functions and ages.

The fundamental element of behavior for Piaget is the schema, a
reliable response to a stimulus. Schema are mobile; with increasing

age the response can be applied to a larger variety of stimuli, even those which are completely novel to the organism. The concept is broad enough to apply to overt behavior patterns as well as internalized thought processes. Although at first the organism may find a new situation beyond its response scope, interest in the new situation will keep the organism attuned to it. Indeed, the child is "fed" by the challenge. The organism adapts to the elements of the new situation by evoking old behavior with minor changes until the schema works reliably for the new situation. Schema are combined and restructured again and again.

Concepts on the order of Piaget's are common stock in the psychology of adaption. Learning elements, motivational elements, and behavioral elements are combined here, however, in a particularly rich way. Unfortunately, they are expressed without parsimony and in a complex logico-mathematical way.

The work of Lewin (1954) has been much admired by social scientists, because of both its sophistication and its specifically stated relevance to long periods of the life cycle. The basic unit of this theory is the life-space, an abstract, phenomenological concept defined as the sum of all the facts that determine a person's behavior at a given time. This highly fluid unit changes from moment to moment because of the properties relevant to the situation; the past enters only as it affects its representative elements in the present. The life space in children is seen as differing from that of adults according to three principles: differentiation, rigidification, and time perspective. Briefly, differentiation refers to the number of regions of the life space which can be clearly demarked from one another. Rigidification is seen as the strength of the boundaries between regions of the life space. Moment to moment changes in external situations do not confuse and blur possible differentiations of the life-space regions. As the organism grows, organizational thrusts reach further into the future, delays are tolerated, and activities are organized into larger time units.

Additional elements not explicitly related to age by Lewin but obviously so related are *needs*, which may grow and shift indefinitely with age, and *tensions* which focus and deploy *energies*. Thus with age, motivations may decrease, tensions may not be exerted upon behavior potentials, or energy sources may be depleted.

An explanation of the period of adolescence in field terms has some usefulness to those who would study adults (Lewin, 1939). He suggests that a fruitful approach is to refer first to typical problem situations of adolescents for hints as to what conditions would increase or decrease those problems. The regions of adulthood are largely unknown to the adolescent, leading to uncertain and random behavior; even the body, once so well known, cannot now be depended upon. There is ambivalence over the entering of new regions and the leaving of old. The "marginal man," on the boundary of new experiences, is full of contradiction and sensitivity. All stages of adulthood beyond the present are full of uncertainty for the person about to enter them; for this reason, adult stages are capable of fitting the adolescent model when a time of transition is involved. Development is seen by Lewin as being identical with behavior, with the same formula. Whatever heuristic value could come from such a similarity has not been exploited (Escalona, 1954).

Of all theorists, no one has been more explicitly developmental than Werner (1948, 1957). His general approach has provided a strategy and a mode of thinking which revolve around concepts of development. Several ideas are worth consideration here.

For Werner, the term development is one of the widest possible generality, indicating a process of change which is equally explicatory of biological change, psychological processes, or social and cultural phenomena. A change can be called developmental when it follows "orthogenic" principles, or in other words proceeds from a state of relative globality and lack of differentiation to a state of increasing "differentiation," "articulation," and "hierarchic integration."

These theory-words encompass the main metatheoretical elements in Werner's thinking. Differentiation is the isolating of experience from large units into discrete sub-units. In a typical developmental sequence, early stages are syncretic or fused, while later stages are more distinct from one another. The transition is never complete and adults may retain the option of thinking syncretically when it seems appropriate. Articulation must accompany differentiation. Separateness must not be achieved by mutilating the whole; the organismic quality of experience is never lost.

The integration which occurs in articulation is characterized by an orderly succession of stages. Werner has, for example, identified stages in the ontogenesis of perception: first, a global stage in which whole qualities dominate; next an analytic stage in which part elements are emphasized; and finally, a stage in which the parts are integrated in respect to the whole. These steps are not only applicable to children; a group of Werner's associates have devised a developmental scoring system for Rorschach cards in adults, showing the same developmental stages (Hemmedinger, 1951).

A person may at any age in life operate on a higher or lower level of differentiation, as befits the circumstances. A more important point for adult years in this theoretical mode is made by Kastenbaum (1965). He suggests that the basic problem of old age is to keep integration at a continuing high level, noting that the increase of the saliency of certain "parts" can be emphasized but often only at the expense of the "whole"; conversely, the problem of making adequate wholes (such as with bodily concerns) may force slighting some of the parts. Dedifferentiation is a related term from Goldstein (1963). Here catastrophic problems of life result in a progressive, systematic disintegration back down the hierarchial steps by which differentiation occurred.

The organismic views of Werner and Goldstein are general

enough to fit a host of measurable phenomena, since miniature or microgenetic changes are treated by the same operations and concepts as are long-term gross changes. Lack of detail and vagueness of conceptualizations are problems of all theories of change; and Werner is not free from such criticisms.

The process theorists have appealed to those developmentalists who are interested in experimental methods in human development (Zigler, 1963). Those who are more interested in development in natural settings are inclined to be disenchanted because of the irrelevance of one such developmental theory to others of its type and because of the difficulty of moving from abstract conceptions to those variables commonly studied in development (Baldwin, 1967). Certainly, the dimensions of retirement seem far afield from the abstract conceptions of such theories.

GENERAL DEVELOPMENTAL CONCEPTIONS

The theories which have been concerned with change over time extending into the later years have provided a springboard for only limited research. If they are general enough to encompass the range of behavior, which seems to expand in a population of aging persons, they are too cumbersome and generalized to provide hypotheses for study. If the theory explains only limited aspects of behavior, a developmental picture of the whole aging organism is difficult to construct.

Theories which center on the earliest years of life, when at least biological change is regular and productive, are not easy to extrapolate to adult years. Tests of all theories have all too often been cases of gathering non-clinical populations to test whether "presumed" data actually exist in samples drawn. In adults there is not even that regularity of biological function which could prove an anchoring point. Neugarten (1966) has shown that the menopause, one of the few time-clock phenomena of the adult life, does not provide a biological unit from which behavioral predictions can be made. This does not at all mean that important biological changes are not taking place and that they are not orderly and predictable. For the purposes of this paper it is more appropriate to say that they are not reflected predictably in molar behavior.

Theory itself has come upon bad days in much of social science. The monumental seven-volume series edited by Koch (1959), organizing a host of lively psychological theories, was concluded by him with a pessimistic view. For him, the "age of theory" has passed and more modest efforts to develop prototheories and clear-cut conceptualizations seem in order.

Anderson in several publications (1956, 1957, 1964) has identified a number of conceptualizations which seem to be of considerable use, not so much as unifying forces which can tie together masses of data but as brakes upon too complacent acceptance of stereotyped styles of thinking. They follow the general vein of system theory (Bertalanffy, 1952). In several ways they give background to conceptualizations which hypothesize that retirement is a period of developmental crisis characterized by disruption and return to homeostasis. Each of these systematic problems has some special application to retirement.

The Open System and the Mechanisms of Change

Development assumes a living, open system in which there are transactions between the organism and the environment, internal and external. Developmental principles have seemed maximally useful for the earliest years, when rather abrupt changes occur in spite of environmental dissimilarities. When the organism is young, change in all areas is so rapid and pervasive that almost all measurements will vary systematically with age. At the end of the life span, more rapid change may again become an expected feature. It is problematic, however, whether such changes are age-related or related to pathology. Von Mering and Weniger (1959) have suggested that the age of pervasive downward change is no earlier than 75 years. Even though measurements downward in many functions are expected, the rate of maintenance or descent is very different for different functions, certainly different for different persons, with intraindividual variability in measured functions often seen to be increasing.

The period of relative stability of the functions under consideration and the measures used in the years from maturity through old age may be an artifact of the functions and measures used. In most cases the conceptual framework of salient variables comes from childhood or early adulthood and measures of them have been standardized on such populations. Just as declines in functions have often been attributed to problems of measurement (Pressey, 1957), the inability of test items to lead toward any hypothetical gains must be pointed out. Most tests of adjustment seem to imply that we reach a level of performance early in adulthood in which further change is neither necessary nor probable, except as regression.

Bortner, in a number of papers (1966, 1967, 1968), has looked at problems of explaining change in adult years. Since a biological substratum is not useful to an understanding of adult life in the same way as with a growing organism, and no other types of variables show consistent change with age, some have questioned whether adult changes are actually developmental in nature or are instead idiosyncratic. Personality psychologists and clinicians agree that change can occur in adulthood but is usually preceded by or accompanied by some degree of conflict and tension resolution. The argument is that these times of conflict and resolution are culturally shaped and normatively related to certain broad bands of the life span. These modal experiences or "crisis stampings"

(Sullivan, 1953) will be similar enough for enough people to begin to take on time relationships. Bortner (1966) protests that such choice points and resolution experiences have not been systematically considered in early and middle adult years, so that a theoretical position on systematic or developmental adult change is premature. The manner in which personality does change affords suitable material for another theoretical orientation; in particular Worchel and Byrne (1964) and Secord and Backman (1961) have shown how the interrelations of self-concept, overt behavior, and the social context can and should produce change over time.

The Chicago school of researchers (Neugarten *et al.*, 1964) has demonstrated that many personality variables show no age relationships during much of the adult years. Those which do show change in these studies are the intrapsychic processes of change in ego function rather than in external, social character. Questions of attitude toward time, of orientation toward safety, and of concerns about passivity are emergent and ever more salient in adulthood (Neugarten, 1964). An interesting support to these findings is provided by Tuddenham (1959), who measured specific traits after many years. Here external behavioral traits (such as aggression, spontaneity, and expressiveness) showed much greater stability than internal psychological functions and content. It is unfortunate that so much of the literature descriptive of adult life is in gross behavioral units.

The material evidence for developmental changes in adulthood is based on very small samples of human beings. The evidence is provocative, not persuasive. Baldwin, in evaluating various theories of child development, has damned us all with the following statement: "With adults we count on any good intuitive knowledge of other adults to keep us out of trouble" (1967, p. 74). Kessen (1960) has suggested that developmental findings, even in child research, have been largely limited to safe areas which can almost surely be shown to be associated with age. One way of understanding personality change in adulthood is by considering the Markov chains (Lohnes, 1965; Halperin, 1966) of sequence after sequence of alternatives in the individual life style; but research here is only beginning to emerge.

In sum, retirement can be seen as requiring more or less extensive change. It is not at all a question of whether change does occur but whether it is predictable and invariant (Emmerick, 1968). Questions of differential rates of change at different ages and their relationship to a challenging event seem scarcely to have been questioned.

Only very limited claims may be made that the present modal retirement age reveals characteristics which make retirement mandatory or even indicated in any compelling way. Even in the face of pervasive physical decline, there is little justification for a view of retirement as a merciful release from increasing pressures in the work situation. It should be obvious that the decision to sever persons from productive jobs is typically based on social demands, not on demonstrated developmental declines.

Directions of Change

A considerable body of theory and speculation (Riesman, 1954; Allport, 1955; Jung, 1958; Murphy, 1961; Maslow, 1962; Rogers, 1963) is concerned with the potential of the human as he moves through the life span. This directional process has often been referred to as a developmental phenomenon, a use of the term directly related to biological theories of maturation. Fromm (1941) has spoken of this later period of life as the time when the "real" character emerges. This entelechy stands in direct contrast to conceptions which stress that maturity is early arrived at, with the rest of the life span a losing effort to maintain earlier gains.

A person who inclines to the latter view would urge persons to shore up their defenses, so that declines would be compensated for, substituted for, or adjusted to. The fact of general physical decline is a real one (Birren, 1964), though it seems certain that functional loss is most deleterious under stress and can be compensated for, and that residuals are adequate for most situations of everyday experience. The case for decline of mental functions is less compelling (Botwinick, 1967). In neither of these cases, moreover, is there a clear-cut picture of reversion to an earlier state. Similarity in total additive score units does not presume equivalence in the units which combine to make up the score.

Somewhere in the second half of life there occurs what has been referred to as a new "prime of life" (Heard, 1963; Donahue, 1968). It has frequently been asserted that human behavioral study has focused on clinical studies of malfunction rather than efforts to show self-actualizing tendencies. When Cummings and Henry (1961) come to the end of their formal thesis of disengagement, they suggest that a person's "last pleasures seem to reside in good meals, an occasional outing, short naps, and long dreams" (p. 227). It is not clear whether this picture is developmentally the end of the life of the personality or is well into one of pervasive disintegration of personality. Butler (1967) suggests that many manifestations seemingly associated with aging per se reflect instead medical illness, difference in long-term personality variables, or sociocultural effects. On the other hand, the chief criticism of those who take the view that self-actualization can continue through the life span is that they have little research data to support their claims (Olds, 1955).

That personality growth can occur throughout the life span in some persons would scarcely be questioned. Wright (1960) has shown that decline in function can trigger growth of new ways of perceiving and acting. Even the prospect of dying has been shown to develop in some people new dimensions of personality (Zinker and Fink, 1966). On the other hand, there is little evidence for clear-cut personality growth in any large segment of the older population.

For the largest number of persons engaged in gainful employment, whether the personality richens or deepens is of no serious consequence, for their jobs do not provide a framework for showing such growth. Some, whose contributions of insight and personal warmth are especially valuable, might be leaving their tasks at a time which denies them and society an opportunity to demonstrate this growth (Pressey, 1966). If it were society's decision, however, to divide the life into successive careers of study, work, and community service, as Secretary Gardner proposed (1967) at the hearings of the Special Committee on Aging of the United States Senate, the question might become vital. It is easy for many to think of the post-retirement years as those especially appropriate for volunteerism, a shorthand expression for unpaid *work*. Some of the most urgent demands of society are those which call upon especial reserves of compassion and understanding. That they are to be found in older persons, not necessarily at the professional level, can be seen in the success of the Foster Grandparent program. Volunteer activities for older persons are too often "busy work" with little dignity and little opportunity to show the skills and attitudes which come from long experience.

Related to the subject of continued growth and the already discussed mechanisms of change in adult life is the question of what, if anything, can promote further personality growth past adulthood. There are those who emphasize that positive personality change occurs in optimal environments (Birren, 1964b; Snygg and Combs, 1959; Rogers, 1963). This point of view, when examined in personality terms, does not so much describe the environment as the ability of the organism to react to it. Snygg and Combs (1959), representative of the self-actualizing school, suggest that adequate personalities are the result of positive experiences; they decry those who proclaim the toughening power of failure, rejection, and humiliation. The very reconstruction and growth of personality, in their terms, always has elements of stress. They maintain that the development of the adequate personality is a goal towards which all struggle but at which none arrives.

Linden and Courtney (1953) make a strong case for the virtue of struggle. They see counterforces as obstacles which yield conflict, giving in in turn to solution of conflict through experience. The implication of this viewpoint is that all personality growth is preceded by some reorganizational demand of the moment. A serious problem is that the nature and dimensions of crisis are individualistically self-interpreted. Prior experiences and their organization are critical in determining whether a situation will or will not be anxiety-producing.

Developmental Stages and the Concept of Crisis

The concept of crisis, or the emergence of new personality dimensions in the face of conflict, is an integral part of some theories of developmental personality trends (Erikson, 1959; Peck, 1956). One of the most quoted principles in texts on human development is that change is "gradual and continuous." Even those who suggest, opposingly, that change is abrupt and saltatory (Zubeck and Solberg, 1954) find it hard to divorce themselves utterly from such a fundamental idea.

The same problem of continuity versus discontinuity occurs in learning theory. Hilgard and Marquis (1961) put the burden of proof upon those who insist upon insightful and sudden change, since almost all learning experiments show a gradual course of acquisition and extinction. Even those who adopt a view of relatively rapid reorganization and change, such as Piaget and Erikson, also soften this view by an insistence that the reorganization goes through smooth transitions. For example, Inhelder and Matalon (1960) defend the presumed discontinuities in Piaget's work by alleging that, in actual fact, the transitions between successive conceptions of the world are gradual and continuous and reveal a trend. Werner (1957) points out that the size of the change is not the important thing; for him there must be no intermediate identifiable stages of a character like the preceding or subsequent ones if growth is to be considered discontinuous.

The concept of crisis or "critical phase" (Hartman, 1958) differs from two other conceptualizations with which it is often confused. It is not an event in the external world which requires the marshalling of adaptive forces; and it is not a "critical period," a unique time at which the plasticity of the organism allows an unusual discrimination of stimuli and permits a particular type of response, so that events may have quite different effects at different times. The meaning used here is rather that of typical danger situations which call into use available psychic energy in a challenging way. It is not that anxiety may not be present in considerable quantity, but rather that the transition situations are characterized by need for new intergrations of strengths. Such crises are marked by considerable growth potential.

It will be remembered that Erikson's theory does not presume that the crises will be ideographic; rather the personality unfolds through phase-specific psychosocial crises. Although the phases of Erikson (1959) and Peck (1956) have shown themselves to be sequentially related in a modest way (Gruen, 1964; Peck and Berkowitz, 1964), adult relationships to age per se are not demonstrated.

Whether or not development passes through phases or stages which are identifiably different from one another is another way of phrasing the same question. There are two ways of looking at it: that the means of successive populations should be significantly different in some salient variable, even though overlap may be considerable; or that there are sufficiently different reorganizations of personality to guarantee that any person could be sorted into the right category. In the studies of life stages by Erikson and Peck, just noted, the method used to assume sequentiality was that of showing higher correlations between adjacent cells in the developmental matrix than in more remote cells. Anastasi (1958) has raised the caution that age-related heterogeneity in a variable to be correlated with another variable will spuriously raise the correlation over a situation of less heterogeneity. Researchers who compare age cohorts should be careful not to make age comparisons without some information on the variability within the age populations they study.

The findings of the Dedham Conference on Development in Children are germane to the problem of stages in adult life. At that time, Kessen (1962) suggested that even those who argue that development is continuous find that the concept of stage helps them to understand the fluidity of change in human behavior; indeed, among all child psychologists the only ones not using some vague-to-precise stage concepts are those who lean to learning theory as an explanation for change. Three kinds of stage are common: stage as a metaphor (the empty nest stage); stage as a paraphrase for age (the forties); and stage as a symbol for an event which is prominent within a period of life (the menopausal stage).

Kessen points out that our problems with stages come from the tendency of American psychology to think in terms of movement from state to state, not being so much concerned with the *processes* of change en route. Harris (1967) has indicated that stages tend too often to be artificially shaped and delineated; intergrades can always be found, since the stage typically encompasses a substantial block of time. The length of time in a stage varies inversely with the rapidity of development. This fact may be a major blindfold to successful thinking about changes in adult life; development proceeds so slowly over so much of the years past maturity that units of change may be smaller than the errors of measurement. Since we measure from state to state, we may miss short intervals of rapid change. It has been customary, Harris says, to consider periods of very gradual change as stages and periods of rapid change as transition.

Some of the cautions which Caldwell (1962) proposed in evaluating the usefulness of the critical period hypthesis are germane to the question of stages:

1. The end of one period does not automatically mark the beginning of another.
2. Behavior criteria, not age, should mark a phase.
3. All possible age periods should be compared for similarities.

In summary, though stages and developmental periodicity are widely used concepts, problems of description of stage properties and method of transfer from stage to stage need amplified and clarified exposition. It would be hazardous to describe retirement as a stage which has more than purely descriptive characteristics. To say that retirement occurs typically in the sixties does not conversely mean that a person who enters the sixties will be entering the retirement stage.

Developmental Tasks

A related conception is that of development tasks, an age-ordered sequence of social duties which are required of a person as he moves through life. As Havighurst (1953) has defined, a developmental task arises at or about a certain period in the life of an individual, and its successful achievement leads to happiness and to success with later tasks. Some tasks arise from physical change, others from societal demands, and still others from pressures of the ego; in fact, most probably arise from various combinations of these factors.

Havighurst has devised a series of broadly defined units which fit certain age periods, freely admitting that these units could be subdivided. The adult stages have been used in considerations of adult personality, both because of their intrinsic value and because of the paucity of alternative approaches. That the majority of the population passes through these task situations is indisputable; that the tasks form an invariant sequence is highly debatable, despite some corroborative evidence from the adolescent years (Schoeppe & Havighurst 1952).

If they are not sequential and do not rely upon the completion of a certain prior task or tasks for successful achievement, then the alternative hypothesis of generalized success at one time creating an atmosphere for further success at a subsequent time (as in level of aspiration studies) is perfectly acceptable. If a task can occupy a station higher or lower in a stage or move from stage to stage, there is a troublesome necessity to show that early success is a requirement for later success. Some adult tasks seem interrelated as steps of progression in a kind of career ladder. For example, "Taking on Civic Responsibility," "Achieving Adult Civic and Social Responsibility," and "Meeting Social and Civic Obligations" seem to be *ipso facto* various progessive elements of a single process which could occur in sequence after entry at any age.

Clark and Anderson (1967) have questioned the conception of such tasks as being development, labeling them instead "culturally defined." Havighurst, it will be remembered, does not deny the cultural implications. The point they make is, however, that these tasks are not *universal* human tasks (an assumption the term "developmental" often implies); whether or where they appear on a development ladder may vary with social custom or cultural change.

Zaccaria (1965) has shown that there are ideographic dimensions to developmental tasks which stand in opposition to the idea of modal societal interactions. He suggests that a given task has a unique meaning to any individual; individuals vary in respect to their general style of approach to task and in the pattern of meeting them. LoCascio (1964) has identified three basic patterns for meeting developmental tasks: the "continuous" (or normatively successful); the "delayed" in which mastery comes late but successfully; and the "impaired" or maladjusted pattern.

Oetting (1967) has considered developmental tasks as useful conceptualizations, not because they are delineations of individual or normative passage through the life span, but because they provide a picture of successive environmental interactions under which growth can occur. If tasks appropriate to age and social conditions are available, personality growth will continue; if not, some aspects of development will be retarded. Oetting sees the need for society to impose not fewer but more developmental tasks, especially at mature ages, to crystallize and give direction to growth.

That retirement is a task of considerable importance in life is undeniable. Whether it can be discharged more successfully before or after some other tasks is difficult to know. If retirement were changed by social decision to a decade earlier, would the lack of now preceding tasks help or hinder the tasks of retirement?

Critical Periods

The concept of critical periods is of particular importance for studying very early life. The basic idea underlying this concept is that there are limited periods in ontogeny during which a stimulus will have a profound effect. The familiar demonstration of "imprinting" in avian organisms (Hess, 1964) is an example. An important element of the critical period is the fact that material learned in such a period is so well incorporated that contrary learning, though subsequently greatly desirable, is no longer possible (Scott, 1962). Kuo (1967) suggests a corollary to the term "critical point" of physics, as, for example, the temperature above which a substance in gaseous form cannot be liquified no matter how much pressure is applied.

This formative but restrictive quality for later experience perhaps is the proper use of the term; yet the concept of "readiness" in education is often used as suggesting an ability to learn well at one period that which is less well learned at another. Whether it could be learned as well at another "teachable moment" with a change in appropriate stimuli and methodology is debatable (Denenberg and Kline, 1964). The implication that such particularly fallow periods are spread over the lifetime is suggested by Havighurst (1953), who says that of all the periods of life, early adulthood is the fullest of teachable moments and of special sensitivity and unusual readiness of the person to learn, adding that it is also the emptiest of efforts to teach.

Kastenbaum (1964) and Anderson (1957) have been quick to point out that the presence of such critical periods through the lifetime must be supported by research. There is no question of an ability to learn late in life; rather the presence of *particular* "moments" at any ages past the very earliest seems to be in question. Bloom (1964) suggested that the greatest change in personality comes when individuals are in situations which are in sharp contrast to the environment from which they have just come, most of such change happening in the first months of exposure to that new environment. If this is the case, then perhaps the oldest years, with their disruptions, may be ones of more "teachable moments" than those of early or middle maturity.

At any rate, retirement may well occur at present as a very "teachable" time for many. Losses in personal and social spheres and changes in self-concept may sensitize the person to opportunities for growth. Alternatively, there may be a greater feeling of self-worth in quitting when one is ahead, before failure is imminent and probable.

Questions of Universality

A question faced in any developmental thinking, and one already traversed here, is that of the generality of developmental phenomena. Anderson (1964) and Allport (1937) are particularly interested in the unfolding of individual lives and the choice points and resolutions which occur in them. For others, a phenomenon must have considerable generality, perhaps universality, before it can be called developmental. Others take a view that distinct subgroups may have somewhat similar developmental patterns.

Riegel (1959) questions the use of personality types in adult life; and indeed American psychology has found the use of personality types rather distasteful. Stagner (1961) has suggested that a type approach to personality is defensible only if we can demonstrate that differences in quality of pattern, not reducible to dimensional scales, can be identified as distinctive in each type. Others, such as Eysenck (1953) or Stephenson (1953), feel that types need not show an all-or-nothing character, but can be used as convenient schema to show relative dominance of some particular patterning of traits.

One important characteristic is that the sample from which identification of types is drawn should be supplemented by the demonstration that these types occur in other samples drawn from the general population and can be identified with success by raters other than those who fashion the categories. This last caution is not clearly followed in many studies. Further, types have more frequently been used as explicative of personality variables than of general behavioral components, even though Cattell (1959) has pointed out that basic personality traits seem to be normally distributed, while behavior styles may not be.

Those who study development in adults have tended to use the concept of types at a time when this concept has been employed relatively little in general research in personality. In fact, our most imaginative, comprehensive, and influential studies in aging use conceptions of type (Reichard, Livson & Petersen, 1962; Neugarten, 1964; Williams and Wirths, 1965). Indeed, their use as compared to the more familiar use of trait is seen as a virtue (Neugarten, 1963).

The use of personality typology in aging is perfectly legitimate and may be very useful. To some extent, however, the concept is not parsimonious. The commonality of change is stressed in Birren's definition of human development:

> Human development refers to the series of changes that individuals *characteristically* show as they progress in time towards maturity (growth and maturation) and through adult phases to old age (aging) [1964a, p. 2]. [Italics inserted.]

It is almost a contradiction of developmental thinking to show that there are different modes of reaction to a major event among different kinds of people, unless by doing so one can show that some characteristic variables differ in groups among their time of onset, rate of resolution, and interrelationships with other variables. At present, differences between types, rather than similarities among them, are exploited. If type styles were to show more clearly the *principles* which underlie elements involved in retirement, there would be no question of their special value. Unfortunately, the number of types is often so great that a parsimonious theory of variable change is too much to expect.

RETIREMENT AND DEVELOPMENT

In this long catalog of developmental conceptualizations, it will be seen that the developmental point of view assumes an immense burden of variables and their relationships. Zigler (1963) has been very critical of the developmental psychologists' preference for "grand designs" and for attempting to explain everything but explaining very little. He contends that developmental psychology is an extremely arbitrary subdivision of psychology, a suborientation of general behavior theory. It may be (and it is here explicitly stated to be so) that the greatest contribution of developmental thinking to general behavior theory is that it calls attention to "state" dimensions which *must* be covered in a theory or a model of whatever nature. Just as learning theory had tended to ignore individual differences, personality theory is extremely timid in making much sense out of age differences.

It is to be expected, and not necessarily with embarrassment, that other theories or modular systems might conceptualize retirement with more "bite" than developmental systems. Still, it is possible to make a series of statements from a developmental point of view which can be of conceptual value to the phenomenon of retirement.

1. *Retirement is not an event but a process.* Even a physiological phenomenon like sexual maturation has components which spread over many years. In the same way, elements of retirement may unfold over an extended period of time. Maddox (1966) cautions that to continue to speak of retirement as though it were a single experience with a predictable consequence serves no useful purpose. As in any process, the study of interrelationships between identifiable sequential elements during the process gives some cues leading toward a more fruitful study of relationships of that total process to others of the life span. Studies of the process of retirement from some preliminary point of involvement to some subsequent point of equilibrium seem a necessary step for understanding the phenomenon of retirement in the whole of the life pattern.

2. *Retirement is related to but not necessarily the focus for other developmental phenomena.* Perhaps because retirement is

often seen as a datable event when other variables related to development are less well-defined, this has had the effect of positing it as the central or salient event of the seventh decade of life. There is no questioning the fact that the circumstances in which work occurs give a focus to many life roles; it does not necessarily follow that leaving work means the alteration of such roles. Britton (1963) and Cumming and Henry (1961) point out that achievements early in one's career serve very effectively as potent social delineators in later life, even in the face of pervasive deterioration.

The centrality of work in most people's lives has often been declared (Friedman and Havighurst, 1954). Ansbacher and Ansbacher (1956) go so far as to insist that the position of aging people in our society is severely threatened because the value of work is almost decisive for the evolution of personality. Such a viewpoint is more often questioned recently. The cross-national studies of three industrial societies (Shanas *et al.*, 1968) show that work may not necessarily be central or dominant as a life variable, since British and Danish retirees have very different attitudes (at least in retrospect) toward work than those from the United States. Maddox (1966) points out that the notion that work is the primary source of meaning and satisfaction in life was once probably more true than in recent decades. Dubin (1956) revealed that only one in ten of industrial workers in his sample gave work as the central social interest of life.

There is a tendency to attribute to moments of crisis special gains or losses in some variable or another. Kagan and Moss (1960) have discussed the "sleeper effect," where correlations between events early in life and those at a point of maturity are higher than those close to the time of later testing. Depressive or facilitative factors are often ignored; a child who is countermanded by an over-possessive mother may seem to grow up overnight when he goes to college. Likewise, losses occurring in the months just past retirement may have been increasingly concealed or minimized by an understanding employer over many years. At any rate, important as retirement may be as a transitional circumstance in later life, it may be less important than aspects of family relationships, physical abilities, economic conditions, or a complex of self-regarding attitudes; retirement is greatly flavored by all of them.

3. *Retirement is related to earlier aspects of the life situation.* Since even well-designed longitudinal studies must make rigorous selection of kinds and frequencies of physical, social, and psychological measurements, we lack a systematic way of knowing the probable salient antecedents of important later phenomena of life. In general, efforts to show meaningful antecedents to later life phenomena are not very successful. For example, Lowenthal (1965) attempted to delineate antecedents to isolation and mental illness in later life (an area where conceptualization is much sharper than with retirement) and found that such obvious psychosocial factors as marital history, employment history, physical illness, or retirement bore little relationship to social withdrawal.

We need more research before we can feel confident about the kinds of experiences to which people have reacted as crises or at least as important periods requiring major reorientation in their lives. The life review, used as a research technique by Butler (1968), seems to be a promising avenue to this kind of needed information. Retirement crisis may be less severe or less meaningful psychologically than earlier crisis which may be more universal.

4. *The work life has its own developmental schedule which may not correspond to other developmental experiences of the life span.* There is a tendency to consider the total experience of work as a unity, whereas in actual fact, the person may have made entry into and out of many jobs, through several job skills on more than one occupational level. Techniques and privileges which are typical

of one stage of a job experience may be atypical for another
Some studies (Benge & Copell, 1947) show a curvilinear relation
ship, with early high morale, lower morale in the middle years
and rising morale later on. These cross-sectional studies tend to
ignore differences in time after entry into the system. The job
morale of older people has been attributed to the fact that person
with low morale tend to remove themselves as early as possible
from situations which they find distasteful (Davidson & Kunze
1965).

Studies of the occupational life cycle which show distinc
evolutional characteristics of the adult work experience (Hall
1948; Riesman & Roseborough, 1955; Becker & Carper, 1956
Becker & Strauss, 1956) have been given little attention i
considerations of retirement. For example, Reif and Strauss (1965
suggest that most research insitutions in their role as purchasers o
scientific talent have already made most critical decisions abou
the person even before he enters the work life; starting from hi
entrance to graduate school, it may take only six to eight years t
determine the kind or level of position the scientist is likely t
occupy for the rest of his active career. The situation is, of course
quite different in those occupations with a career ladder. Th
second career is a phenomenon of increasing frequency; the pat
of the two careers of a single individual are usually strikingl
different.

In sum, the work experience may be made up of man
discernible elements with developmental change in each of them
themselves paralleling a life with many continuities.

5. *Retirement is related to other problem-centered behavior an
follows sequential steps in resolution.* A tendency in research ove
time is to go from antecedent to consequent conditions, ofte
glossing over the very series of events which give the reason fo
study. In support of developmental theory, there is some evidenc
to suggest that units of process follow some general development
laws.

Reaction to stress is a component part of the whole life span. One aspect of stressful situations, often ignored, is that the severity of the stressor is probably less important to successful resolution than the clarity with which the stressor can be perceived. Breen (1963) has suggested that those situations which are clear-cut and recognizable are better adjusted to than those which may be more severe but are less easily identified.

The steps in adjustment to retirement have not been so carefully documented as those in bereavement, unemployment, or family illness. In studying family adjustment to alcoholism, for example, Jackson (1956) has identified these sequential steps:

1. Attempts to deny the problem
2. Attempts to eliminate the problem
3. Disorganization
4. Efforts at reorganizing the problem
5. Efforts to escape the problem
6. Reorganization without the spouse
7. Equilibrium

Hanson and Hill (1964) have compared institutional disasters with family (and, by extension, personal) crises. Disruption after institutional crisis is not prolonged; a general euphoria follows, with reorganization soon achieved. In family crises, however, the period of disorganization is longer; there is no overcompensation, and a much slower rise follows to eventual equilibrium.

There are probably meaningful antecedents to *each* sequential aspect of resolution in the retirement experience. Pre-retirement preparation should consider all of them, rather than preparing only for concerns which occur after cessation of active employment. The point of recognition that one will perhaps never achieve the confident dreams of young adulthood may be more difficult to anticipate, conceptualize, or prepare for than the point of departure from daily work.

6. *Retirement is still not a modal crisis in the later years.* Without minimizing the potential of retirement as a modern

societal problem and as an anxiety-producing experience for many persons, the tendency to consider retirement as the most important condition of the later adult years must be considered carefully. That it is an emergent pattern cannot be questioned (Donahue, Orback, & Pollak, 1960). Indeed, work can be terminated for so many reasons that a unitary meaning to retirement may be impossible to find. Many persons (perhaps one-third to one-half) leave work because of ill health (Palmore, 1964); many continue to work well into old age (Stein and Travis, 1961); and many, particularly women, do not technically enter or leave the work force at all. In these terms, retirement is not universal; indeed, even as a social problem it lies at the level of incidence of divorce, alcholism, or physical handicap; it certainly does not even approach universality.

Further, although retirement is of great significance in our society, whether it is the capstone, the basis, or just another event in the last decades of life needs to be answered. Neugarten and Garron (1959) found that forty-year-olds were just as concerned over increasing dependency and loss of income and health as those in their sixties. Williams and Wirths (1965) found the work life central to only one out of six within the sample they studied. To focus the development of so much of the life span upon one circumstance, no matter how well couched in descriptive terms, puts a heavy burden of explanation on a single conceptual unit.

7. *Substitution for values lost through retirement is not equivalent to growth precipitated by retirement.* An attractive and practical way to deal with the problems of retirement is to find reasonable substitutions for whatever satisfactions work and the world of work supplied. The meanings, values, and products of work might be varied, as Friedman and Havighurst (1954) and Levy (1963) have pointed out; but psychological, sociological, and economic equivalents might be found for any of them. Indeed, social planning has largely attempted to furnish these equivalents

in terms of income, social participation, and time ordering. Social planning has been less successful in finding substitutes for feelings of self-worth and creativity in post-retirement years (Morris and Binstock, 1966).

If, as some developmental theorists insist, irreversibility as a developmental phenomenon does exist and growth in personality can occur past retirement, a strategy which facilitates growth may be in order, rather than substitutions for deprivation. The circumstances of retirement may even be a signal for unveiling dissatisfactions which heretofore it had been possible to suppress or ignore, or alternatively, an opportunity to increase conflict by these disruptive behaviors so as to make life more exciting or involving. Buhler (1961) points out that homeostasis does not imply stresslessness but rather a satisfactory level of stress, or what von Bertalanffy (1968) has called equilibrium. Allport (1960) has made clear that human personality has a tendency to go beyond steady states and to strive for elaboration and growth even at the cost of considerable disequilibrium. A social strategy for increasing planfulness (Miller, Galanter & Pribaum, 1960) and for increasing the dimensions of experience (Fiske & Maddi, 1961) may provide more help over the long haul than concentrating on a system of substitution. If retirement is a signal for a new developmental stage, unique tasks with new organizations and perceptible characteristics must be devised.

Sorokin (1950) has indicted us all when he comments that the very issues regarded by men as involving their noblest sentiments and their highest values have hardly been touched by the scientific method. J. W. Gardner (1967) has commented:

> Unfortunately, the conception of individual fulfillment and lifelong learning which animates the commencement speaker finds no adequate reflection in our social institutions. For too long, we have paid pious lip service to the idea and trifled with it in practice [p. 136].

If it is possible to think of the personality as having the potential throughout life to emerge in new and different, though equally valued, ways of expressing itself, then we have the burden of identifying the means by which such change can be achieved. Society, and in particular its most articulate and powerful representatives, probably lack in belief that much growth can occur in older people. It will be difficult to cast aside the idea that the best we can do is to "rot and rot," particularly in the face of such noticeable deterioration of the biological organism. No contemporary course in preparation for retirement is likely to have useful material for coming to grips with the sense of self in the later years.

The frequently heard statement that preparation for retirement should begin early in life is only partly true, since possible growth of personality in the later years almost surely needs some trigger of reality to set it off. Retirement may be that impetus. The *technique* of continuing self-development through later years has no curriculum as yet; and it is sorely needed. And, just as very limited potential gains are worth trying rehabilitation, just so very limited growth can be prized. We must divest ourselves of our Olympian models and make ourselves sensitive to the possible growth in personality which is taking place around us.

8. *Retirement is a primitive social solution to developmental change.* While granting without question the point that retirement may often be premature and economically wasteful to society, the reality is that it is also an effort to fit the societal demands to changing capacities. Some important, irreversible, biological changes will certainly come to all persons at some period of late life. There will be behavioral changes related to them; it is difficult, however, to show clear-cut interrelationships, due to the imprecision of measurement of global behavior and to the complexity of the factors involved. Eventually, the decline in the capacities of the individual will make previous outputs more

difficult or even impossible. At some time it will be kinder to the person to accept the fact of lessened output or to make societal adjustment to no output at all.

In earlier times, when retirement was likely to be cataclysmic, work was terminated because of sickness or accident. Retirement is earlier and earlier, paradoxically, at a time when more persons are healthy at a given age. The fact is that retirement is a societal decision, serving an *anticipatory* function. Flexible retirement is seen even by its proponents as requiring a set of criteria relative to the ability to continue work (Mathiason, 1953) to achieve any administrative acceptance. Criteria which are objective are not available and subjective criteria represent only another societal decision.

It has already been stated that there is a developmental, not a totally idiosyncratic, nature to aging. It is not that events will occur at a certain time in life nor even that there is an invariant sequence of events occurring within a range of years. As Birren (1960) has suggested, an accumulation of events may be built up over time without the events being ordered in any regular sequence. In addition to a collection of physiological losses, a collection of psychological perceptions may emerge randomly and periodically through the life span. Perceptions of finitude, of a lessened attractiveness, of goals, and of personal productive potential as compared to those of younger colleagues may be as potent and legitimate reasons for retirement (or for adjustments which make continued work possible) as biological elements. The basic meaning of retirement is that of stepping back rather than stepping out.

It is probably a very different thing to quit work as a person still productive in a society which will not hire him, as the victim of an economy unable to hire him, or as a man too sick to work. Whether work is seen as man's eternal punishment or as the focus of the innate productivity of man, leisure life must be granted its good, too. Developmentally, some progress will have to be made toward analyzing the effects of stopping work at a time when potential remains to continue that work. A far larger range of variables than those used now would be in order. The work world is a jungle in its own right; an organization needs productivity and some individuals have it. Man energy and machine energy can be usefully studied as equivalents in many disciplines. When work can be considered as a prescription to achieve some good for mankind, we may assign persons to worker or non-worker states to achieve the highest good.

MARGARET CLARK, Ph.D.

Margaret Clark is Senior Research Anthropologist and Director of Subcultural Studies in the Adult Development Program of the Langley Porter Neuropsychiatric Institute, and Professor in Residence in the Department of Psychiatry of the University of California School of Medicine at San Francisco. She received her Ph.D. from the University of California, Berkeley, and subsequently worked on several applied anthropology research projects in medicine and public health.

Dr. Clark has conducted field research on American Indians and on Mexican-Americans in the United States and has been instrumental in promoting anthropological studies of adult life and aging patterns. She is the author of *Health in the Mexican-American Culture* (1959) and of "The Anthropology of Aging, a New Area of Studies of Culture and Personality" (1967), and co-author of *Culture and Aging* (1967) and of "Mexican-American Aged in San Francisco" (1969). Currently Dr. Clark is engaged in research on intergenerational conflict and aging adaptation in three subcultural communities of San Francisco.

4: AN ANTHROPOLOGICAL VIEW OF RETIREMENT

MARGARET CLARK

Although there have been increasing numbers of reports in the anthropological literature about the status and activities of older people in different societies around the world, there has been little examination of cultural factors influencing retirement from active work and the effects of this change on older people. Even a cursory examination of the ethnographic literature from non-Western societies provides at least a partial explanation of this dearth of attention. The fact is that retirement, in the form it has come to assume in our own culture, is a rarity in tribal and village societies, as well as among most culturally distinct ethnic enclaves within Western nations. Even within Euroamerican society, retirement as a social institution is a relatively new phenomenon. Historically, even within our own culture, formal retirement from office has been primarily a characteristic of bureaucracies—of complex organizations such as the military, the civil service, schools and universities, and large commercial and industrial enterprises—usually those whose employees are organized into labor unions.

With the growth of urban-industrial societies in many parts of the world, however, economic and demographic changes are taking place that are introducing the institution of retirement into more and more cultures. Although it is a task better undertaken by a historian than by an anthropologist to document these changes, there is an emergent need for some systematic conceptualization about cultural influences bearing on work and retirement, especially in comparative studies.

This chapter will first discuss the problem of arriving at a useful cross-cultural definition of work and retirement and some of the characteristics of each of them that can be seen to vary from one society to another. Second, the chapter will describe differences in content and emphasis of social anthropology and psychological anthropology, suggesting ways in which each of these two approaches to cultural data may contribute to work and retirement studies. Finally, it will present a behavioral model developed within the field of psychological anthropology and demonstrate how such a model may assist students of retirement in developing systematic cross-cultural investigations.

THE PROBLEM OF DEFINITION

In some sense it is almost impossible to define retirement without first defining work. That is, retirement implies the absence rather than the presence of certain activities. In order to designate an individual as retired, then, we must know that the activities he is now engaged in are not defined in his society as work, at least for that particular person. In a society such as ours, distinctions become complex when we look at the cabinet maker who retires and takes up golf as a hobby, compared with the golf pro who retires and takes up woodworking as a hobby. There is nothing inherent in either of these two activities *per se* that leads us to define one clearly as work and the other as non-work or play. In no society is there a true dichotomy between work and play in terms of the nature of the activities involved. The major characteristic shared by the professional cabinet maker and the professional golfer is that both receive money for their "work" based on the rationale that each is performing a valuable social function, whereas their "play" during retirement is regarded as amateur activity, pursued for its own sake and the pleasure it provides the player, rather than as a service to society.

Clearly, then, the nature of the activities an individual engages in is not a useful distinction between work and non-work. Neither is the payment of money or other remuneration for services a useful cross-cultural criterion—for the worker in a subsistence economy may have no services to render beyond his own economic unit, nor a surplus of produce to trade or sell to others. Similarly, productivity does not distinguish between work and non-work; much activity in a complex society produces no goods or wealth. A philanthropist may work hard in giving away to other members of his society goods or wealth he has previously accumulated. The priest, the judge, the shaman, the politician, the teacher—none of these is involved directly in the production of goods or wealth, but certainly all of them are defined as working members of their respective societies.

Although in many of its dimensions work must be defined in culturally specific terms, two characteristics of work do seem to be pan-cultural: (1) work provides an ascribed status position and its accompanying role within the society; and (2) work yields social rewards in terms of remuneration—in money, goods, services, power, or prestige. Characteristics that differ dramatically from one society to another include the socially acceptable reasons for termination of work, the magnitude and direction of status change at the point of retirement, and the discrepancies in social and economic rewards available to worker and non-worker.

Cessation of work in most preliterate societies occurs only when the individual, regardless of age, has lost his physical or mental ability to engage in socially useful activities or is so defined by his culture. Prior to that time (as during senescence) the usual pattern of change in work behavior is simply a shift from one form of employment to another. In our society we would call this the notion of the "second career." In more complex cultures, and particularly in those of urban-industrial societies, we find many elders who stop engaging in socially useful activity for reasons other than loss of health or ability. This type of retirement—that of the "healthy aged"—is not limited to industrialized nations. (Pre-industrial Japan and India are two exceptions.) However, within the Western world, as a historical product of urban-industrial life, retirement of "healthy aged" is becoming more and more a modal pattern.

For the purposes of this paper, then, retirement is defined as the termination of gainful work—that is, of activities one of whose aims is that of obtaining wealth, profit, or other social rewards. This definition explicitly excludes the notion of the second career. The latter does not seem to have the same implications for society and for the individual that retirement has, although the effects of an occupational change of this sort are sometimes quite marked.

Defined in this way, retirement can be examined in any culture (1) in terms of its history, form, function, and meaning as a social *institution*; and (2) as a set of culturally derived *personal meanings* to the individual within a society. The concepts and methods of social anthropology are well suited to the first of these areas and those of psychological anthropology to studies of the second.

THE ANTHROPOLOGY OF RETIREMENT: SOCIAL AND PSYCHOLOGICAL APPROACHES

There are two discrete bodies of anthropological theory that are germane to the phenomenon of retirement of older people from gainful employment and the variable character of that phenomenon in different societies. One of these is the perspective of social anthropology and culture history, and the other is that of psychological anthropology or culture-personality studies. This chapter is concerned primarily with the second of these approaches, although it will deal briefly with the other perspective.

Traditional cultural anthropology has always had as one of its major tasks the description of typical or modal ways of life of diverse peoples of the world. The goal of the field ethnographer has been to record and analyze a range of observed behavior among members of a society and to determine the common behaviors learned and shared by all or by identifiable subgroups of the individuals of that society. The resulting modalities or central tendencies have been called the patterns, themes, or institutions of a culture. These have been viewed as having an objective reality apart from the individual behavior from which they are abstracted. Thus Kroeber (1948) wrote of the "superorganic" and the "superindividual" nature of culture. His view was that the essential processes of culture, and the institutions and practices of ideas constituting it, have a persistence and can be conceived as going on outside the societies that support them. He further stated that the manifestations of culture were best conceived in relation to each other rather than in relation to individual behavior or personality.

Leslie White has carried the notion of the "superindividual" in culture still further, preferring the term "culturology" to that of "anthropology" on the ground that what he is concerned about (and, by implication, what other anthropologists *should* be concerned about) is the science of culture, which is more appropriately approached from the standpoint of history than from that of personality or individual behavior. His position is that the individual is neither the creator nor determinant of culture, but merely a "catalyst and a vehicle of expression" (1949, p. 75).

With the growth of the field of psychological anthropology, the more traditional approaches of historical ethnology were found to be inadequate for the study of certain classes of problems. Hallowell (1955) was an early spokesman for this point of view. He questioned the notion that a social or cultural environment could be defined in terms of some "objective" reality external to the individuals such properties or structures are said to environ. "Without further analysis it is implied . . . that this environment, as described by some objective observer, is the actual environment to which the individual responds. . . . Presented to us in this form, these cultural data do not easily permit us to apprehend, in an integral fashion, the most significant and meaningful aspects of the world of the individual as experienced by him and in terms of which he thinks, is motivated to act, and satisfies his needs" (pp. 87-88).

A number of anthropologists during the 1950's, perhaps spurred by social psychologists such as Henry Murray, developed this idea further. For example, Spiro (1951) concluded that the concepts of culture and personality represented a false dichotomy. While from a genetic point of view this is surely so, the theoretical constructs most useful in the analysis of cultural dynamics are inappropriate and inadequate in attempts to describe the components of interaction between the individual and his environment. The converse, however, is probably *not* true, despite the protests of Kroeber and White. Culture theory rests on generic concepts (such as style, innovation, diffusion, syncretism, and configuration). While culture-personality studies cannot be *based* on such holistic concepts—since the phenomena for analysis in the latter are on a lower level of abstraction—the *findings* of culture-personality studies can be, and have been, used in cross-cultural comparisons which aid in the development of broad culture theory.

The utility of the data of psychological anthropology in the development of culture theory should come as no surprise to general anthropologists. They are familiar with the fact that anthropology, at least in the American school of Boas and his students, has been a largely inductive science. Kroeber himself, drawing upon meticulously garnered data from folklore, linguistics, kinship, religion, and technology, derived the theory expounded in his *Configurations of Culture Growth* (1944) by inductive methods. There is no apparent logical reason why data from psychological anthropology should not ultimately be put to similar use. To this end, however, the field requires theoreticians with sufficient knowledge and interest to deal with perceptual, cognitive, and affective categories of data as imaginatively as in the past they have contemplated potsherds, the concept of zero, the patrilineal clan, and the glottal stop.

I am not suggesting here that the origins of cultural forms and social institutions can be discovered by an examination of psychological data. Bruner (1964) has stated this problem quite clearly:

> . . . (S)ome social and cultural anthropologists . . . say that anthropologists should not be concerned with either psychology, personality, or individuals, even in a cross-cultural framework. They fear that the psychological anthropologist will offer naive explanations of social institutions and events in terms of individual motivation—for example, that war is caused by man's aggressive instinct—without reference to the complex historical, political, and economic factors which precipitate warfare in any given instance. The modern student of culture and personality, on the other hand, well aware of the excesses of his predecessors and of the cautions of his critics, contends that the psychological dimension is an essential component of human existence, and further, that adequate understanding of relationships among men or their cultural institutions must include statements about what goes on within an individual's mind—about what he thinks and feels—with due attention to irrational unconscious processes as well as to the rational conscious ones. It is the acknowledgment of the importance of unconscious and cognitive processes which characterizes culture and personality research [pp. 71-72].

Although most of the early work in culture and personality (as in the early writings of Sapir, Benedict, and Mead) was of the broad configurational type that has been so roundly criticized by subsequent writers, there has been a trend in anthropology within the past decade towards collection of more detailed and comparable phenomenological data. This sphere of inquiry has been variously labeled "world view," "the behavioral environment," "existential value-orientations," "ethnoscience," and "subjective culture." Whatever the designation given to the dimensions of this conceptual nexus between personality and culture, it is within this framework that we must examine the cultural patterning of *meaning*. And it is from studies of meaning that anthropology can contribute most significantly to an understanding of phenomena such as work and retirement as they relate to individual functioning.

At this point in time, however, the phenomenological approach in anthropology is just beginning to yield systematic studies. Ultimately we will no doubt have available to us theoretical models which will enable us to make comparable studies of the meaning of work and retirement, as of other social phenomena. Later in this paper I will suggest some phenomenological categories that seem to me to be most promising in such investigations. Until now, however, we have had to rely largely on the data and constructs of social anthropology for what knowledge we have of work and retirement in various cultures.

The Social Anthropological Approach to Work and Retirement

Social anthropology (which might as appropriately be called comparative sociology) deals with variations in the social substructures of human groups, their development, form, function, and interactions. Although the following list is not meant to be exhaustive, there are several major differentials in social organization that seem to bear directly on considerations of work and retirement. These are: (1) the size and composition of the economic unit within a society, and the relationship of that unit to the economic base of the group being studied; (2) the presence of formal age grades in the culture, with an accompanying division of labor; (3) residence patterns; (4) sex differences; (5) the concept of "career" as an inherent part of the social identity of the individual and the relation between occupation and prestige within the culture; and (6) kinds of property rights and rules of inheritance.

Looking first at the nature of *the economic unit* within a society, we find that in a subsistence or semi-subsistence economy, the size of the economic unit is fairly large—certainly larger than the nuclear family—and is usually based upon an extended kinship group. In such a society, produce or profit accrues to the whole economic unit, and the labor involved is distributed among its members. The second career, which I have mentioned above, is the modal pattern of work change among healthy aged throughout most tribal and peasant societies (Simmons, 1945). It ordinarily consists of the older person's relinquishing a central role in the main productive activities of the society and substituting supportive or ancillary activities. As a member of the economic unit, the older person continues to receive subsistence, but ordinarily the relative amount of profit acquired or produce received by him depends less upon the kind or extent of labor he performs than it does upon the culturally patterned prerogatives of old age. In subsistence or semi-subsistence economies, then, work is available for all reasonably healthy adults. The anthropological literature is full of references to such work. Holmberg (1961), for example, reported: "Retirement is a word unknown to the peasants of the Andes. Healthy people continue to labor, although in reduced form, just as long as they are physically able to do so. Appropriate to the older members of the household are such tasks as weeding the fields near the house, scaring the birds away from the fields when the crops are maturing, minding the house when the younger members of the household are away, tending distant fields or herding animals or going away on a trading expedition . . . . Often an aging couple will pass their fields to their sons and daughters, reserving a right to a share of the crop for their own subsistence and the maintenance of an independent household" (p. 89).

To a limited extent, the second career is found within contemporary industrial societies as well. In Western societies this shift usually carries with it some form of remuneration, but ordinarily such earnings are smaller than those formerly acquired during a fully productive adult career. For example, we see the retired policeman working, at a lower wage, as a private night watchman; the former schoolteacher as a part-time insurance salesman; the former steelworker as a shop janitor; the former contractor as an apartment house manager; the emeritus professor as a part-time consultant. The second career, however, is not a modal pattern in American life; such jobs are simply not available in sufficient numbers to supply gainful employment to all healthy Americans of more advanced age who want to work. In an economy based on wage labor, there is greater competition for employment. In such circumstances, the older individual today finds himself competing with young apprentices, unskilled adults, or the physically handicapped for jobs requiring little physical strength and little specific experience.

The effects on the retirement status of the elderly of conversion from a subsistence to a cash economy seem to be variable, even within a single society. Hughes (1961), for example, writing of the St. Lawrence Island Eskimos, reports: "With the greatly increased exposure to the culture of the Alaskan mainland over the past twenty years, some serious inroads are being made into the position of middle-aged and elderly people. . . . Respect for age is lessening with the 'emancipation' of the young through education and through increased job opportunities (or at least job aspirations) which do not require tutelage from one's elders in the ways of animals and ice. . . . However, the old people maintain their usefulness to their village and especially to their families" (p. 95). The author cites a new development which makes it additionally profitable to be old and nominally retired in this society: Many elderly Eskimos are now eligible to receive monthly old age assistance payments. In a poor society in the process of change from subsistence to a cash money system, these monthly checks give the aged a great deal of power and prestige within their family units.

A second factor that appears to have a definite relationship to the employment of older people—at least in primitive societies—is that of *age-grading*. Simmons (1945) found, in a survey of tribal societies, a positive correlation between the existence of age-grades and the continuation in office of aged men. The association was most marked in stable agricultural societies having well-organized government facilities, irrespective of the system of family organization. It is important to realize, however, that in the non-industrial societies studied by Simmons, relatively few tribesmen lived long enough to become "elders," and it was therefore an easy matter to find positions for them in political, religious, or ceremonial offices.

In urban-industrial societies, however, there is a very different situation, even though there may be an emergent age-grade system. There has been a phenomenal increase in the number of older persons in Western society. In 1830, only one American out of 25 was 60 years of age or older; in 1960, one out of eight. To be sure, there are still occupations for a minority of the aged in any society. Our culture continues to employ a sprinkling of elder statesmen, mature artists and writers, wise judges, and emeritus professors. These are the people in our society who correspond to the "village elders" of simpler societies. The great bulk of the aged, however, are excluded from formal occupational roles of any kind in Western urban societies.

The consequences of retirement in a particular culture may be mitigated by the assignment of even non-occupational roles specifically to the aged. The availability of such activities in a culture has been found to provide reasonably satisfying roles for the elderly, enhance morale, and heighten prestige (Simmons, 1945). These beneficial effects are present even when the activity involved serves mainly a personal rather than a social function. For example, Rustom (1961) has described the importance of ceremonial and religious observances for the aged in Burma. He points out that during the last stage of life, men and women both retire from economic activity and are expected to devote themselves to religious duties, including the performance of good deeds, observance of holy day feasts, and meditation. It is expected that the aged will be disinterested in worldly affairs, be sustained by their families and "eat in tranquility." Barring ill health or senility, this is generally regarded as an extremely happy period of life, during which the individual does not lose influence within the family or community, but is relieved of economic responsibilities.

There is some evidence to suggest that the growth of a consumer-oriented leisure class among American aged may have some functions in our society that religious, political, or other non-economic activities have for elders in non-industrial societies. Some current research on American retirement communities suggests that, at least for some members of certain social class groups in the United States, leisure activities within age-segregated communities may serve a useful function in maintenance of morale and social involvement of the elderly (Wood & Bultena, 1969).

The retirement community phenomenon suggests another social variable that may influence the consequences of retirement in various societies, that of *residence patterns*. Simmons (1945) demonstrated that, at least in preliterate societies, the extended family residence provides an opportunity for the aged to perform auxiliary economic roles, and these are shown to be positively correlated with prestige of elders, particularly among women. Since a great deal of research has been done by gerontologists on the social and psychological consequences of varying residence patterns, I mention it here only to suggest that cross-cultural investigations might add to our knowledge in this area.

Sex differences in reactions to retirement is another area that could be studied profitably by social anthropologists. We know that the nature and meaning of work and retirement in most societies vary enormously with the sex of the individual. Until recent decades in the United States, relatively few women have been employed outside the home. The assignment of work within the home to women has led to a situation much like that of the elderly in general in preliterate societies, where cessation of labor generally results only from loss of ability to perform, and is therefore more rational and acceptable to the aged individual than is forced or arbitrary retirement. Now, however, with the entrance of more women into the work force outside of the home, sex differences in attitudes toward work and retirement may begin to fade. Some research suggests that work may be becoming more important to women now, and retirement therefore more stressful. In fact, Lowenthal, Berkman, and Associates (1967) found that retired women in their San Francisco sample were more likely to be psychiatrically impaired than were retired men. Much more research is needed on sex roles in various cultures, the meaning of work, and the consequences of retirement.

The relationship between *work and prestige* within a culture is a very potent determinant of the nature of retirement. We know, from students of Western cultures—particularly in the middle classes of Western Europe and the United States—that almost nowhere else has there been such an elaboration of the work morality. Although I will have more to say about this in subsequent pages, it is worth alluding to here as well.

It is important to remember that most American social scientists are themselves products of the American middle class (or of laboring or mercantile families of Western and Central Europe). We have acquired a strong belief in the value of work from our traditions, and it is often difficult for us to perceive that this value may not be shared by people from other backgrounds. Yet, even as recently as 50 years ago, popular British novels were full of descriptions of the *loss* of prestige that a family of the landed gentry or minor nobility suffered if one of its members were forced to take employment or "go into trade." The "nobility of labor" is a concept that is quite recent in Western civilization. In cultures in which prestige is ascriptive rather than achieved, individual status is unrelated to work. A man is honored for who he is, not for what he does—in very general terms. Only in societies where work has moral and ethical value attached to it is retirement such a demeaning event.

Many other social factors, such as *rules of inheritance and control of property*, likely result in cultural variation in attitudes towards retirement. A classic example of this was found among certain groups of the Irish peasantry in the first third of this century. In that society, quite elderly farmers continued to control property and engage in active farming until they themselves decided to pass title to their land on to their sons (Arensberg, 1937).

A great deal more research by social anthropologists is needed if we are to have reliable information on the correlates of retirement and its meaning in various cultures. As other anthropologists have remarked, ethnographic data on the aged are sparse, in part due to lack of interest on the part of ethnographers and in part to the fact that non-industrialized societies rarely have very many really aged members (Arth, 1968). We know something about the roles and status of the aged in varying cultures, but of the realm of attitudes and concerning the aged retired, we have virtually no information. It is this area that I will turn to now.

The Approach of Psychological Anthropology to Work and Retirement

Information on the social anthropology of aging is very sparse indeed. The probable reasons for this paucity of data have been discussed elsewhere (Clark, 1967). We have perhaps even less information on the aged and the aging process from students of psychological anthropology. Simmons (1945) extracted from the ethnographic literature available 25 years ago at least some data on the major sociocultural correlates of the status of elders in primitive societies. His unparalleled and valuable work, however, did not deal at all with the phenomenology of aging, that is, with the culturally patterned content of perceptions, beliefs, attitudes, or sentiments of older people in various societies. These data simply do not exist in the ethnographic record in any systematic way. All that can be done here, therefore, is to suggest categories of problems which seem to require cross-cultural investigation if we are to develop an anthropological theory of the meaning of work and retirement.

The model presented here is a slight modification of an analytic system devised by Hallowell (1955) for the explication of what he called "the behavioral environment of the self." In introducing the model, he states that the individual in human societies must be provided with certain basic orientations in order to act intelligibly in a world that he can apprehend. Hallowell calls these basic orientations collectively the "behavioral environment of the self in any culture," a concept that enables the observer to "appraise and reorder culturally given data to bring into focus the actual structure of the psychological field of the individual" (pp. 88-89). In other words, the individual learns through the vehicle of culture to perceive and react to the world around him in terms of that culture's definitions of the nature of reality. Hallowell lists some of the major dimensions of culturally defined reality, or "common instrumental functions" which every culture provides its members, as these: (1) self-orientation; (2) object-orientation; (3) spatio-temporal orientation; (4) motivational orientation; (5) normative orientation.

In this discussion, spatial and temporal orientions will be discussed separately, since, with regard to aging, work, and retirement, they seem to operate as discrete factors. Within each of these areas, the role of work and the impact of work-loss or retirement as cultural variables will be discussed.

Self-orientation

As Hsu (1961) has remarked, "personality" is differently conceived and defined by psychological anthropologists and psychologists. He suggests that while the emphasis by psychologists is placed on the individual and the idiosyncratic, the anthropologist looks for the shared characteristics of the psychic processes of members of a group or subgroup. Kaplan (1968), in a general and excellent discussion of definitional problems in culture-personality studies, comments on this distinction, but makes a case for the utility of data on both "core" and "social" personality in cross-cultural studies. I agree with Kaplan that certainly both orders of personality characteristics may show cross-cultural variability. However, it seems to me that most anthropologists, lacking intensive training in clinical methods, would be on more familiar ground if they followed Hsu's advice. In this discussion, then, I will not deal with individual variability within cultures, but with shared group characteristics.

While there is good evidence that the phenomenal self—the self-image—is overwhelmingly a product of culture, there is little specific information on the role that work and the work-concept have in the constitution of personal identity. I am not speaking here of the extent to which work is *valued* by members of one society compared with another, but of the degree to which, in a given culture, an individual's very ability to conceive of himself as a meaningful entity is based on his past, present, or future occupational role.

Psychoanalysts have consistently stressed the importance of work in personality integration. Freud himself wrote that "Laying stress upon importance of work has a greater effect than any other technique of living in the direction of binding the individual more closely to reality" (1930, p. 21, fn.). Erikson, in his work on stages of psychosexual development, has postulated that industry and work identification are the critical factors in ego development during adolescence and young adulthood (1960).

Anthropological work on this problem seems quite appropriate. For example, would we find a less fragile sense of self among children and adolescents born into a culture like that of traditional Hindu society with its hereditary occupational castes, in which the child learns in the first few years of life that he is a Jat, a Chamar, or a Brahmin; and that he and his ancestors and his descendents all have the same work-identity and the same place in the total scheme of things? Would such a person be less likely to undergo an identity crisis in adolescence, such as is so commonly reported in our own society? Would resolution of such crises, even if they did occur, be more predictable than in our society?

It is difficult to discuss self-orientation without making reference to the relationship of the self to others. Although the next topic is a discussion of object-orientation, let me simply say here that the human individual grows up in a world of linguistically created objects (including other people) and comes to define himself in relationship to them. Self-perception is first predicated on kinship, and the child learns to respond categorically in the human environment on the basis of culturally defined status and role. Some anthropologists have postulated that identity is inseparable from the roles one is assigned. The individual continually asks his environment for a definition of his own nature. He carefully examines the behavior of others towards him in order to be convinced of who he is. As Becker (1962) has put it: "The child derives his identity from a social environment. The social environment remains *to his death* the only source for validating that identity" (p. 85, italics added).

While we know that development of the work role is important in the constitution of the self-perception in adolescence and young adulthood, we need cross-cultural data on the extent to which there are identity problems associated with retirement and loss of the work role in later life. From some of our own previous research (Clark and Anderson, 1967), we discovered numerous elderly subjects in San Francisco whose retirement from productive work resulted in a weakened self-concept. As we observed, many of these people seem to be in mourning, sometimes unable to recover from the loss of employment and the significant activity accompanying it and, most poignantly, sometimes inconsolable over the partial death of something within themselves. One subject said, "I was a different person when I was 50. My energy was different. I wanted to work and had the ability to." His only response to the question on current self-image was: "Now I'm a pensioner." Sometimes the self cannot be perceived as existing outside of an occupational role: the image of the working self is vital; the unemployed self has a moribund quality. One subject could not get beyond this description of himself: "I was a waiter *in my life*." By clear implication his life is no more.

In other industrial societies, like those of Japan and other Asian nations, there is also retirement as we have defined it in this paper. Yet we have little data concerning the adequacy of cultural provisions in those societies for a continued self-orientation in the non-working years.

Object-orientation

In Hallowell's scheme for the components of the behavioral environment, the category of object-orientation is one of the broadest and most inclusive. He uses the term to specify the orientation of the self to a diversified world of objects—both person-objects and thing-objects—which are "discriminated, classified, and conceptualized with respect to attributes which are culturally constituted and symbolically mediated through language" (p. 92).

The primary task of culture in this area is to provide the individual, by means of cultural (linguistic) taxonomies, with an ordered, predictable world in which the (anxiety-prone) individual is firmly oriented" (p. 84). The proposition that "objective reality" for the individual is not merely reflected in but actually determined by linguistic structure is the basis of what has been called the "Sapir-Whorf hypothesis." The dominant thought was expressed by Sapir 20 years ago in one of his essays on language: "Human beings do not live in the objective world alone, nor alone in the world of social activity as ordinarily understood, but are very much at the mercy of the particular language which has become the medium of expression for their society. It is quite an illusion to imagine that one adjusts to reality essentially without the use of language. The fact of the matter is the 'real world' is to a large extent unconsciously built up on the language habits of the group" (in Mandelbaum, 1949, p. 13). Whorf (in Carroll, 1956) greatly expanded this original pronouncement, concluding that "facts" said to be perceived are a function of the language in which they are expressed, and that the "nature of the universe" is a function of the language in which it is stated (see Black, 1968).

Hallowell resists the temptation to subdivide this category of orientation to objects according to polarities such as tangible-intangible, animate-inanimate, human-nonhuman, or natural-supernatural. Such polarities, he claims, are themselves cultural conventions of the observer, and the metaphysical propositions upon which they are based are implicit or explicit dogmas regarding the boundaries of reality. These dogmas may not be applicable in a culture very different from that of the observer. In other words, the "social" relations of the self may be far more inclusive in one society than ordinarily conceived by members of a different culture. The self in its relations with other selves may transcend the boundaries of social life as "objectively" defined. As Hallowell says, "In some cultures the social orientation of the self may be so constituted that relations with deceased ancestors, or other-than-human selves become much more crucial for an understanding of the most vital needs and goals of the individual than do interpersonal relations with other human beings" (p. 92).

It may be in some societies (and even among certain religious subgroups within Euroamerican cultures) that perceived relationships with the "supernatural" world—with deities or spirits of the departed—may provide meaningful and rich areas of relatedness that sustain aging individuals as they begin to lose other roles such as those of kinship and work. We know very little about the inner psychic life of devoutly religious older people, even in our own society. Many social scientists, as members of secular subgroups, may fail to perceive the "reality" of an individual's relationship to the supernatural and underestimate its importance. Such subgroup differences raise the larger issue of generational differences in object-orientation or cognitive mapping.

Although whole generations of psychologists have worked on the problem of cognition, anthropologists seem to have discovered the concept only within recent years. Cognitive mapping (or so-called "ethnoscientific" investigation) is now becoming a fashionable pursuit among anthropologists of various persuasions. Although these studies are too nascent to have yielded much useful theory for the culture-personality field, it is worth mentioning that cross-cultural studies of native information systems may ultimately add to our knowledge of the behavioral environment of the self.

Kastenbaum and Cameron (1969) have recently reported some research which indicates that cognitive mastery becomes an increasingly important determinant of decisions to act as age increases. This finding suggests an additional problem that retirement from active work may pose in individual adjustment, and how this problem may vary from culture to culture. In a simple, fairly homogeneous society where the aged continue to work and be integrated in some fashion into the larger society, there is likely to be a greater similarity of object-orientation and of "cognitive maps" for young and old. However, in a culture like ours, which is characterized not only by withdrawal of the aged from the world of work, but also by rapid culture change and the obsolescence of former information systems, the cognitive orientations of young and old may vary dramatically. McLuhan (1964) has suggested this in his *Understanding Media*, although he seems to think that universal communications systems will integrate rather than isolate people from each other. This is an area, it seems to me, where cross-cultural research could formulate and explore some new and significant problems, provided data are collected from subjects of various ages, and age-group and generational comparisons are drawn.

Let me return now to a discussion of the social component of the object-orientation sphere. The relationship of work and retirement to social orientations has been the focus of a great deal of research in social gerontology. Research has shown that occupational role and its concommitant status underly a large segment of the social identity of the individual. Work is a vital part of much of social life. It provides the individual with a reference group, it reinforces kinship obligations and expectations, it provides a shared frame of reference with respect to action goals, and it helps institute communication patterns.

There is probably an enormous cross-cultural variability in the relative weight of work and the work role in the quality of social relationships, but this problem has received virtually no anthropological attention. There is clinical evidence, however, that the psychosocial emphasis on work in American society is intense. For example, Deutscher (1968), a psychoanalytically trained psychologist, has recently reported: "My interest in the significance of work in adult life began with the realization that three of every four patients I see make it the focus of their need for therapy. They report unhappiness and suffering from their lack of work effectiveness" (p. 882). He states his main thesis as follows: "Involvement with meaningful work helps to establish and maintain adult life in adult form. It is not that one works when one is an adult—but that working, for an adult, maintains his personality structure with its capacity for intimacy, relatedness, productivity, and participation in community life and concerns . . . . Work has social reality; the work a man does gives him a contributing place in his community, and defines his sense of status and prestige. Through his occupation, man makes a bridge between his family and the outside world. And his work status shapes his actions as the head of the household within the family" (p. 883). Whether there is as much pathology associated with work problems in non-industrial societies is a matter that has received no anthropological attention, but I would speculate that there is considerable cross-cultural variability in this matter.

Before leaving the topic of object-orientation as a category for research in culture-personality studies, let me emphasize that cultures determine also the patterns of an individual's relationship to the world of artifacts, tools, animals, food, land, property and other wealth, as well as persons in the supernatural world (gods, culture-heroes, ancestors, and spirits). The retirement transition may represent marked changes in the individual's access to these and in the nature of his behavior towards them. Thus, in some cultures, the social interaction patterns predicated upon the work role may give way to and be replaced by a manipulation of artifacts, closer interaction with animals, or greater preoccupation with food, property, or other wealth. The stereotypes of the miserly recluse and the late-blooming handyman and inventor are well-known figures in American culture. As reported above, the retired in some Buddhist traditions—like the Burmese—are expected to relate more and more to the spirit world and gradually relinquish their concern with the realm of living people and tangible objects. The Hindu cultural ideal for the third stage of life, as set forth in the Asrama system, is Retired Life in the Forest: "According to (the laws of) Manu, 'When a householder's hair turns white, and he sees his sons' sons, he should become a hermit, either leaving his wife to the care of his children, or taking her to the forest with him'... thus entering the third stage, ... (Vanaprastha), during which the individual prepares to renounce completely all worldly relations. In practice, an elder of the family may retire to a separate room in the house, spending his time in religious study and meditation. When spiritually prepared, he enters the fourth stage, that of Complete Renouncement of worldly attachments (Sannyasa). It is in this stage that he becomes a wandering religious mendicant" (Rowe, 1961, p. 104). By contrast, elders in societies such as the African gerontocracies become increasingly socially-oriented with age, occupying more and more significant social, political, and economic roles. The effects of these differences in object-orientation on the self-system in old age are only beginning to be described by anthropologists.

Spatial orientation

The relationship of animal behavior to the uses of space has received revived attention with the publication in recent years of

The Territorial Imperative (Ardrey, 1966). The use and conceptualization of space, however, has unique significance for the
human animal. Hallowell (1955) has asserted that "Spatially, like
temporally, coordinated patterns of behavior are basic to the
personal adjustment of all human beings .... Without the capacity
for space perception, spatial orientation and the manipulation of
spatial concepts, the human being would be incapable of effective
locomotion, to say nothing of being unable to coordinate other
aspects of his behavior with that of his fellows in a common social
life .... (W)e know that variations occur, between one culture and
another, with respect to the selective emphasis given to the spatial
relations and attributes of things, the degree of refinement that
occurs in the concepts employed, and the reference points that are
selected for spatial orientation" (p. 184).

As early a writer as Poincaré claimed that the concept of space
can be understood only as a function of objects and all their
relations, and that space cannot be perceived independent of
objects. Later psychologists have emphasized that there is not a
specialized "spatial sense," but that space perception, by its very
nature, is intersensory; it requires the interactions of several sense
modalities, including vision, tactual, and kinesthetic components.*

We know almost nothing about cross-cultural variations in the
perceptions and utilization of space. The recent development of
the field of proxemics (Hall, 1963) has concentrated almost
exclusively on variations in social space and interaction patterns.

---

*That cultures vary in conceptions of space and distance was made clear
to me a few years ago when I accompanied an old Navajo medicine man on
a trek to gather jimson weed for a curing ceremony. The place was "not
far," I was assured. After a two-hour hike across rugged reservation terrain
(which included climbing a bluff and fording a stream), we finally reached
the spot which was "not far." Yet, one of my elderly subjects in San
Francisco went to the considerable trouble of moving her residence because
her first apartment had been "so far" from the neighborhood grocery store
five blocks away. Both of these elderly people were in good health and had
no locomotor difficulties.

Some questions that seem to call for research involve changes in territoriality and in kinesic patterns through the life span. We suspect, although there is no systematic data on this point, that work is primarily instrumental in the development of important motor habits that become largely automatic with practice. Great distress may accompany disruptions of spatial relationships that implement these motor habits. If the hammer in the workshop, the broom in the closet, the salt box in the kitchen, or the vital reference book on the study shelf are "misplaced," conscious effort and energy must be expended to locate them, and largely unconscious motor habits are disrupted. Work may also determine the transportation patterns (and problems) characteristic of a particular milieu. And, in turn, ease or difficulty in transportation of self and goods may influence self-awareness in relation to the overall social environment. While architects, city planners, and students of urban development have done some research on personal and social space within Western urban societies, we need more cross-cultural data in this area.

Impressionistically, at least, we know that spatial relations and territoriality change with retirement in our own culture. When activity patterns change drastically (with shifts in transportation modes habitually used, routes used in getting to markets and public places, and perhaps changes in living quarters) following retirement, more conscious effort must be exerted in order to avoid accidents and perform self-maintenance tasks. I suspect that spatial reorientation is harder for the older individual to effect than it is for a younger person, especially in the face of sensory and memory decrements. There is some evidence that, among the aged, well-established motor patterns often are used to compensate for decline of conscious memory in physical activity. None of these problems has received any cross-cultural attention—and very little even in our own society.

Temporal orientation

Time orientation, as Florence Kluckhohn (1950) has demonstrated, is one of the fundamental variables in cultural definitions of reality. The relationship of time and self "is one of the necessary conditions required if any sense of *self-continuity* is to become salient. Human beings maintain awareness of self-continuity and personal identity in time through the recall of past experiences that are identified with the self-image" (Hallowell, 1955, p. 94). This psychodynamic imperative has been the subject of much writing in psychoanalysis and ego psychology and has been summarized by Becker (1962): "Self-esteem . . . is an aspect of self-consciousness that permits the self to handle not only present anxieties *but past and future ones as well*. It had to come into being as a component of action, because the ego binds time and fixes the pronominal animal in a world that can be remembered and anticipated. As soon as the individual can project himself into a past and a future, a new problem is posed. The ego is tasked to avoid anxiety *at the imaginary point in space-time*, and not only in the present . . . . A Hindu may drag an untouchable body uncomplainingly through life, with the precious inner conviction that in a future incarnation his true value will be rewarded" (p. 81).

The culturally constituted variations in the relative value placed on past, present, and future are among the best-known and studied concepts in cross-cultural phenomenology. Western civilization, and most especially American culture, has reified and elaborated the concept of time to an unparalleled degree. I will not elaborate here on the significance of this fact of culture history for the aged, since I have discussed it in considerable detail elsewhere (Clark and Anderson, 1967). Let me simply summarize by saying that, in a study of the temporal dimension of self-concept, a present-orientation seemed to have more positive adaptive value for a sample of aged subjects studied in San Francisco than did an emphasis on either past or future projections of the self. This finding held even in the face of a reported modality of future-orientation among younger Americans studied by Kluckhohn and Strodtbeck (1961).

Although there are innumerable research problems which could be fruitfully pursued in the relationships between retirement and temporal orientation, let me mention just two that seem particularly worthy of note in cross-cultural studies. The first of these has to do with the temporal dimension of social reciprocity. The American patterning of this relationship is perhaps best illustrated by a joke that was in circulation a few years ago. One man approached another, a friend of his, for a loan. The friend, reluctant to lend the money, was taken to task by the man making the request, who reminded his friend of the numerous instances in the past when he had stepped in to save him from social, physical, or economic disaster. "But what," asked the friend, "have you done for me *lately*?"

The humor in this story seems to rest on the fact that in our culture, although we feel a little awkward about it, past services rendered or aid given does not bind the recipient for long to a demand for reciprocity. The past is somehow unreal to us, and we speak often of "water under the bridge." In other cultures with different temporal orientations, strong sanctions may persist into the present, and even to future generations, for good or ill done in the remote past—even to ancestors. These differences in cultural orientations can readily be seen to have considerable significance for the support of aged parents or grandparents by the young, and probably are intimately related to the ways in which "dependency" is defined and treated within a society. We lack cross-cultural studies of this problem.

A second area related to temporal orientation in which cross-cultural research might be productive has to do with the relationship of discontinuities in work and activity patterns to memory loss. This notion was suggested in a paper by Neisser (1968), a psychologist, on cultural and cognitive discontinuity. In a discussion of cross-cultural differences in childhood amnesia, Neisser refers to the work of Benedict on cultural discontinuities:

> The cultural determination of such differences as that between work and play has been eloquently stated by Ruth Benedict . . . 'We think of the child as wanting to play and the adult as having to work, but in many societies the mother takes the baby daily in her shawl or carrying net to the garden or to gather roots, and adult labor is seen even in infancy from the pleasant security of its position in close contact with its mother. When the child can run about, it accompanies its parents, still doing tasks which are essential and yet suited to its powers: and its dichotomy between work and play is not different from that its parents recognize, namely, the distinction between the busy days and the free evening . . . the child is from infancy continuously conditioned to responsible social partici- pation, while at the same time the tasks that are expected of it are adapted to its capacity. The contrast with our society is very great.' When we become men, we are admonished to put away childish things—and with them, childish pleasures, attitudes, and thought. It is little wonder that we put away childish memories in the bargain. In terms of the hypotheses we are considering here, would we expect more continuous societies to suffer less from infantile amnesia than we do? [pp. 361-362].

This observation seems to have some potential relevance to memory loss in old age. Does the cultural discontinuity of total retirement, with all the phenomenological shifts it generates, have any causative connection with the widespread loss of memory reported—even in the absence of demonstrable brain damage— among elderly people in Western societies? Would a "second career" modality be less likely to result in "senile amnesia"? This is an area which might be well explored cross-culturally through cooperative work of anthropologists and psychologists.

Motivational orientation

From the anthropological perspective, motivational orientation consists of the culturally patterned elements of ego-involvements. It is the organization of shared goals and values with reference to the satisfaction of individual needs. There are three major components, at least, of motivational orientation that have engaged psychological anthropologists. The first of these is the nature or content of action goals as a configuration—that is, the extent to which various goals prescribed by the culture are complementary or conflicting, comprise a coherent functional value-system, and are shared by various subgroups within the society. The second is the relevance and adequacy of action goals to individual need satisfactions. The third, which is of a somewhat different order, is the cultural provision of action modalities or mastery styles deemed appropriate in the society for the attainment of goals.

In view of the vastness of the psychological, psychoanalytic, and anthropological literature on motivation and its dynamics, any attempt at systematic discussion of it is beyond the task of this paper. Many volumes have been written on the development and dynamics of ego-involvements, the role of anxiety in human motivation, the hierarchy of human needs, and the culture history of value systems. Here I would like to make only a few suggestions regarding cultural factors in the motivational orientations to work and retirement.

From a cross-cultural and/or historical perspective, work has always had a somewhat ambiguous place in human life. The reasons for this become a bit clearer if we define work as an instrumentality and not as a terminal value. There seems to be some confusion on this point in the literature. The physicist's definition of work as the expenditure of energy, whether by manpower, animal power, or the forces of nature, seems much too general to be of use in behavioral studies. While it is certainly true that the expenditure of energy is a universal human phenomenon, we sometimes call this expenditure work, sometimes play, sometimes sexuality, sometimes art or worship, sometimes aggression, and sometimes random activity. It seems more useful to consider work to be that form of energy release or activity that has as one of its goals creation of produce or other wealth.

A seeming human universal, from the most primitive societies to the post-industrial Western civilizations, is that men invariably work more than they must simply to subsist. As Herskovits (1948) once said, "A question that inevitably arises when the productive cycle is being investigated, is why men work. Men work, of course, because they must. But this simple answer by no means suffices. 'I began this paper,' says Hogbin, . . . 'by stating that these natives depend for their subsistence on tillage and collection. Though this remains true, they have many additional motives for the practice of agriculture and gathering of the fruits of the forest: food has been associated with personal prestige, status and vanity; with the desire for immortality; and even with aesthetics' " (p. 274). Thus it would seem that while even primitive peoples work more than they "must," it is not the work itself that is valued, but the symbolic meanings attached to what work is thought to provide.

If there are other means available to an individual for obtaining these terminally valued things, work, as here defined, may not be a strongly motivated activity. This may explain in part why there have been so many historical shifts within Western cultures in attitudes toward work. As Lowenstein has recently said, "The essential characteristic of Paradise is absence of work. That is the view of the author of the Book of Genesis. It is shared by some sociologists who believe—or more accurately, dream—that some day work will be eliminated by technology" (1968, p. 893). Toynbee (1938), in writing of work in the history of the Western world, says that "In Hellenistic days work was 'deconsecrated' by its identification with slavery, that it was 'reconsecrated' by the Church in the Middle Ages, and that now it is being 'secularized,' to the detriment of man." He goes on to say that, as long as work had a religious motivation, man needed no other incentive. Now, however, work has become "demonic" in that it has come to be pursued obsessively for its own sake. In other words, for many individuals in contemporary Western society there has been goal-displacement, with the means of work becoming viewed as an end in itself.

At the time of this writing, however, comments about the compulsive attitudes of Americans towards work—whether with sacred or demonic motivation—begin to sound a bit out-of-date. Maddox (1968) has summarized some research indicating that, with the weakening of the Protestant ethic, work in America today does not provide the central focus of life and source of rewarding social relationships that it did a few decades ago. More people retire early, if given that option, and fewer people (only one in ten, according to one survey) report that their principal social relationships are work-connected.

This development raises another issue with respect to work motivation and the consequences of retirement: namely, that the nature of most work in an industrial society, although it is a strong cultural focus, renders it unrelated to and inappropriate for the satisfaction of individual needs. Work does enable man to subsist, but that has never been a sufficient incentive, as Toynbee has said. Much of the work of a society with a highly developed division of labor has no relevance to such other motivations as achievement, autonomy and self-reliance, social status, and feelings of competence and effectance. Here we have a problem that has been a characteristic of our national life since long before the present age of automation.

In the first few pages of *Walden*, Thoreau deplored this situation among his fellow New Englanders in the mid-nineteenth century and regarded it as a dehumanizing tyranny:

> Actually, the laboring man has not leisure for a true integrity day by day; he cannot afford to sustain the manliest relations to man; his labor would be depreciated in the market. He has no time to be anything but a machine . . . . Talk of a divinity in man! Look at the teamster on the highway, wending to market by day or night; does any divinity stir within him? His highest duty to fodder and water his horses! What is his destiny to him compared with the shipping interest? Does not he drive for Squire Make-a-stir? How godlike, how immortal, is he? See how he cowers and sneaks, how vaguely all the day he fears, not being immortal nor divine, but the slave and prisoner of his own opinion of himself, a fame won by his own deeds. Public opinion is a weak tyrant compared with our own private opinion . . . . The mass of men lead lives of quiet desperation [1960, pp. 10-11].

Thoreau's classic commentary sounds not unlike a paper by Swados, "The Myth of the Happy Worker," published a full century later: "The plain truth is that factory work is degrading. It is degrading to any man who ever dreams of doing something worthwhile with his life; and it is about time we faced the fact . . . . Almost without exception, the men with whom I worked on the assembly line last year felt like trapped animals. Depending on their age and personal circumstances, they were either resigned to their fate, furiously angry at *themselves* for what they were doing, or desperately hunting other work . . ." [1960, p. 202].

There are conflicting theories about the relationship of work satisfaction to attitudes towards retirement. The unhappy worker may have no major conflict about retirement—in fact, if his subsistence needs are provided by a welfare society, he may welcome his release from long hours of meaningless drudgery.

(Maddox, 1968). As Herskovits has said, "Herein lies one of the most difficult problems of an industrialized society, where the means of production are no longer in the hands of the worker, and where specialization of labor has been carried so far that this identification with the finished product is not possible. It is only under such circumstances that labor becomes distasteful, and where release from work is envisaged as the requisite to desirable living" (1948, p. 274).

Other writers (see discussion in Maddox, 1968) have suggested that individuals who are dissatisfied and alienated in retirement are those whose earlier work life was "disorderly" and unrewarding. In other words, the personal and social resources built up by an individual during a successful work career may enable him to develop a viable self-image and greater personal and social resources that will persist even after retirement.

It would appear that much more research needs to be done in the area of work and inconsistencies in motivational orientations, both in Euroamerican society and in cross-cultural settings, before any coherent anthropological theory of retirement can be developed.

Before leaving this topic, I would like to touch briefly on the third aspect of motivational orientation, that of mastery styles. Gutmann (1964; 1967; also see Chapter 10 in this volume) has been the most systematic student of this problem in the field of research on aging. In his cross-cultural investigations, he has found some common developmental trends from a modality of active mastery among younger men towards either passive mastery or magical mastery styles among older men. Gutmann's data derive largely from projective materials. While these are interesting and valuable to the psychological anthropologist, they would perhaps be more revealing of culture-personality dynamics (as contrasted with developmental processes) if they were related to other kinds of ethnographic data. For example, it may well be, as Gutmann suggests, that there are universal age-trends towards passive and magical mastery.* What we need to know further is the extent to which these styles have available institutionalized means of expression in one culture as opposed to another. I suspect that such an analysis would reveal that some cultures emphasize and sanction active mastery, regardless of age, and provide few if any institutional forms for the effective expression of magical mastery. If such a culture exists, we might suspect that it would regard such age-changes as undesirable, or even pathological. Others might value and reward such age-linked personality changes. This is another area for fruitful collaborative research in psychological anthropology.

Normative orientation

Norms and standards are intrinsic features of all cultures, and all cultures provide their members with a normative orientation, standards by which the individual can judge his own behavior as well as the acts of others. Normative orientation is a necessary corollary of self-orientation, in that the individual must be motivated to consider whether his acts are right or wrong, good or bad. The result of this appraisal is, in turn, related to self-esteem or self-respect and to the individual's perception of the appraisal of others (Hallowell, 1955).

The early anthropological literature on cultural norms made some assumptions about homogeneity that seem somewhat naive to modern students of culture and personality. Wallace (1961) has addressed himself to this point in some detail. He asserts that there are available to the student of culture and personality two major, and somewhat antithetical, conceptions of the nature of the

---

*There is some additional empirical evidence from recent cross-cultural studies on coping styles and work orientation that supports this thesis. (See, for example, Diaz-Guerrero, 1967.)

relation between cultural and personality systems. These conceptions emphasize, respectively, the *replication of uniformity* and the *organization of diversity*.

In the former approach, he states, the anthropologist is interested in the way in which individuals by virtue of their common culture come to behave in the same way, to have learned the same things, and to share a uniform character. This approach has led social scientists to devise such concepts as "basic personality structure," "modal personality," "national character," "residues," and "core values." These concepts have been among the most widely criticized notions in the field of anthropology, and attempts to define and utilize them have resulted in widespread intellectual travail. (See, for example, Blake and Davis, 1968.)

The second approach suggested by Wallace, that of organization of diversity, emphasizes rather the range of habits, motives, personalities, and customs which coexist within the boundaries of any culturally organized society. Since socialization is not a perfectly reliable mechanism of replication, "culture shifts in policy from generation to generation . . . and is characterized internally not by uniformity, but by diversity of both individuals and groups, many of whom are in continuous and overt conflict in one sub-system and in active co-operation in another" (p. 28). In other words, culture may be thought of as a set of policies and contracts between and among groups of people "to organize their striving into mutually facilitating equivalence structures" (p. 28). This latter approach goes much further than the first in revealing the reasons for and the dynamics of culture change, as well as the heterogeneity of behavioral and characterological norms within a single culture.

Wallace's formulation was anticipated to some extent by Linton's exposition of role and status in the development of personality structure. He, more than perhaps any other anthropologist, promulgated the idea that any behavioral act could be evaluated only in terms of the role that the actor was playing and the status he was occupying at the time. Norms, then, could not be defined or have any meaning without reference to role/status considerations. (Even such "general" norms as prohibition of murder or rape would have to be set aside in the case of the execution of criminals or the ritual defloration of maidens, where these behaviors are sanctioned role-expectations of certain statuses within the society.) From the point of view of the individual, then, self-judgments of behavior as good or bad, weak or strong, must be related to the normative role-expectations assigned to the status he is occupying at the time of the behavior.

It has often been said that the retirement years in American culture comprise a "role-less role." In the absence of work, in the loss or attentuation of kin relationships, in the withdrawal from community and civic concerns, and in the relinquishing of memberships in voluntary associations, the retired individual finds himself without role-peers or reference groups to supply him with norms and standards by which he can evaluate his own behavior. Since norms are functions of roles, we could anticipate the role-less individual to suffer from the affective states we associate with normlessness or anomie.

In technologically simpler societies, as many writers have already described, there are important auxiliary productive or social functions that may be served by the relatively small number of people who survive into old age. In such societies, cumulative wisdom has real social and economic value which it lacks in societies characterized by a rapidly changing technology. In other societies, too, there is anticipatory socialization for the role of the elder, so that eventual retirement from productive labor is marked by entrance into a new set of status expectations. Thus, the young member of an African gerontocratic society knows that if he survives, he will inevitably accede to the status of elder, which carries with it clearly defined obligations, duties, and prerogatives. But where there are no clearly defined role-expectations for the aged, anticipatory socialization is absent. This has been the case among American aged for several decades.

There is some evidence, however, that a new set of norms and goals is becoming institutionalized for the retired in American society, at least in urban areas. There seems to have been a shift in our culture within the past ten or fifteen years from a work morality to an activity morality. Activity of any sort is presently valued over non-activity. Furthermore, this activity need not be defined as work; it need not be reimbursed by income nor contribute to any general social goal. It is moral to "keep busy"; those who are inactive are made to feel useless and worthless. There has been a transmutation of the "idleness" of the aged into "leisure-time or retirement activities." Leisure, then, as long as it is marked by some activity, has become a value in American life, as it has long been in Japan (Miller, 1968).

If this is, in fact, a growing trend in American life, then we can anticipate the "institutionalization" of retirement activities, with the development of special groups of older people who share them, criteria for admission to the groups, special buildings or other sites devoted to their pursuit, norms concerning the ways in which they will be organized and conducted, a meaningful rationale for participation and positive sanctions—including social recognition—for proper performance. This "institutionalization" of retirement activities does indeed seem to be occurring among the more affluent aged (Wood & Bultena, 1969), most conspicuously in planned retirement communities.

As Miller (1968) has pointed out, we are just now beginning to legitimatize leisure activities, and so far the justifications proffered have been that they relate in some way to culturally manifest economic goals (such as potentially lucrative hobbies as handicrafts or coin or stamp collecting), or at least with latent implications of being useful or gainful in some way (such as adult education or development of a skill or talent).

There are, however, other culturally manifest goals; one of the

most highly sanctioned of these is independence. The rapid
development of the new leisure activity or play morality for the
aged in our society may be related to strong cultural sanctions for
both social and emotional independence. The American elder who
can be happily disengaged from younger people while pursuing an
active (and preferably a potentially lucrative) retired life is coming
to be perceived as the "well-adjusted" older citizen. In time, his
role may become institutionalized, and anticipatory socialization
can then be inaugurated.

The major difference between the sort of role that seems to be
developing for American aged and that of elders in non-Western
societies is the resulting segregation of the former from younger
members of society. We do not yet have adequate research to
evaluate the long-term effects of age-segregation on self-image and
morale. There may be inevitable loneliness in such a role, with
what Wallace (1961) calls "chasms of mutual ignorance" between
age-groups and failures of understanding between individuals.
However, even if such a role has serious deficiencies, it may help
in reducing the emotional and social deprivations of occupational
retirement.

An additional value that seems to be emerging in our society is
that of "self-actualization." Most of the present generation of
elderly Americans will probably be unable, because of their earlier
conditioning, to avail themselves of this value in justifying their
non-productive years. Among younger Americans, however, with
their emphasis on self-knowledge, meditation, "expansion of the
consciousness," encounter group participation and sensitivity training, the value placed on development of the inner life may be
greatly enhanced. This value has long been central to the aged role
in Buddhist and Hindu cultures; in generations to come, it may
provide status for the retired in our society.

SUMMARY

This chapter has attempted to apply a model of the behavioral environment of the self, as developed in psychological anthropology, to the problem of work and retirement in cross-cultural perspective. It has described the several dimensions of interaction between the individual and his culture that may be related to the phenomenon of retirement as it has emerged in urban-industrial society. Self-image, social relationships, orientation in time and space, motivation, and values may all be seriously disrupted by retirement, given the central focus of work in Euroamerican society.

With the decline of the Protestant ethic, work morality and economic sanctions, however, we may anticipate a lessening of retirement stress and a greater cultural ratification of new activities and roles for the aged in our society. Before we can assess the effectiveness of these new roles in terms of individual function, however, we need more systematic cross-cultural studies of both workers and retired individuals in their behavioral environments. Assessment of the quality as well as the quantity of life after the working years may be possible using such an approach.

ROBERT N. BUTLER, M.D.

Dr. Butler received his medical degree at Columbia University. His psychiatric residency and research training were taken at the Langley Porter Neuropsychiatric Institute of the University of California Medical Center, at the National Institute of Mental Health, and at Chestnut Lodge.

His interest centers upon the natural course of adult development and upon the possibilities of introducing change. Although he is a psychoanalyst, Dr. Butler's work has ranged from physiological studies to legislative proposals. He is coauthor of *Human Aging: A Biological and Behavioral Study* (1963) and has written extensively on gerontology, drug effects, psychotherapy, and creativity. To ego psychology he has contributed the postulates of "the life review" and "autodidacticism."

Presently Dr. Butler is research psychiatrist and gerontologist at the Washington School of Psychiatry. His teaching appointments include George Washington University Medical School and the Washington Psychoanalytic Institute. He consults for the National Institute of Mental Health and St. Elizabeth's Hospital and is a member of the Board of the National Council on the Aging. Dr. Butler's current research projects include memoir studies of creative persons after middle life, a follow-up of the National Institutes of Health Human Aging Studies, a protective services demonstration, and studies of the life cycle.

A balletomane, Dr. Butler was a member of the Founding Board of the National Ballet, the first resident ballet company in the nation's capital. He was an Elected Member of the Washington, D.C., Delegation to the Democratic National Convention in 1968.

5: A LIFE-CYCLE PERSPECTIVE:
PUBLIC POLICIES FOR LATER LIFE

ROBERT N. BUTLER

This chapter looks at the institution of retirement in relation to what is known about relevant stages of the human life-cycle. It uses the nature of man as it changes during the course of life to provide a frame of reference for considering policy regarding the older worker and retirement. Within this framework, it suggests policy alternatives which can be evaluated in terms of their effectiveness in meeting personal and social needs.

How can individual and social needs most effectively be met through policies respecting work and leisure? In particular, given the characteristics of persons in the latter half of the life cycle, what societal arrangements for this period will most benefit the individual and society? Public policies often are established without regard to empirical evaluation or even social theory. However, both the executive and legislative branches of our government recently have shown interest in examining the nature of retirement before developing policies and programs (Special Committee on Aging, 1968; Carp, 1968).

THE LIFE-CYCLE PERSPECTIVE

Biological

Biologically the life cycle is characterized by a more or less regular sequence of events related to time: conception, gestation, growth, puberty, adolescence, maturity, and aging. These time-linked phenomena are not yet fully understood. The corpus of knowledge, from genetics to gerontology, is limited. Aging remains especially mysterious. Biological processes or stages may be accelerated or retarded. They may evolve unevenly with each other or with psychological and cultural processes. Biological delays may result from chromosomal defects (Turner's or Klinefelter's syndromes) or from "normal" heredity. Consider the genetic contribution to longevity, as articulated by Pearl in his Total Ancestral Index of Longevity (1934). Progeria or leprocaunism may illustrate pathologically induced accelerated aging. And environmental factors can influence the timing of biological events. Nutrition may account for the earlier menarche (by seven years) of the female today compared to 100 years ago (Tanner, 1961).

Psychological

Psychologically there are also sequences of events from conception to death which interrelate with both biology and culture. At least six psychological aspects of the life cycle can be identified.

In the forefront is the fact of death, the finitude of life, which has variable impact in intensity and timing on experience, behavior, and adaptation. So far as is known, only humankind possesses an *awareness of death.* Creative people may have a more profound realization of the brevity of human life which serves as a motor for their creative expression (Butler, 1967). For a variety of historical-cultural reasons (for example, the Bomb), young people appear to be discovering death earlier. The individual may view death as part of a continuing process or as a terminating event.

Thanatologies exist (Eissler, 1955). Religion has been called the great psychotherapy of death (Hall, 1923). Existential philosophers place death center stage (Kaufmann, 1956). The question of why time and death have become major foci of present-day literature, philosophy, and culture is itself important to examine (Meyerhoff, 1955). Even if this preoccupation is excessive in our era, the roles of time and death must eventually be accorded some position in human psychology.

Second, the *sense of the life cycle* as an unfolding process of change seems, clinically, to be important to adaptation throughout life, perhaps especially in later life. An "average expectable life cycle" is a counterpart to Hartmann's (1964) "average expectable environment." We do not know to what extent the normative, modal features of this sense of the life cycle account for change and adaptation. The sense of the life cycle transcends the individual's life and includes a sense of history and of the interconnection of generations. Sponsoring the young and contributing other forms of legacy—leaving one's tracings—represent an ethics of futurity which is generally a post-meridian development.

Psychopathological issues around death (excess fear or denial) and around the sense of the life cycle (excess preoccupation or denial) are undoubtedly secondary to personal history or present context. For example, fear of death may be more pronounced in a structureless, person-less environment. However, some concern about death is ever present. In clinical assessment and therapy, death and the sense of the life cycle must be considered simultaneously with the history and the present context. They should not be subjected to facile reductionism and attributed to historical "castration anxiety" or to contemporary fears of pain or of being a burden. The problem of life's termination and the sense of the life cycle are genuine psychological variables.

A third major facet of the life-cycle perspective is the *sense of time*—human time, as Bergson distinguishes it from scientific or objective time (Meyerhoff, 1955). The sense of time is made possible, as are all the facets of the life-cycle perspective, by memory. The sense of the life cycle also requires awareness of the immediate future and of the steps intermediate before death.

This aspect of the life-cycle perspective may be related to several problematic developments. Time-bound behavior, seen in extreme in the obsessive-compulsive patient with his procrastination on the one hand and his compulsiveness on the other, illustrates one kind of disturbance in the sense of time. The depressed patient, with his sense of the increased duration of time, illustrates another disturbance. The older person who has not resolved the problem of time may experience "time panics" or refuse help because he does not know whether he can ever reciprocate. "Anniversary reactions" are still another example of the problematic sense of time. They may be likened to the "diseases of reminiscence" (Breuer and Freud, 1955) or to late effects of experiences in concentration camps (Chodoff, 1963).

On the other hand, a normative sense of time is reflected in tranquility or serenity. According to Neugarten (1967), in middle age there normally is a reversal in the sense of time, following which time is counted toward death instead of from birth. The sense of time may not fully explain these behavioral patterns; indeed, it may be the dependent variable. However, the life-cycle perspective requires exploration of the roles of time and the sense of time.

The fourth aspect of the life-cycle perspective is the *sense of life experience.* This is the awareness of seasoning, of broadened perspective, and of growth. This "knowing what life is all about," at least for oneself and one's immediate relationships, comes only with the progress of the life cycle.

A fifth facet of the life cycle from the psychological point of view is the accumulation of a body of *knowledge of age or time-linked changes.* What is to be expected? What is typical of persons at a particular point in the life cycle? Who is offpace? What can be attributed to the situation, and what to the life history and personality of the individual? This fifth facet is clearly related to the sense of the life cycle, for it is the body of knowledge which helps develop that sense.

The psychological life cycle may have a sixth facet, *the idea of stages or phases*. A corpus of knowledge of time-linked changes and a sense of the life cycle may suffice, but knowledge about stages may be involved also. There would appear to be no doubt of the existence of developmental stages in childhood. Freud (1956), Piaget (1948), and Erikson (1963), as examples, offer schedules of development but all tend to consider it derivative and determined by preceding stages.

No stage theory offers an adequate account of life from conception to death. Contemporary psychoanalytic theory ends with the achievement of adulthood. Erikson's psychosocial theory offers two points beyond early adulthood. Jung (1933) formulates post-adolescent stages but in a loose, incomplete manner. Benedek (1950, 1959) has considered parenthood and the climacterium as "developmental phases." The menopause, through its long history of blame for middle-life depression in women, has been given a vague place in the psychological, psychiatric, and psychoanalytic literature which could be construed as stage-oriented. In the main, however, the life of man is truncated in contemporary theory. Psychological development is presented as complete with early adulthood.

There is legitimate debate regarding the value of the concept of stages, and even regarding the occurrence of psychological changes after the achievement of adulthood. Does adult man have the capacity for change? While no one would seriously deny superficial variations in personality and mental content, questions remain. Are not the basic personality traits crystallized? Is not adult psychological organization so established that tendencies toward change are offset by stabilizing mechanisms? Partial changes do not refute the fundamental immutability of character if they are predictable outgrowths. On the other hand, natural events and psychotherapeutic interventions are believed by some to produce fundamental reconstructions in personality. Outcome studies of psychotherapy remain equivocal. The answer to the question of its relationship to fundamental change may be long forthcoming.

Inasmuch as operational definitions of "basic changes" do not exist to the satisfaction of all, it may be sufficient at this time to say that psychological changes of some unspecifiable order occur after the achievement of adulthood. Here the concept of stage may be especially useful. A psychology of parenthood, of middle life, and of old age, as examples, may be demonstrable. This would contribute to solution of the problem of consistency versus change in adult life, and to that of measuring the influence of various interventions.

At the very least, mental content and the nature of problems change. Issues to be resolved occur predictably at various points along the course of life. These may be met so silently that no one observes them. Denial, resignation, non-appraisal and non-decision may set the stage for later crises. However, these life-course issues offer opportunities for reappraisal, reorganization, and renewal. Here again, knowledge of normative issues and their resolutions may contribute to building a psychology and a psychopathology of the life cycle. Only in light of them can we speak of fulfillment or successful resolution.

Recurrent elements

In one sense, the aspects of the life-cycle perspective discussed above—the awareness of death; the sense of the life cycle, of time, and of time-linked changes or stages; and the accumulation of experience—are superordinate. They parallel the course of life and do not refer to external events or accidents. Certain other psychological elements are part of the life-cycle perspective. These additional elements seem to be recurrent rather than constant. They are discontinuous but inevitable, and in some measure they are predictable in regard to time.

Renunciation-and-restitution is the great recurrent issue of life. It is inevitable because loss is inevitable. On four occasions loss is predictable: at resolution of the oedipal complex, at separation from the family of orientation, at separation of progeny, and at the deaths of parents.

Disengagement theory (Cumming and Henry, 1961) should be considered in life-cycle terms. Disengagement has been criticized as a theory of aging because of the extent of which disengagement may be explained as a consequence of fulfilling role expectations, as a result of medical and psychiatric disease, and as due to social adversity such as arbitrary retirement (Tobin and Neugarten, 1961; Kleemeier, 1964; Maddox, 1964). That disengagement is an inherent process peculiar to old age remains to be definitively demonstrated. It would appear to be an example of the broader phenomenon of renunciation, of the necessity to relinquish goals or objects and reach out for new ones.

The process of giving up objects and taking on new ones is characteristic of the flow of life. Young people, for example, must give up parental attachments and seek new ones. However much difficulty the young may have in finding new object relations, this is a problem of poignant dimensions for the elderly.

The *sense of self* is another recurrent issue. Although identity is essentially continuous, it is subject to counterforces in ways that the formal psychological aspects of the life cycle are not. Anti-identity forces, elements operative against the maintenance of identity, are especially salient at certain points in the life course. Identity is the consolidation of personal history, to which the individual may be captive and because of which he may have made compromises, reduced aspirations, and diminished innate potentialities. Maintenance of the contemporary identity is not *per se* adaptive. Indeed, it is reasonable that identity should change. Adolescence is the first major occasion for revision, middle life is the second, and old age the last.

Whatever the boundary conditions imposed by the past and its consequences, alternatives are present. Realization of these options goes hand in hand with the recurrent struggle of identity against anti-identity. The search for lifeenhancing activities or persons delineates the process of exercising options. This is vividly observed in the autodidactic searching for renewing experiences. Autodidacticism is rarely seen in full form except in creative people (Butler, 1967) and then, often, only in their area of interest.

Finally, a word must be said about *lack of recovery from childhood*. The Freudian theory of libidinal or psychosexual development, Piaget's stage theories of cognitive and moral development, and the psychosocial schedule of Erikson all imply stoppage or fixation in the face of obstacles, and its salience in later development. Maturity, however defined, is so rarely achieved that the fact of unrecovered childhood is a feature throughout life. It may have continuous or recurrent effects. The extreme form of recurrence is regression, either in relation to specific life-cycle processes such as marriage, parenthood, and retirement, or in response to accidents and diseases.

Culture

In America and in Western culture generally, there is an abiding belief in the myth of the perfectibility and reparability of man, individually and collectively. Condorcet's (1960) optimistic view of the progressive perfection of man provides the most definitive statement of this questionable idea. If this view were not so pervasive in Western culture, man might rarely suffer the consequences of the failure to recover from childhood.

History gives evidence of the sense of the life cycle and recognition of stages in the course of human life. Terms for childhood, adolescence, middle age, and old age have existed as far back as is known. Aristotle referred to youth, middle age, and old age, finding middle age the period of greatest interest, in keeping with his preoccupation with moderation. Shakespeare wrote of the seven ages of man. Rousseau offered his own division of the life cycle.

But despite everyday language and the comments of philosophers and writers, stages of the life cycle, as lucid and compelling concepts, are recent. Aries in his *Centuries of Childhood* (1962) offers evidence regarding the evolution of the concept of childhood. Adolescence has emerged culturally within the last two hundred years. In this century, old age has emerged as a concept, probably because of increased survivorship (Butler, 1968a).

Historical conditions, then, would seem to have shaped both the psychological and cultural awareness of periods of life. Possibly these historical developments are in transit. Perhaps the cultural visibility of stages is a passing phenomenon, and a suggestion of low-order sophistication. Perhaps appreciation of the *process* of the life cycle is a higher-order phenomenon. Then the study of stages will be but a step in man's appreciation of the course of life. "Stages" are visible because they have some sharpness of delineation. With increasing knowledge these "stages" may be seen for what they are: markers along the way.

The Oriental conception of the life cycle seems to be distinctly different from that of the West, and this difference seems to derive from the conception of the self (Hummel, 1967). The Oriental considers the individual, the course of his life, and its outcome, death, to be *within* the process. Thus life and death seem more natural and are more acceptable. In Western culture, man stands *without* the process and endeavors to explain, predict, and control nature. Because of the greater individualism or narcissism of Western man, he has greater difficulty in accepting death, which he tries to delay and deny.

PUBLIC POLICIES

In view of what is known about man in the latter part of the life cycle, what policy changes might assist society to better meet his needs and its own?

Life-Cycle Redistribution of Education, Work and Leisure

Education, work, and leisure could all be distributed throughout the life cycle rather than each being concentrated in a distinct period: childhood, middle life, or retirement. To support such a redistribution of activities, a life-cycle system of income maintenance and credit would be required. Monies available would vary in accordance with needs during the life cycle (Kreps, 1968).

Kreps predicts that by 1985 the Gross National Product (GNP) will exceed $1.5 trillion, reaching about two and one-third times the present level. Taking into account population increase, at such a rate the per capita GNP would rise from a little over $3,000 to almost $6,000, an 80% increment. If this happens, society will have several choices which include a 22-hour work week, a 27-week work year, retirement at 38, or placement of one-half the labor force into educational programs.

Distribution of education, work, and leisure more smoothly throughout the life cycle may have advantages to the economy and to the individual. Kreps found that in certain Western European countries there was no trend toward early retirement comparable to that in the United States. Instead the work year was being shortened. The functions of leisure for the individual include freedom to pursue interests. Present concentration of leisure in the period of life most subject to illness and disability reduces the opportunities for such pursuit. Increased attention should be paid to the advantages, to the individual and to society, of various patterns for redistributing education, work and leisure through the life cycle.

Flexible retirement

Retirement from work may not be an inevitable phase of human development. It may be a culturally evolved phase which may or may not be desirable. Pre-industrial, agrarian economies have not provided old people automatic retirement. If pastoral, the society usually takes care of them; if nomadic, it may abandon them. Retirement may be inevitable in industrial and post-industrial societies, as a means of avoiding disruption through death (Blauner, 1966). Society avoids dependence upon those with high death-risk; that is, society disengages from the old.

Retirement may also have the legitimate function of protecting society against the errors of older people with mental and physical disabilities. However, disease rather than age is the critical variable in determining competence. Because of social-economic forces, and because of deficiencies in scientific knowledge, retirement arbitrarily determined by age has been the prevailing practice. Information requisite for appraisal systems adequate to support flexible retirement policies is not available. Perhaps flexible retirement should be a social goal, and effort should be made to develop techniques for evaluation of continuing competence.

Another function of retirement is the protection of society against the perpetuation of outdated policies, skills, and ideas. However, retirement is not applied where there is most at stake. Society is not protected through the forced retirement of those who have the most critical decisions to make regarding matters of individual life and death, and those of grave national importance. Physicians, judges, and politicians are not subject to arbitrary retirement (Butler, 1968b). Society is not protected from disruption by their deaths, from their errors, or from their outmoded views.

Probably physicians, lawyers, judges, teachers, and career executives in government should be required to undertake continuing education and undergo periodic relicensing examinations. Perhaps chairmen of Congressional committees and executives of governmental Departments should be required to rotate from their positions every five years, and executives in the private sector should be encouraged to do so. For the good of society, continuity and stability in the performance of important functions must be balanced against obsolescence in the performers.

Cultivation of leisure

Public education should move toward cultivation of the use of leisure for advancing human sensibilities towards people, the arts, and learning. Beginning in childhood there should evolve a sense of leisure, characterized by a receptive relation to one's inner life as well as to outer stimuli. Imagination, the capacity to be alone, and comfort with time are among the critical ingredients in leisure.

The industrial revolution is making the culture of leisure a possibility. However, free time is not the same as leisure. To those who suffer psychologically in the absence of responsibilities and to those who have no interests, retirement may be disquieting rather than rewarding. Some studies appear to demonstrate that, statistically speaking, retirement is not necessarily a cause of psychological problems. Nevertheless, the clinician sees many people for whom retirement participates in the genesis of depression, apathy and paranoid states as well as those in whom it precipitates behavioral and mood changes not of pathological dimensions.

Maintenance of economic status

The practical realities of life for retired persons must be considered. Income, health care, and housing are inadequate for them today. One-third of the 19 million elderly persons in this country are living below the poverty line. Even if the older person is willing and able to work it is difficult for him to find jobs, in part because of bias toward age, in part because of the obsolescence of his skills. Yet job earnings account for one-third of all income among the aged. Fifty-five percent of the elderly live in the centers of our cities, often in dilapidated housing.

Despite Medicare, many cannot afford necessary medical help because Medicare covers only 35 percent of their health bills. Over 75 percent have at least one chronic health problem. One out of four has some hearing loss. Physical problems and hearing and visual limitations curtail mobility to stores, medical and other necessary facilities, and social and recreational activities. Provisions should be made for economic security, decent housing, and high quality health care. Then at least what is known as important and possible in the maintenance of adaptive status will be accomplished.

Life-cycle education

Public schools, colleges, and universities should expand opportunities for life-long education. Re-training, new career directions, new skills, and preparations for meaningful leisure are important goals of such programs. Knowledge about the life cycle should be taught, and education should include proper preparation for life-cycle events and issues. The study of survivors should be incorporated in the pedagogy of the young, and adaptive traits identified and learned. The new syllabus should include material about retirement, death, and other facets of the course and flow of later life.

Social usefulness

Psychologically the older person has to come to terms with a sense of uselessness. In order to provide meaningful roles for the elderly, the skills of older people must be matched with community needs. To accomplish such matching, a local health and welfare council might keep registries of retired persons and their skills, and of various community needs, and provide transportation expenses and minimum wages for the elderly persons. Such an operation would integrate the various programs which have been more or less successful, such as Operation FIND, SCORE, Foster Grandparents, and Greenthumb.

However, in keeping with the life-cycle perspective, any such program should apply to persons of all ages. Excessive fragmentation of the life cycle, whether in social participation, housing, or medical care is inadvisable on both mental health and social grounds. From a practical point of view, fragmentation is generally more expensive. Medicare may be cited as an illustration. In the absence of a compulsory, comprehensive medical-insurance program for people of all ages, impairing conditions accumulate into old age, at added cost in money as well as in human comfort and effectiveness.

Ethic to the future

Consideration must be given not only to the older person's participation in the present, but also to his sense of, and commitment to, the future. Values change in the course of the life cycle, and interest in the future becomes most salient in later life. Society should facilitate expression of the later-life concern with the future, and use of the life experience and accumulated knowledge of retired people for the advantage of future generations.

Man's relation to posterity has been recognized since time immemorial but has not been institutionalized. Consider four attitudes toward the future. There are the nihilistic who say, "Let the world end with me!" There are the bitter who, like Mark Twain, feel that, "The future does not worry about us, so why should we worry about the future?" There are those who try to conserve the *status quo* in the future. There are those concerned with leaving traces, a legacy to the future and to later generations. These several attitudes—nihilism, cynical indifference, maintaining the *status quo*, leaving a trace—delineate different ways of handling grief concerning the loss of the self.

The writing of memoirs is an expression of concern with the future, an effort to leave a trace. At present, memoirs are essentially fortuitous. The National Archives contain documents and records of national interest, but the life histories of those responsible for such documents and records are not collected. A program could be established for obtaining the private memoirs of persons who have made significant contributions to public life. When to release such material would be the decision of the memoirist, a control which might reduce the defensiveness or self-justification in autobiographical material published during an author's lifetime. Consider, for example, how political figures might write about one another if they were writing for posterity rather than for immediate publication.

It would be useful to focus on decision-making. The public should be appraised of the mental and physical health of past leaders—King Ludwig, Adolf Hitler, Woodrow Wilson, Franklin Delano Roosevelt, as examples. Harold Lasswell long ago (1930) stressed the relationship between psychopathology and politics. The collection of memoirs should not become a mental health station nor a vehicle for character assassination. It could be a growing reservoir of data pertaining to the elements in decision-making, including psychological and psychopathological factors. This would help in developing retirement policies for persons in positions of great power.

CONCLUDING REMARKS

This paper suggests that knowledge about the cycle of human life is one framework for consideration of alternatives in social policy. Some scientists would object that science cannot be used to make practical suggestions without subverting its neutrality. Others would argue that public policy decisions, usually made on the basis of insufficient evidence, should be informed by current scientific knowledge. There are indications that public policy judgments in recent years are being influenced by scientists and by scientific findings. There is a good chance that scientific studies will have some place in the development of social policy.

The life-cycle perspective suggests that there should be retirement policies, in the plural. Especially important is the alternative of distributing leisure throughout the life cycle, and the consequent necessity to redistribute work, education, and financial support. There is need to create a variety of roles for those who elect retirement, and those whose health or competence requires it. One might refer to a civil right of leisure, that is, to freedom from guilt when not working. This would entail a social reconstruction toward a culture of leisure in its best sense. Such a culture cannot be tacked on at the end of life, but must involve a continuing social and individual commitment.

In spite of centuries of effort, society has not found completely satisfactory arrangements to reduce the disruptive effects of death. Nor has man built entirely constructive arrangements for meshing the generations. Means for the transmission of values, skills, and knowledge require extension and refinement. Man has not capitalized fully upon the inherent desire of the individual to "leave his mark." This interest in the future might well be channelled and recorded so that future generations can benefit from the lives and experiences of those before them.

R. MEREDITH BELBIN, PH.D.

After taking his Master of Arts and Doctor of Philosophy degrees at Cambridge University, England, Dr. Belbin remained in Cambridge as a research worker in the Nuffield Research Unit into Problems of Aging. Subsequently he became a Research Fellow of the College of Aeronautics at Cranfield. During this period he identified himself, in turn, as classicist, experimental psychologist, gerontologist, and industrial engineer. After leaving Cranfield, he spent ten years as an independent management consultant, writing and lecturing on a variety of management subjects and in several countries.

Dr. Belbin then returned to his former interest in aging, through a commission by the Organization for Economic Cooperation and Development, to review industrial and scientific data pertinent to the training of older workers. The results of this review were reported in 1965 in the series *Employment of Older Workers.* There followed another assignment with the Organization for Economic Cooperation and Development to conduct demonstration projects in the training of older workers in the United Kingdom, Austria, Sweden, and the United States, the results of which were published in 1969 in the same series.

At present Dr. Belbin is Industrial and Research Consultant to the Industrial Training Research Unit of University College London, in Cambridge. The Director of the Industrial Training Research Unit, Eunice Belbin, Ph.D., is his wife. Dr. Meredith Belbin's major leisure-time interest is hybridizing clematis.

R. MEREDITH BELBIN

The condition of retirement is now taken for granted as being the proper lot of those in later maturity. Easily forgotten is the fact that retirement represents in some ways a rebuttal of an intimate involvement in society that evolution has done much to shape. People have always aged but only recently have they retired. Old age is not normally endured as a luxury by nature. The span of human life outstrips the capacity to engage in the primary economic activities of the tribe, outlasts the ability to procreate, and exceeds by fully a decade the period necessary for the nurture of the last-born offspring.

This apparent *overmaturity* in human beings has gained a special value which has no exact counterpart amongst other species of primate. Almost universally in primitive and primaeval society, older people are seen as agents in the transmission of culture—upon which man's survival and preeminence depend—in repairing and fashioning tools, in teaching the young, and in acting as overseers in cultural rites (Simmons, 1945). It seems evident that this extension of the life span to encompass social roles has conferred survival value on society itself. Even in senescence man may be viewed as having developed specialist characteristics of a functional order. His disposition to dwell on long-past events would be an invaluable asset in preliterate society by extending the memory reach of the whole tribe.

Literacy and its dominating influence in education and training have now radically changed relationships between age groups. Older people have lost their special identity of function. A new form of mass social contract has come into being, retirement whereby older people receive economic support from, but are relieved of reciprocal obligations towards, society.

If retirement had come into being simply as the fulfillment of the universal desire for leisure, it might be supposed that those who were highest in the social hierachy would become the first claimants of an early retirement, and those who were lower would tend to retire later. Taylor's study (1968) of occupational differences in retirement trends suggests rather the reverse. His survey concentrated on men aged 65 and over who held regular full-time jobs in designated occupations between 1957 and 1962 but who were not working at such jobs in 1962.

Three occupational groups can be distinguished: those with low retirement rates, those with medium retirement rates, and those with high retirement rates. The low retirement group includes professional and technical workers (31%), managers, officials, and proprietors (43%), and farmers and farm managers (49%). The middle group is comprised of clerical workers (53%), sales workers (54%), and farm laborers and foremen (55%), while the high retirement group consists of service workers (59%), operative (60%), and craftsmen and foremen (65%). Persons engaged in higher status occupations probably exert more influence over their own retirement rates. They retire less readily than those in lower-ranking occupations. But as Taylor observes: "In the employee society reasons for retirement are increasingly a function of occupational organization and of social organization. They are decreasingly a function of individual choice" (p. 373).

A prima facie case exists for the view that pressures toward early retirement arise less from the self-interest of those reaching late maturity than out of the changing needs of society combined with a loss in the economic and social utility of older person roles. The pressures to retire people from the labor force at an even earlier age seem to outweigh pressures to reduce labor force participation by other means, such as a shorter work week or extended vacations. If these pressures continue, more serious consideration will need to be given to their long-term effects. Suppose that the retirement population continues to increase rapidly in size. What changes in retirement phenomena can be expected in the next two decades? What are likely to become the principal problems of mass retirement? What challenges will they pose for retirement strategy?

LONG-TERM RETIREMENT TRENDS

A few predictions may be made. First, a number of problems which currently receive a great deal of attention are likely to recede. This will apply especially to income, housing, and medical care. This prediction depends on nothing more than on extrapolation of current trends. Perusal of data on retirement incomes in North America and Western European countries shows a steady growth in governmental and private pension arrangements. Not only are the incomes of pensioners rising but more especially there is increasing coverage of the elderly population. To this must be added the benefits arising from a steady accumulation of wealth. Pensions will increasingly be augmented by investment income. In addition, retirees will continue to benefit from the accumulation of possessions during their lifetime, which will reduce the extent of their need for consumer durables. No prediction is offered on whether the rate of income rise for retirees will be faster than for the active population.

Housing for retirees is also likely to improve due to increased knowledge of the needs of older people, due to improvement in social services, due to growth in special housing projects and due, above all, to the rise in affluence.

Finally, health services for retirees are likely to become more effective and at the same time more comprehensive and embracing in character. Retirees have been subject in the past to the pincer effects of reduced income and increased need for expensive medical treatment. However, most countries of Western Europe now have socialized or semi-socialized medical programs, and the elderly have become the first beneficiaries of socialized medicine in the United States.

A number of new phenomena are likely to appear on the retirement scene. The most notable of these will be retirement migration. This is already favored among the more prosperous members in a few countries, regions of which are subject to an unpropitious climate. Migration retirees are more likely to be persons formerly in itinerant occupations and those formerly addicted to far-ranging vacations. Their numbers will be swollen due to the positive influence of rising prosperity and the negative effects of lack of opportunity for continuation of pre-retirement roles in their home areas. Retirement migration already exists on an interregional basis within countries; it will extend increasingly to international migration. These trends are currently masked by the way in which demographic statistics are compiled. New research tools will be required to take account of a host of problems that will surround the migration retiree.

The main focus of study and effort is likely, however, to switch to the crucial problems of retirement living. Attention will center on disorientation, lack of adjustment, and striving to find satisfaction. A large inactive population tends to breed a malaise to the extent that it becomes concentrated and separated from kinsfolk (both through migration of offspring and retirement migration); that it is discriminated against as an identifiable minority group by the surrounding active population; that it perceives its own high death rate; that at the lower end of the age scale increasing numbers of less competent employees are retired, so giving retirement an unfavorable image; and that the norms of retirement behavior become blurred with the steady loss of acknowledged "senior citizen" roles.

This set of predictions is difficult to check because many intangibles are involved. However, it seems clear that concern with the principal problems of retirees in the future is likely to shift towards their psychogenic needs.

IDENTIFYING NEEDS IN RETIREMENT

While needs in retirement are highly personal, two can be postulated as deserving study because of their generality and their independence of economic, social, or cultural factors.

Retirees often express themselves "as loath to go downhill." The first need, then, is that retirement should be organized so as to allow human capabilities to be retained even though capacities are lost. The elevator, spectacles, the hearing-aid, the automobile with power-assisted braking and steering offer substitutes for the diminished power of the senses and muscles. But advancing technology has contributed nothing to meeting the problems of the decline in mental capacity and in the interpersonal skills upon which human contact depends. The retention of mental power and abilities might enable the retiree to remain a "grand old man" even if he is confined to a wheelchair. The benefits of success in psychological aging are likely to be shared by the retiree, his family, and his associates.

The second objective should also meet support. It is that retirement should promote satisfaction. Satisfaction can be measured and related to a variety of factors, and the implications can be examined for planning retirement programs.

Maintaining Skills and Capacities

There is little direct evidence on how retirement living affects the maintenance of capacities. Indirect evidence offers some useful pointers.

A fair amount of research has centered on the relationship between age and intelligence with special reference to the rates of decline among groups at different levels of intelligence. It is well established that those with initially low intelligence display the greatest relative amounts of decline with age, and those with high intelligence, least (Raven, 1948; Owens, 1953; Bayley & Oden, 1955; Jones, 1959).

This phenomenon is opposite to that normally observed under laboratory conditions if aging can be likened to a form of stress, the effect of which is to impair performance. Subjects with high performance tend to show a greater drop in performance levels under stress, and low performers show least drop. This is to be expected since higher scores offer more room for deterioration. Intelligence follows the opposite course when subject to impairment by aging. It has been suggested that high intelligence is better maintained because the exercise of intelligence facilitates the capacity to think intelligently. This is akin, perhaps, to the effect of physical exercise in maintaining physical fitness and physical agility.

What is more problematic is: How far do the effects of mental and behavioral exercise extend? Also: Have they consequences of a general as well as a specific character? Here a limited amount of evidence presents itself from some different aging trends found among various occupational and life-style groups.

An early study was carried out by Gertrude Ehinger (1931) who compared the motor ability of 181 factory women with that of 152 educated women who were living "cultivated" lives. The ages of both groups lay between 25 and 50. Both were given the same five tests described as including: Walther's discs, cutting out, beads, dotting, and tapping. It might be supposed that manual workers would display higher manual skills than non-manual workers and therefore would achieve superior scores. The opposite was the case. The performance of the cultivated women was superior to that of the working women in all tests with the exception of the discs which "resembled a form of activity with which all factory women examined were familiar." Decline in scores with age was found in three of the tests. Declines were sharper and occurred earlier among the factory women. They were evident at 30 in the case of the factory women against 35 for the educated women. Ehinger concluded that the age curve in decline of abilities varied with the type of life led by the subject.

A similar conclusion was reached by a later French worker (Clément, 1969). Clément compared certain abilities—memory (using the Wechsler memory test), intellectual efficiency (using a coding test), reaction time, and strength of grip—among two occupational groups who had spent their working lives as factory workers and as teachers in state schools. These two groups were further subdivided by age to form younger groups 28-35 and older groups 48-55. The two occupational groups were of different intellectual levels with no overlap between the groups: The teachers had a mean I.Q. of 120 with a range from 110 to 135, and the factory workers had a mean I.Q. of 100 with a range between 90 and 110. In comparing the younger workers with the younger teachers, and the older workers with the older teachers, it was noted that the teachers achieved superior or highly superior scores on all tests. The decline with age in the performance of teachers was also less on all tests except that of reaction time (where there was high variability among teachers).

A central question was whether the greater age decline among factory workers could be attributed to the effects of the initially low intelligence of the factory workers or to the restricted working lives and leisure activities that characterized the factory group. To throw light on this point, Clément made a further subdivision of the group according to whether or not the workers possessed the *Certificat d'Études Primaries* (a diploma taken at the end of primary education which all the factory workers had undergone). Clément found that there was a similar decline of performance with age for factory workers who possessed the C.E.P. certificate and for those who did not. His contention is that the slope of decline with age is influenced less by initial intelligence than by the nature of the working lives of his subjects (which was similar for his two factory subgroups, i.e., with and without the C.E.P. diploma). Clément sees the main reason for the difference between the losses with age shown by the teachers and factory workers as being the unduly fatiguing work of the latter.

However, Clément also cites evidence to show that, while the factory workers engaged in routine and passive leisure activities, the teachers lead generally active lives. An alternative explanation then, is that the faculties of teachers are better maintained on account of their more diversified existence and the favorable effect which this exercises on their capacity to make high-order responses in an unaccustomed test situation.

Some further evidence about the way in which different age trends show themselves in different occupational groups arises from a study by the Unit for Research into Occupational Aspects of Aging in Liverpool, England (Heron & Chown, 1967). This Unit applied a substantial battery of tests to about 300 men and 240 women aged between 20 and 79, with a view to establishing norms of relationship between age and function, and studying the interrelationships between the measures. Subjects were recruited so as to fall into one of five occupational classes as defined for work in the field of audience research. Significant correlations were found between scores and class (with age held constant) in 22 cognitive and psychomotor measures. Heron and Chown state: "In all cases where a difference in scores between occupational classes is found, the higher occupational classes obtain the higher or better scores" (p. 67).

Some insight into the reasons for these differences was made possible by examining the cognitive scores of subgroups within the different occupational groupings. These subgroups were matched in the Mill Hill vocabulary test, a useful means of gauging previous intellectual attainment since this test shows high stability with age and little loss of score with impairment of intelligence. Among these matched subgroups the fall in performance with age in other cognitive functions was greater in the lower ranking occupations. This was taken as an indicator that occupational experience and activity influence the rate at which cognitive functions decline.

It is difficult to postulate any alternative hypothesis. It may be that, while subgroups were matched for previous *intellectual attainment*, those in the lower occupational groups were nevertheless of lower *initial intelligence*. Even so, most of the tests have no correlation or only low correlations with intelligence test scores.

More positive evidence in regard to cognitive functions as related to the degree to which activities are maintained *outside* an occupation has been provided by a study of 89 candidates between the ages of 22 and 60, taking a home study Coal Preparation course (Belbin & Waters, 1967). Candidates were asked the question: "Have you studied any subject since leaving school?" Forty-five had continued *some* form of education and 44 had not. In each of four age groups the "continuers" achieved better scores on the theory test than the non-continuers. While the non-continuers had percentage scores of 53.6, 57.0, 53.1, and 48.5 in the 20s, 30s, 40s, and 50s, the scores of the continuers were 71.3, 71.5, 69.4, and 62.3, respectively. The two groups were similar, however, on the marks of their practical examination, on their school-leaving ages, and on the range of their occupational grades. Nor was it the content of the "further education" which assisted the passing of the theory examinations. In very few cases was it relevant. Art, Commerce, First Aid, History, Music, Public Speaking, Wireless Telegraphy, and Trade Union Laws were typical of the subjects studied.

We need now to take all these data into account in the formulation of a hypothesis about modifying influences on the decline of functional capacity with age. Most abilities are tied to a greater or lesser degree to physiological variables which are adversely affected by advancing age. However, it does not follow that performance declines at the same rate as the prime physiological function that is involved in performing. For example, performance in an inspection task does not follow the decline with age that has been established for visual acuity. Decline can be, and often is, offset by compensatory adjustments, by refinements in skill and technique. Performance on tasks of only moderate complexity will depend on subsystems, on particular repertoires of skill that can be brought to bear in the situation. There seem fair grounds for supposing that these subsystems have a certain transferability and that they can be used to enhance performance in apparently unrelated tasks. Activity would be conducive to their maintenance.

This hypothesis would carry implication about the future: The elderly members of a society committed to early retirement would be more likely to display the behavioral characteristics of the aged than would a society in which retirement was postponed. This tendency would be modified, however, to the extent that active leisure can be introduced. This modification by active leisure, in turn, emphasizes the great need for retirement planning.

Satisfaction in Retirement

The previous section suggested that activity may be especially important in retirement as a means of saving the human mechanism from impairment. It might be contended, however, that this would not be universally acceptable as a goal. Some people might prefer to "go along with aging" rather than attempt to resist it by appropriate strategies. This might be justified by some belief about how satisfaction in retirement is best achieved. The whole subject of satisfaction in retirement now needs to be considered, for this is unarguably a *prime* goal. What evidence, then, do studies of satisfaction in retirement have for retirement strategy?

A key issue is whether retirees should endeavor to involve themselves in an active life or should plan a progressive withdrawal. The latter might be seen as the natural and preferable choice if one was to accept the implications of the disengagement theory (Cumming & Henry, 1961). According to this theory there is an increasing tendency for older people to withdraw from social interaction and for this process to be characterized by its mutuality. The aging individual becomes more preoccupied with himself and less concerned with the outside world, while society begins increasingly to exclude the older person and so maintains its vitality.

Disengagement leads to changes in personality which can be recognized and related to measures of adjustment or satisfaction. Reichard, Livson, and Petersen (1962) studied 87 elderly men, rating them on 115 personality variables and on "adjustment to aging." Three personality groups were found to have high adjustment: One group characterized as a "mature" group had an active and constructive approach to life, a second "armored" group struggled in a defensive way from becoming dependent on others and resisted idleness, while a third "rocking-chair" group took life easily and relied on other people. It could be said that two of these groups were "engaged" while the third tended towards disengagement.

More specific evidence on the relationship between engagement and satisfaction came from the Kansas Study of Adult Life (Havighurst, 1968). Personality, Role Activity, and Life Satisfaction were related for 59 adults between the ages of 70 and 79. Eight typical personality groupings were identified, each with characteristic degrees of Life Satisfaction and Role Activity. A clear pattern established itself for groups with high degrees of Role Activity to have high Life Satisfaction. The exception was one group comprised of three people. These formed the *successful disengaged*. They had low activity levels, having moved away from role commitments as they had grown older, but they had high Life Satisfaction and strong feelings of self-regard. As personality types they were regarded as integrated though disengaged and holding a "rocking-chair" outlook on life.

Havighurst sees personality "as the pivotal relationship between level of activity and life satisfaction." The small proportion of interviewees who were judged to have successfully disengaged may have been predisposed by personality, but the successful nature of their retirement style may have been due to unusually supportive and favorable environments.

Personality may be important in old age insofar as it relates to religious outlook: This may serve to overcome the sense of futility, to provide goals by meeting religious observances, and to give meaning to the final and uneventful years of life. Moberg (1965) has reviewed several studies which show an association between religious commitment and good adjustment. The evidence also shows that while religious commitments tend to strengthen with age, church attendance tends to fall. Good adjustment increases with *participation* in religious activities and is highest among elders and leaders. But in another study (Barron, 1961) only 39% of interviewees affirmed that religion gave them most satisfaction in their lives. Worry about getting old was almost as prevalent among those who found religion comforting as those who did not.

It is possible to reconcile these various data by postulating that it is not so much religion and religious belief as *activity* in religion which is instrumental in producing satisfaction, and that this forms part of a wider tendency for activity in general to relate to good personal adjustment and satisfaction.

One problem of relating satisfaction to life style is that the expression of satisfaction tends to be governed by conventions. We do not know, for example, whether identification with a religious creed exerts pressure to declare life satisfaction. To do otherwise would be tantamount to a loss of faith in the personal value of the belief held.

If the expression of satisfaction is governed by conventions, so also may be the expression of dissatisfaction and the attribution of its causes. Szewczuk (1966) has found the "feeling of futility" to be the most frequent cause of dissatisfaction in old age. It is followed by bad health and approaching death. Other dissatisfactions may be masked by the umbrella term, a feeling of futility. For example, sexuality is known to decline slowly with age. Growing numbers of married couples eventually become sexual drop-outs, and by the age of 65 or 70 about a third of married interviewees no longer engage in regular coitus. For many partners this has become a source of dissatisfaction and depression (Rubin, 1965). His evidence also suggests that this decline is due less to the inevitable consequences of physical aging than to poor compatibility and to deep-seated attitudes that devalue sexual behavior in later life. Much interview material reveals not only that loss of sexual activity is often disturbing to old people but also that recovery of activity in favorable circumstances is a source of much happiness.

Another potential source of satisfaction or dissatisfaction concerns work itself. Most studies of attitudes toward retirement have shown that the majority of retirees accept retirement as a desirable condition, although this varies with income, the health of retirees, the elapse of time since retirement, and even with whether the retiree is interviewed in winter or summer (see Martin & Doran, 1967). There is, nevertheless, the possibility that acquiescence in retirement may be a matter of bowing to the inevitable. Evidence about the relative satisfactions of work and retirement could be more convincing where a *real* choice is offered.

This is typically the case with voluntary retirement. In one study, emeritus university professors were invited to engage in a research role within their university (Roman & Taietz, 1967). The response to the invitation seemed to depend on whether their proposed role corresponded to their pre-retirement role. Fifty percent accepted when this was the case against 25% where this was not. The former seems a high rate of response when it is considered that the majority of those declining were already carrying on their profession in a non-university setting, were in poor health, or were over 75 years of age. Only a minority of 15% were fully eligible but did not avail themselves of the opportunity. Thus, on balance, the preference favored continuation of the pre-retirement work activity. Roman and Taietz cite this high involvement rate as evidence of the way in which the opportunity structure modifies our notion of the disengagement theory.

The opportunity structure may apply also to the domestic environment. In a carefully controlled study, Carp (1966) set out to answer the question: Can old people be changed by altering the environments in which they live? Applicants for a new public-housing facility for older people were interviewed at the time of application and again 12-15 months after moving into new residence.

> The change in environment brought about was almost unanimously satisfying and associated with more favorable attitudes about themselves and towards others, in signs of improved physical and mental health and in more active and sociable patterns of life . . . . Social activities increased most markedly and gave the greatest satisfaction. Groups formed quickly about hobbies or other pastimes and they were maintained. Friendships flourished. There were a few romances, one leading to marriage within the first year . . . . The quality of relationships with family members improved following the move, regardless of whether there was more or less contact [p. 107].

Altogether there were 15 indices in the sphere of mental health and favorable adjustment which showed statistically significant gains in score. Unsuccessful applicants, initially similar to successful ones, showed little difference in scores over the same period.

Another means of changing the opportunity structure is through reactivation therapy. Szewczuk (1966) explored this approach with 13 subjects, a small sample of people from his earlier survey who, like the majority of respondents, had given the feeling of futility as the main reason for dissatisfaction with life. Activation began by exchange of ideas on various topics of interest to the subjects, followed by an attempt to engage them in a new form of interest. The new activities comprised establishing an apiary, raising rabbits, collecting herbs, looking after and reading stories to children, writing an autobiography, and collaborating in a research study in an old people's home.

Eleven of the 13 subjects showed an evident gain in self-respect and alertness, and recovery from depression. Szewczuk's studies led him to the following conclusions: "Inaction is not a necessary and irreversible phenomenon of old age; preservation of normal activity depends on the conviction of one's usefulness to others and engagement in new forms of activity facilitates adjustment to the general process of aging" (p. 126).

The concept of reactivation gains added importance from Havighurst's theory (1961) of the *equivalence of work and play* which states that to a considerable extent people can get the same satisfactions from leisure as from work. Havighurst's study of the use of leisure time by older people examined not only their favorite activities but the reasons why these gave satisfaction. These satisfactions were compared with those derived from work. There were many similarities: "a chance to be creative," "contact with friends," "service to others" and so on. The rank order of basic satisfactions in work and leisure activities was also similar.

If reactivation is to play an important part in retirement philosophy, special attention may need to be directed towards the "missing" satisfactions previously obtained from work.

CONCLUSIONS ON OBJECTIVES

An overview of retirement patterns in terms of maintenance of capacities and in terms of satisfaction and personal adjustment suggests that two retirement archetypes present themselves.

The first consists of low activity, a routine way of life, and a high measure of adjustment to a specific and restricted environment. The behavior of retirees will be heavily dependent on previous learning. New learning will be shunned and there will be a consequent loss of perceptual effort and discrimination. Loss of discriminative ability, in turn, will be instrumental in lowering performance in a wide variety of measures of ability, skill, and capacity.

This style of life may also hasten irreversible physiological deterioration, perhaps for the reasons enunciated by Smith and Smith (1965): "In cybernetic theory, learning involves changes in the detector neurons and systems of receptor and sensorimotor control. To become functional early in life, such neurons must be activated. To retain their precision of control, they must be reactivated repeatedly. We believe that aging involves deterioration of neuronic control which proceeds more rapidly if the cybernetic control systems are not used" (p. 359).

The retiree whose life conforms to the first pattern may yet count as one of the successfully disengaged. This will depend on the outlook of the individual and the supportive nature of his social environment. The degree of success may also be influenced by his personal attitude to religion, which can provide him with a goal and life style fully acceptable to the ego during an inactive existence.

The second archetype pattern is built on a high level of activity and typically includes the people Havighurst has characterized as *successful reorganizers*. Their successful adjustment to their environment demands interest in new learning and the maintenance of learning capacity and is likely to be encouraged by a pre-retirement life style in which learning skills have been fostered and maintained. This group is likely to have well-preserved abilities and to enjoy a high or medium-high satisfaction in retirement.

The evidence that has been reviewed suggests some grounds for directing retirement strategy towards an active retirement. The success of this strategy will be seen to depend on three factors:

1. *The provision of opportunities*. An active retirement is likely to remain an empty phrase for the majority of retirees until there comes into being amenities, institutions, and social programs in which retirees find it satisfying to participate.

2. *Willingness to take advantage of opportunity*. This is likely to be influenced not only by the personality and previous experience of the trainee, but by social attitudes and norms. Here the image of what is acceptable as a retirement style may have an important bearing on the extent to which retirees take advantage of those facilities available to them.

3. *Capacity to prosper (respond adequately) in that environ-*

ment. Encouraging retirees to engage in highly activating pursuits carries the disadvantage that the demands may be set above their level of accomplishment. Failure to progress in these pursuits may cause retirees to retreat into the shelter of disengagement. Hence any form of activating facility or pursuit provided for the benefit of older people needs to be accompanied by carefully designed induction procedures or training programs.

All three points may be illustrated by taking a case from the field of recreation. Little active thought has been given to the forms of recreation and of games that are of ideal design for older people. Nevertheless, enough is known from gerontological research to lay down certain desiderata. These are:

(i) Physical exercise should be involved but should be free from hurried and snatching movements. The exercise should be available all the year round.

(ii) The activity should not be subject to the constraints of speed stress. The older player must be allowed to play at his own pace.

(iii) Accuracy is desirable as a special feature of the game. The studies of the relationship between age and skill by Welford (1958) have shown consistent evidence of the preference of older performers for lower speed and higher accuracy. (Accuracy is commonly emphasized in skills which center on aiming.)

(iv) Demands on short-term memory should be avoided if possible.

(v) The game should offer great scope for strategy so that wisdom could be put to good use.

(vi) The game should offer a high ceiling in skill and achievement so that continued learning would be possible over a long period and there would be a minimal risk of tedium.

One game which answers all these requirement is pool or

snooker, which, nonetheless, encounters typical objections. Good tables are scarce although they could readily be provided in clubs and institutions. The image of the game is clouded over by association with low-class billiard halls and misspent youth. New players would tend to be discouraged because the skill of a novice falls far short of that of a moderate player. The difficulty in the case of beginners applies to almost all games that fulfill some or many of the requirements which make them ideal for older people, such as golf, darts, bowls, croquet, bridge, and chess. Hence training methods designed for older people may be as important for recreational activity as they have proved for industrial occupations (Belbin, 1965, 1969), with the same effect, that of enabling older people to become active again. Other difficulties, too, can be overcome, given adequate resources and with the drive that can be generated from a clear recognition of priorities and objectives.

At this stage the main problem is perhaps to translate general objectives into more specific programs. What choices are open to a retiree who wishes to cultivate a retirement life of the second archetypal pattern? The following are suggested as the main possibilities, starting with the most activating:

1. *Taking up a new career*. Successes in this field are found especially among people with "transferable" skills. For example, businessmen and executives sometimes prove successful in setting up small-scale enterprises devoted to a long-standing specialized interest such as propagating rare varieties of plant or breeding cage birds.

2. *Learning a new subject*, especially one which is to be put to use. A typical instance is when grandparents with a daughter living in a foreign country learn a new language so as to keep up with their grandchildren.

3. *Carrying on business as an entrepreneur*. Welford has suggested (1968) that entrepreneurial activity is more activating for

older people than are most other types of occupational activity since any failure to maintain a high level of discrimination is likely to result in rapid loss of position. A favorite form of entrepreneurial activity among retirees is in the buying and selling of objects d'art.

4. *Maintaining an occupational skill in a new setting.* Charles Odell (1965) has suggested that retirees should participate in Peace Corps activities and endeavor to make use of their skills and expertise in serving other nations. This specific suggestion can apply to only limited numbers of people. However, activities of this type might be greatly extended since they can be combined with travel and recreation.

5. *Carrying out part-time work.* Le Gros Clark (1966, 1968) has proposed a variety of ways in which part-time work can be provided. One well-proven method is for firms to set up communal workshops for their retirees. Extensive use is often made of scrap materials. In some instances retirees engage in repair work or cope with surplus orders, and in others they are allowed to sell their products outside. Small subsidies often suffice to enable programs to prosper, even in the case of handicapped and disabled people. In some towns in England agencies have been formed for the employment of older people in the normal labor market, and there is a brisk demand for people with particular skills to fill in temporary jobs or to engage in regular part-time work as in keeping the books for small businesses. In most cases "work" of this sort is seen to have three components: economic, recreational, and therapeutic.

6. *Pursuit of new recreations and cultural interests.* Few research studies have been carried out in this field, and this may be due perhaps to the point to which Kleemeier has drawn attention (1964), namely that: "Society views leisure with suspicion and rejects it summarily as a way of life. Western culture is better geared to and better understands work" (p. 184).

7. *Participation in new forms of social organization.* Here

Retirement Clubs and Fellowships have an important part to play. The basis of such organizations needs, however, to become richer and more varied if any appreciable proportion of the retired population is to be enrolled.

Pursuit of these programs seems worthwhile if the contention is accepted that cultural and recreational enrichment can have far-reaching consequences in promoting mental health in retirement, and in offsetting or slowing down some of the behavioral and mental changes associated with aging.

RESEARCH IMPLICATIONS

Any attempt to develop strategies for retirement will demand some feedback of information on how effective given strategies are. Is there confirmatory evidence that one retirement strategy leads to more retiree satisfaction than another? Or that various retirement strategies exercise different effects on the preservation and decline of psychomotor abilities?

The growth of retirement communities, each with its own amenities, opportunities, and associated cultures will increase the possibilities of comparison between different forms of retirement living. The scope may be increased still further by international cross-cultural study.

Progress much depends on the development of methodology in a few chosen fields:

√1. Since satisfaction is a prime objective of retirement living, standard scales will need to be developed for the measurement of current satisfaction and for determination of the sources of satisfaction. These measures will need to be related to the assessment, in retrospect, of satisfaction throughout earlier periods of life, and to the sources contributing to satisfaction during those earlier periods.

2. There is a need for a standard psychomotor test battery that

can be used as a measure of "mental health" and in terms of which deterioration and preservation of functions can be described.

3. Research into retirement strategy demands longitudinal studies. If comparisons are to be made between retirement groups, it will be necessary to find a means of comparing individuals at entry, since different retirement communities are liable to attract or possess people who differ widely in their initial personal characteristics. One fruitful possibility may rest on *matching*. While populations may differ, for example, in their average years of schooling and former occupations, meaningful comparisons become possible by taking similar individuals in dissimilar communities.

Research into retirement strategy is essentially long-term but may be seen as a key area if "preparation for retirement" is to rest on sure foundations.

WILLIAM L. MITCHELL

In 1962 Mr. Mitchell retired as United States Commissioner of Social Security, after 40 years of government service. Subsequently he was called back to work by the American Association of Retired Persons to conduct a study of retirement-preparation programs in federal agencies.

Mr. Mitchell was educated in the public schools of Port Washington, New York, and at Georgetown University's School of Foreign Service in Washington, D.C. After several years with the United States Department of Commerce, promoting foreign trade, he served as Southeastern Regional Director of the National Recovery Administration. In 1936 Mr. Mitchell began his career with the Social Security Board (later named the Social Security Administration). In 1955 he received the Distinguished Service Award of the Department of Health, Education and Welfare, and in 1968 the Medal Pour le Mérité of the International Social Security Association.

He has led a number of official delegations of international conferences on social security and social welfare and is a member of several professional organizations in those fields. He is the author of *Social Security in the United States* (1964), the United States Social Security section of the *Encyclopedia Britannica* (1963), and *Preparation of Retirement* (1968). Whether in the work force or in retirement, Mr. Mitchell is an accomplished water-color painter and an avid golfer.

7: LAY OBSERVATIONS ON RETIREMENT

WILLIAM L. MITCHELL

At the outset this should be identified as the layman's chapter. This leaves the author unhampered by facts not known to him when making assertions. As layman he claims no other than a passing acquaintance with the literature in the field, and he is not bound by the discipline of the professional in the use of precise terminology.

WHAT IS RETIREMENT?

The "retirement" we are attempting to characterize, at least in this chapter, is the situation which occurs when, to all intents and purposes, a career of gainful employment is permanently interrupted in upper middle-life. There are those for whom retirement began at birth. Others retire only to begin a new career. This chapter is not concerned, except incidentally, with either. Our focus is on the more typical situation. In it the new role of non-worker must be assumed. There is a change. The person moves from a life that is work-centered to one of leisure.

The group discussions which preceded the writing of this and other chapters were focused on "conceptualization of the retirement crisis." The word "crisis" functioned like the proverbial red flag. It precipitated energetic differences of opinion. To the layman, "crisis" ordinarily means something dramatic, probably an impending catastrophe. Retired people seldom think of retirement as a crisis in this sense. Retirement is neither momentary nor necessarily dramatic. To laymen, "crisis" may also mean the precursor of an abrupt and decisive change. It may be the fever that precedes death or recovery, a "critical period" of unknown duration during which the course of the future hangs in the balance. Certainly retirement is not a single decisive moment in experience. It would be a serious mistake to use the term "retirement crisis" in that sense, if one of our purposes is to establish a realistic concept of retirement as a basis for the conducting of research.

It is true that retirement usually occurs on a fixed date. This may be a "day of crisis" for some, but certainly not for all who retire. Retirement is a variable period of time. The beginning and the end remain to be determined. Retirement is not a period of fixed duration nor one that is the same for everyone. Still, it is an interval of time, not a momentary transfiguration.

It is risky to try to generalize regarding any aspect of retirement. The most variable variable probably is the retiree himself. Even a simple question like, "When does retirement begin?" can only be answered in general terms with many qualifications. Is it the day of the wrist-watch presentation and the last pay-check? For some, yes, but how about the fellow who much earlier sets a future date-certain and at that time begins to think and function in terms of retirement? How about the pensioner who promptly starts another career? Another who is called back to his old job?

When, if ever, does the retirement process end? Is it when one gets used to his new way of life? How about the man who says "I retired last year but I'm busier now than I ever was" or "I'm making more money than I ever did?" Is he still retired? Lack of a definitive ending, perhaps, is why retirement and aging tend to telescope. One begins to speculate on whether retirement is a state of mind, a way of life, an economic or social condition or, as is more likely, a complex of them all?

Retirement vs. Aging

Because most people retire in their sixties, there is a tendency to equate retirement with aging. Perhaps this is unavoidable to some extent, but retirement has characteristics of its own. True, the event of retirement usually occurs in or past middle age, but many other events do too, and in many of these the factor of aging is incidental. Actually, there is no more reason to associate retirement with aging than there is to regard a sabbatical year as aging. Gerontology has been an important field of research for quite some time, but the study of retirement, as such, has been neglected. The medical, psychological, social, and economic implications of retirement take on greater significance as our population grows and ages, and as retirement age lowers. It is high time that retirement be dealt with as a major, modern-day phenomenon rather than as a poor relation of geriatrics.

Social and Economic Retirement

Retirement as a mass, social and economic problem and one too large, 'costly, and complex to be solved simply and within the family is of relatively recent origin. Our agrarian forebears gave little thought to retirement. For most, retirement was the result of some crippling incapacity or old age. Then the retiree became the ward of the family. But the advent of the wage economy and the trek to the cities changed that. No longer could the wage-supported family, commonly living in an apartment or small home, take on—without serious sacrifice—the permanent burden of a non-contributing member.

Step by step, industry began its halting acceptance of an

obligation to deal with this situation. The principal device it employed was, and is, the pension. Government did likewise when the social security legislation was enacted in 1935. During the same period, organized labor became interested and expanded its influence on a rising scale. At present a union contract can hardly be found that does not contain important provisions dealing with retirement. Both government and industry are vital factors in the process of retirement. That being the case, the employee does not function alone on his retirement plan but is a partner in a program over which he exercises only partial control.

The purposes of the employer's retirement plan for his employees frequently are quite different than those of the retiree's plan for himself. However, both plans may serve common ends. For example, the employer may be motivated more by fiscal and management pressures than by humanitarian and social considerations. His actions may be taken to accomplish tax advantages, satisfy union demands, or maintain balance in the age distribution of his employees. Nevertheless, they may contribute to the welfare of the prospective retiree. Then the interests of both are served. On the other hand, rigidly inforced retirement ages and seniority policies, and inadequate pensions may cause feelings of insecurity, resentment, and dependency.

Fringe benefits such as retirement pensions and health insurance have become commonplace in modern employment and compensation practice. In fact, fringe benefits may constitute a substantial percentage of labor costs. Whether they are an unmixed blessing in the process of retirement has yet to be established. Undue emphasis on the pension itself may have a corrosive influence on many employees in undermining the homely virtues of independence, self-reliance, and initiative. Should this be so, the effect on adjusting to retirement could be unfortunate. On the other hand, the advantages of the advance planning which might be triggered by this stimulus could offset any possible disadvantages.

A case can be made for the hypothesis that the employer starts the process of retirement for many employees at the time they are hired. It is then that the pension plan is emphasized as a "plus" in the wage offered and as an evidence of a considerate, forward-looking employment policy.

The effect of the pension plan on attitude toward retirement may thereafter be magnified if the employer periodically distributes to his employees reminders of their retirement benefits and obligations. One of the obligations, however delicately stated, may be that plans to retire at a fixed age should be made. Whether the overall effect on the individual is good or bad is debatable. This practice, which is common, should be evaluated as part of the retirement process, in terms of the effect it is likely to have on the individual.

The same is true of other features of employment policy and its implementation. It may be particularly important to assess the impact of unfunded pension schemes that terminate benefit rights if an employee is separated before retirement age or if he resigns to take other work; periodic letters that warn of impending retirement; and the availability of a training program for retirement preparation.

The retirement process is also involved in the situation brought about by the loss of a job and inability to find other work. Permanent loss of income because of disability causes another and even more complicated type of retirement. Still another is the retirement of the self-employed. Retirees with these and other less typical backgrounds offer interesting research possibilities. For example, do the self-employed adjust more readily to retirement? They seem to. If they do, why? Is it because, as a group, they are more self-reliant and resourceful? Is it because they have greater control over the time and circumstances of their retirement? Research endeavors must take into account the differential effects on the retirement process of the circumstances of entry into retirement.

PEOPLE IN RETIREMENT

So much for the retirement situation. The observations which follow will deal with how people react or adjust to the situation. The word "observations" has been used advisedly. These observations are not offered as hypotheses. Rather they are theories or assumptions resulting from personal experience and observation.

Sine Qua Non

The heading may overstate the case but not by much. It introduces the premise, not too profound and perhaps even trite, that good health, adequate income, and friends—in that order—are the three most important factors in a successful retirement. Agreeable activity, spiritual interests, a philosophic outlook, versatility, and who knows what else may be cited. They are all important. But which of the three basics could be displaced by any other factor?

Good health, as used here, means only the absence of disabling disease or of a permanent or long-term disability, mental or physical. We are not thinking of Superman or even Popeye with his spinach, just of the person who usually feels well and thinks straight. The income needed is only an amount which is secure and which bears a reasonable relationship to pre-retirement earnings. It may be defined as that which will support the retiree and his dependents "in the manner to which they have become accustomed." Friends do not need to be many but must be of the all-weather type, those who share common interests and who are close enough to be confidants. Generally the retiree blessed with good health, adequate income, and friends carves out a satisfying existence in his retirement.

Attempting to identify the factors which contribute most importantly to a successful adjustment may result in neglecting the fairly obvious fact that, except for some shift in emphasis, the factors which make for successful retirement are the same ones that make for satisfaction in life at any stage or age. While this conclusion is fairly manifest, nevertheless it seems to be over-looked by many professionals who study and write in this field. Suppose, for example, we were to conceptualize the marriage crisis instead of the retirement crisis. Certainly the adjustment process would be seriously complicated by poor health or poverty. Lack of friends might be less of a handicap, but only while the stars were lighting up the honeymoon. And so it would be in meeting the other critical phases or events in life. The retirement period may present one significant difference, particularly when retirement occurs in the later years. A phase of aging which we might call later maturity or approaching senility may cause a rise in resistance to change and a lowered capacity to adapt. For this reason it may be impractical to consider retirement completely apart from aging. In addition, advancing age is associated with less favorable conditions.

Health as a factor in retirement adjustment

In our judgement, too much emphasis has been placed upon the effect of retirement on physical health. Of course, good health helps in adjusting to most anything, and certainly we would not want to depreciate its importance; but to suggest that the rigors of retirement adjustment will undermine physical health is largely nonsense. (We have yet to see our first case of diabetes, or even dandruff, caused by retirement.) The chances are rather that a person, relieved of the pressures of a regular job and reinforced by more rest, regular meals and greater freedom for enjoyable pursuits, will improve in physical health.

Mental health may be something else again. But even the mind of the average person accustomed, as it must be at retirement age, to the task of adjusting to change, can be expected to meet the demands of this new test. However, people who habitually have been highly sensitive and easily upset may have their tensions magnified by even the prospect of retirement. Within the acquaintance of almost everyone there are people with this trouble, and we would not minimize their problem. A personality defect existing in earlier life may even be accented in retirement. We have no doubt that the incidence of serious mental disturbance rises during retirement years, but this may and probably does occur more because of advancing years than anything brought on by retirement. Perhaps the stress which some contend is placed by retirement upon physical health reflects the concern of physicians, psychiatrists, and medically oriented researchers whose experience is mainly with sick people.

Income significance

It would be laboring the obvious to stress adequate income as an important factor in successful retirement. The fellow who said, "I've been rich and I've been poor, but believe me, rich is better," summed it up quite well. In this writer's study of preparation for retirement programs in the federal government in 1967, every reporting agency that had a program listed income and finance as its number one discussion topic (Mitchell, 1967). This, of course, was in response to the expressed choice of the trainees. When retirement is voluntary, financial security is the first prerequisite to an affirmative decision; when the retirement is mandatory at a fixed age, the concern is always, "Will I have enough to get by?" When retirement drops the income to levels which require drastic lowering of living standards, the effects may be very serious. It is then that we see the results in strained family relationships (twice the husband and half the money), withdrawal from social life, loss of status, rise in anxiety, unhappiness, and declining health. The adjustment may be the more severe because it comes at an age when it is more difficult to adapt. When poor health is added to financial difficulties the results are often devastating.

There doubtless have been studies made which document our thesis, but all of this has been observed in our personal experience. Here again, we want to make the point that the re-ordering of financial and budget plans which often is necessary at the time of retirement is due typically to retirement, not to aging.

The importance of friends and associates

By coincidence, when this was being written a government employee-relations officer called to request a copy of our new handbook on preparation for retirement (Mitchell, 1968). He said, "We have a pre-retirement program but we seem to be missing something quite fundamental. There's hardly a day that we don't have one or more of our former workers in here who gives every evidence of being a lost soul now that he is retired. They are obviously at a loss for something to do, and seem to be looking for some kind of comfort and understanding from their former associates." This situation, repeated many times in our experience, does not so much indicate inability to find substitute activity for former work as it does the unconscious reliance that so many people place upon their work for satisfying activity and upon their work associates for social contacts. Gregarious and outgoing people rarely think of this as a problem and for them it usually is not, but even they may find that the friend at the workbench or in the next office is not the friend in retirement.

It is possible for some to foresee the problem and to do something about it before retirement. The classical methods of engagement in church, clubs, and social groups all help but, as in the control of drug addiction, the person with the problem must want to do something about it and make the effort. In our experience, whether because of personality quirks, inertia, failure to recognize the problem, or something else, relatively few of those who should make the effort do so. They wait until retirement arrives with its abrupt and pressing need of friends.

The Retiree: Man or Mouse

We have already alluded to the hazard of generalizing about people in retirement. People do not lose any of their individual characteristics in retirement. Some personality traits, both weak and strong, may become more or less accentuated; but none is lost. Also, individual adjustment may reflect the impact of the family situation, educational level, health, financial status, environment, and other external or acquired influences. However, to find out why some succeed in retirement and others fail, we do not need case histories on each one. Some rough categorization is possible. A simple grouping would be: those who have no trouble adjusting, those who never adjust, and all those in between.

For purposes of research this simple grouping would have to be done (and perhaps has been done) ex post facto. The trick would be to identify the successes and failures and find out what makes them tick or fizzle. Another possible approach would be to relate success or failure in retirement to life styles. Both types of study would doubtless prove useful in testing the validity of present theory. Considerations apart from personal characteristics would necessarily have to be taken into account in such studies.

So much has been made of the trauma suffered by some in making the retirement transition that we tend to regard the retiree as a problem and retirement as a sort of bête noire. In our judgement, the picture thus presented is highly distorted. It is misleading and has tended to make retirement adjustment more difficult. After all, the average person has been faced with the problems brought about by change all his life and has usually accommodated to them without resort to the psychiatrist's couch. He is a man, not a mouse.

The average person—the solid citizen type—in our experience is the man (see later comments about women) who occasionally thinks about retirement in middle-life or possibly earlier when the subject is brought up in the discussion of pension rights as an inducement to accept a job offer or as an objective in buying life insurance. He becomes more concerned as time passes but this concern is largely with prospective *economic* security. It is only a year or two before actual retirement that he begins to sense the significance of some of the more subtle questions he may have to face. This is the time of ambivalence. It is the time when the happy contemplation of the joys of a life of leisure is tempered by sobering thoughts such as: What will I do with my time? Will we really have enough to live on? Suppose I get sick? But the typical retiree has met all these uncertainties before and, barring misfortune, he will meet them successfully again. He does not lose his ability to adjust just because he has substituted a pension for a payroll. He will construct a new and rewarding life. In our opinion, this will happen at least as often as not. He is representative of our "in-between group" in the previously mentioned simple grouping.

Then we have what might be called the "preferred retirement risk group." In it are people whose personal and economic problems are minimal and who want nothing so much as to get away from the nine-to-five rat-race, to get to that Shangríla in Florida, or to indulge themselves in long-denied pursuits of their own choosing. The people in this category are, in general, naturally adaptable, resourceful, and well-adjusted. There is reverse trauma (if there is such a thing) among members of this group. A new and satisfying life opens for them. They never had it so good. They will make it on their own.

Exclude the two groups above described, and we have left a core of problem cases. They are the ones who, in the vernacular, have "shot their wad." They have "had it." They exist but they do not really live. They consume but they do not produce. Some of them probably are beyond recall but others, given the proper help and stimulus, doubtless have a latent potential for achieving the satisfactions both of retirement and of later life. How to deal with this group, and particularly with those who seem to have but little potential, is a high-priority research field. These people are the wards of the professional.

Now a further word about the solid citizen type. The first phase of his new retirement life is one of relief and relaxation. His dormant or repressed interests and talents are revived. He is now free to indulge himself as seldom has he been able to do before. Travel, sports, hobbies—there is time for all if the pocketbook, the muscles, and a few other restraints permit. But then, after a few weeks or months, the "good life" begins to lose its zest. Intervals of disinterest and boredom become more frequent. He feels that he is wasting his time and that he has lost status. He begins to feel a little ashamed. Many times he has had to answer the question, "What are you doing with your time now?" The question usually implies, "What are you doing that is worthwhile?" The answer becomes increasingly embarrassing.

At this point our average retiree will decide to resolve his conflict by seeking more rewarding activity, and in this way to regain some of his partially lost feeling of status and prestige. The way in which he works out his problem will be influenced by temperament, life experience, and what might be called environmental pressures: community and church service invitations, job offers, budget stringency, and just happenstance.

If his goals usually have been material ones, he will look for employment for pay. If he is the sociable, benevolent type, he will seek satisfaction in volunteer charitable, spiritual, or political service. These and his other retirement objectives are not mutually exclusive. In fact, there is a marked tendency for them to merge. The pleasures of recreation, travel, puttering, and just loafing will not be abandoned but will tend to become the gap-fillers. Our average retiree, failing to find and to adapt to more socially acceptable and, shall we say, more sacrifical types of activity, will tend to gravitate into the problem category.

Woman's Work Is Never Done

We would not venture an opinion on the relevance of our previous observations to women in retirement, except to suggest that they may be pertinent in the case of single, career women. The situation of these women would not appear to be basically different from that of men, single or married. The housewife, on the other hand, rarely goes into what we call retirement. Her life, however, may undergo considerable change when her husband retires. Frequently there is a complication we might call the "husband underfoot syndrome." The number of jokes about this problem attest to its seriousness. To the parties concerned, it is no laughing matter. Unless it is resolved with intelligence and understanding, it can have serious family consequences.

[In case of the married, non-career woman who works, retirement usually does not seem to have the impact that it does on men. The chances are she took a job more for a little extra money, or for something to do. On the other hand, men, in addition to making a living, are concerned also with the social or status value of work. When employment stops, the non-career women just starts being a housewife again. This reasoning also applies to some extent to the career woman. She does not have to explain or justify her retirement to her friends. Moreover, she can take on payless, humanitarian activities in her retirement without the loss to ego which men often feel. However, it must not be overlooked that the single woman finds quite often that, in her career, she has isolated herself from the companionship that might contribute importantly to successful adjustment to her retirement.

Our opportunity for observing the retirement of women in situations other than those cited above, such as husband and wife both working, widow, and the women with children, have been very limited. As a generalization, women appear to have less of an adjustment to make to retirement than do men, and temperamentally they adapt more readily. This probably accounts for the fact that the machinery of retirement is geared primarily to the needs of men. Perhaps this should be looked into further.

PREPARATION FOR RETIREMENT

Surprisingly little research has been done on the effectiveness of training programs in preparation for retirement. The purpose of such programs is, of course, to assist the trainee in his adjustment to retirement when the event takes place. The extent to which programs accomplish this goal is still a matter of surmise and opinion. It is recognized that adjustment is a personal matter and is not easily influenced or aided in seminars or by the method most commonly used.

Studies have been made to determine the kind of people, by sex, educational level, work experience, et cetera who make the best and speediest transition. These have obvious implications for retirement preparation programs. It is only within the past year or so that serious, professional research has been undertaken to evaluate training techniques and subject matter in order to determine which contribute most to retirement adjustment. The United States Civil Service Commission has completed a sample study of employees nearing retirement age, and of previous employees who have been in retirement for varying periods of time. It demonstrated an overwhelming need and sentiment for pre-retirement training and prompted a reversal in the negative policy of the Commission's attitude toward such training.

Some employers object to retirement-preparation training on the ground that it may tend to undermine employee morale, divert their job interest, and reduce production. There may be something to this. However, the popularity of retirement training has been growing rapidly ever since the conclusion of World War II. An educated guess is that in the past 20 years the percentage of large industrial employers doing retirement training or counselling increased from 10-15% to about 60-70%. The latter figure is the percentage disclosed in 1964 by a sample study made by the National Industrial Conference Board (Mitchell, 1964). Also, according to this study, counseling in industry is done more frequently individually than in groups. This seems strange. It appears, however, that about one-half of these companies limit their counselling to information on their own pension plans and Social Security.

The study made by this writer showed that in the federal government not more than 20-25% of those retiring had access to any kind of training program worthy of the name. Little evidence was available as to how helpful it was to those exposed to it. There is no questioning the fact that retirement confronts the average person with an array of difficult personal problems, many of which might be dealt with helpfully through counselling and training. Probably the most important aspect of pre-retirement education is the stimulus it gives to planning. There is little doubt that there is a demonstrable relationship between sound pre-retirement planning and success in adjustment.

Much so-called "pre-retirement training" is really preparation for aging, not for retirement This can be bad psychologically and it can detract from the presentation of material which is more pertinent to retirement and of more practical use to the trainee. For example, reduced income in retirement will probably require the retiree to overhaul the family budget and change his investments and insurance. There may be family and living readjustments, the sales or purchase of property, and the consideration of employment opportunities. These are all subjects which may be taught and are likely to be important at the time of retirement. On the other hand, discussion of the *physical* disabilities of the aged which are not specifically related to retirement is out of place and could not be expected to improve the retiree's atttitude toward retirement. Hints on physical health for the aging can be reserved for a later time.

We have already observed that resourcefulness and adaptability are very important to retirement adjustment. Whether they are qualities that are instinctive or learned we do not know, but we do know they are difficult to teach, particularly in maturity. Pre-retirement training would be vastly improved if trainees could be helped in strengthening these qualities.

PUBLIC POLICY: SOME OF ITS IMPLICATIONS
FOR RETIREMENT

The interaction between the economy and retirement is a matter of important political concern. Changes in the economy that affect retirement are on one side of the coin and the impact of retirement on the economy is on the other. The effect of political action in either area can be very significant. Therefore, the retiree—past, present, and future—has a large stake in the formulation of national policy and in the enactment of legislation on both areas at all levels of government.

Since this book deals primarily with retirement rather than with economics, let us consider an example or two of how the character of retirement responds to economic change, particularly changes brought on by political action.

In this country as late as the 1920's, official government policy opposed public programs supporting retirement as a way of life. A person was expected to provide for his own retirement out of savings. The pioneer's dedication to the work ethic and to the virtues of thrift, rugged individualism, and family responsibility for its members still dictated public policy. However sound and desirable these public attitudes were at the time, they had to give way to the demands of the economic disaster which exploded in 1929. The plight of the older person was especially serious. He was the first to go as jobs dwindled, and his savings melted away.

It was then that public policy in regard to retirement turned full circle to the support of a national program designed to encourage and facilitate retirement. The objective, of course, was to get the older worker out of the labor market. He was helped financially to do so. This was expected to alleviate the overall employment situation and, together with the other features of the Social Security Act, to pump new purchasing power into the economy.

Basically, objectives of the public action were economic, but the social and psychological effects were of great importance. It is questionable that many Congressmen voting for a compulsory system of social insurance gave much thought to the giant step they were taking toward institutionalizing retirement. This legislation influenced a profound change in the public attitude toward the retiree. Consider also the psychological advantages to people nearing retirement of a guaranteed, secure (even though small) income made possible by their own contributions. Surely those features of the legislation which were basically intended for other purposes turned out to help in easing adjustment to retirement.

Public assistance, also a part of the Social Security Act, operated differently. The retiree on public assistance lacked the assurance of benefit continuity. Moreover, he was given the impression (unfairly, we might say) that he was "beholden." Thereby his retirement adjustment was made more difficult. This point is illustrated by the wistful humor of an incident recounted by Helen Hall of Henry Street Settlement House fame. One day at the House a little old lady was being teased about the attention she was being paid by a fellow visitor of the opposite sex. She admitted her affection for him but added, "You know, John is on public assistance and I am too. I'd like to find someone who is on Social Security." The source of income in retirement appears to be important. Charity and, to a less extent, non-contributory benefit programs are humiliating. Contributory or insurance-type programs have much better status and tend to bestow that status on the beneficiary. Investment income is best of all non-employment incomes.

Here is an example of another retirement situation involving public policy. Professional people and the self-employed (including medical doctors who feared an involvement in "socialized medicine") lobbied for years against coverage under social security. Among their arguments was the contention that they seldom retired and thus would be forced to pay for protection they did not need. Another but unpublicized objection had to do more with status, exclusion from the mob. Incidentally, their opposition did not help retirement establish itself as a socially acceptable way of life. The eventual resolution of the controversy was the enactment of the "Keogh Bill," essentially a tax measure which permitted tax deductions to self-employed persons for premiums paid on retirement plans providing annuities of not more than $2500 per year. In the final analysis, the upshot of all this was that retirement received a prestige boost from an influential group who in turn obtained a tax break.

Another example, this one in the labor field, involves the well-known Taft-Hartley Act. Its original purpose was to provide a legal base for collective bargaining. When it was passed, no one thought of its special relevance to retirement; but its use in that connection became clear when the courts ruled that fringe benefits, including pensions, were subject to collective bargaining.

Then we have the growing trend of early retirement. Early retirement for people in hazardous occupations has been common practice for years. But now we are experiencing a progressively lower retirement age as a concomitant of our expanding economy, which continues to produce more than we consume, despite a rising population. This portends not only an expansion of the retired population and wider age distributions, but possibly also an improved economic and social status for them. It appears that public attitude has already been conditioned to lower retirement age and is reflected in current agitations for a lower age requirement for Social Security eligibility. This is not to suggest that earlier retirement is the only method of absorbing increased leisure. Shorter working hours and longer vacations also will be among the choices.

In conclusion, perhaps the inference to be drawn from these examples is that persons in the retirement period are still groping their way toward a more identifiable and acceptable status. For the present, they are being buffeted by the vagrant winds of social, economic, and political action. The status of this period of life has improved and will continue to improve despite occasional diversions, detours, and dead-ends. If it is to be an acceptable and satisfying phase of the life span it must provide dignity, security, opportunities for rewarding service, and a gratifying social life. Certainly the retiree can be helped in the achievement of these ideals but, within the limits of his capacity, he is responsible for his own destiny. He should be kept aware of this. He is not a ward of society; he is part of society.

ETHEL SHANAS, PH.D.

Dr. Shanas is Professor of Sociology at the University of Illinois at Chicago Circle. She is the author of *The Health of Older People* (1962), co-author of *Old People in Three Industrial Societies* (1968), co-editor of *Social Structure and the Family* (1965) and of *Methodological Problems in Cross-National Studies in Aging* (1968). In addition she has contributed numerous articles to professional journals.

Ethel Shanas has served as Secretary of the Gerontological Society and as Secretary of the Executive Committee of the American Branch of the International Association of Gerontology. She is a consultant to various governmental agencies and research organizations. In 1960 she was Chairman of the Research Committee for the White House Conference on Aging for the State of Illinois. In 1969 she was Rapporteur of a United Nations Conference on the Elderly.

8: ADJUSTMENT TO RETIREMENT:

Substitution or Accommodation?

ETHEL SHANAS

Retirement, that is, the giving up of work, is a major event in the life of men and women in industrial society. Just as entering the work force heralds the beginning of economic self-sufficiency for most people, leaving the work force is also a beginning—the start of a different sort of life in which leisure rather than work becomes preeminent. Retirement is now widespread in the United States and its influence on the individual and society is pervasive. Therefore it is surprising that retirement as a social event, an occurrence affecting both the individual and society, has had only limited attention in the sociological literature (Maddox, 1966).* With few exceptions, an individual's leaving work and its resultant effects on him and those around him have been considered as primarily economic rather than sociological problems (Streib & Thompson, 1958). In contrast to the limited attention sociologists have given to retirement, they have studied in some depth the

---

*An excellent statement is given in the paper by Maddox. He points out that while the economic literature on retirement is voluminous, the sociological literature is limited and seriously deficient in theoretical constructs.

worker, the work place, and the world of work (Nosow & Form, 1962).

/ The present paper deals with the adjustment of the individual to retirement. Two approaches to the study of adjustment are outlined. Each of these approaches stresses a different process: one, substitution; the other, accommodation. For brevity these approaches may be identified as the "substitution theory" and the "accommodation theory." Neither of these positions, as it is presented here, is a formal theory of retirement. On the other hand, the tacit acceptance of the presuppositions of one or the other of these two approaches, substitution and accommodation, has served to organize and give direction to a variety of research enterprises.

In the discussion which follows, we will first review various usages of the word "retirement" and indicate how these usages imply different referrents of the term. Then we will consider the two "theories" of adjustment to retirement: the substitution theory and the accommodation theory. The presuppositions of each of these theories, the kinds of research questions raised by each theory, and some of the research findings which result from these differing approaches will be presented.

RETIREMENT; A VARIETY OF USAGES

The word "retirement" is used in a number of different ways, each of which implies a specific meaning. "Retirement" is commonly used to describe an event or a crisis period, or a stage of life. The exact meaning given to the term depends upon who is using it, whether he be an economist, a psychologist or sociologist, or a worker or employer.

/ The most rigorous definition of retirement is made by the economists. Generally when economists refer to a person as retired they mean either that he is totally absent from the labor force or that he works so few hours each week or so few weeks during the year that he can no longer be considered part of the labor force. The usage of the term "retirement" by workers and employers approaches that of the economists.

In common parlance retirement is used to describe the giving up of work, an event. Thus, we speak of the number of persons who retire each year, or query persons as to whether they are looking forward to retirement, that is, to leaving work.

Psychologists and sociologists often add another dimension to their use of the term "retirement." In addition to retirement being an event, it is seen as a special kind of event which heralds a critical period in the life span. For example, we speak of individuals experiencing "retirement shock." In this usage of the term, "retirement" is seen as a crisis. When retirement is viewed as a crisis, a temporal dimension is added to its meaning. It is no longer a single event. It is conceptualized as a process with a beginning, a middle, and some sort of final resolution.

In addition to being used to describe both an event and a process, "retirement" is also used to describe a stage of life or a social status. In this usage, "retirement" is the period of life which follows an individual's career as a worker. When we speak of someone as "retired," then, we are describing a stage of life, not an event or a process of change.

Because of the various usages of "retirement," the same person may be described as having retired at a given date, that is, as having experienced a given event; as "adjusting to retirement," that is, as undergoing a process of change; and as "retired," that is, as having a given social status. All of these usages of the term "retirement" are widespread and each of them has different referents. This paper is concerned primarily with retirement as a process of adjustment. It considers two ways in which the process may take place.

ADJUSTMENT TO RETIREMENT–THE PROCESS
OF SUBSTITUTION

Retirement, the giving up of work, emerges as a widespread practice only when the level of living within a society is such that persons can be supported by society without themselves being workers. To give up work at a set age and to spend the remainder of one's life in retirement, then, is a recent phenomenon.* In the United States retirement was formally recognized and given an institutional setting with the passage of the Social Security Act in 1935. The Act provided retirement insurance payments for a selected group of workers. With time, the provisions of the Act have been broadened so that all but a few workers are covered by government social insurance provisions.

Although studies of workers and of the level of employment have a rather long history, studies of retirement and of its effect on the individual have a comparatively short history.** Serious consideration of retirement as a social event began in the late 1940's with work of Robert J. Havighurst, Eugene Friedmann, and their associates (Friedmann & Havighurst, 1954). Havighurst began to study older people in the mid 1940's. As he considered the aged in American life Havighurst was impressed with what he saw as a new phenomenon: An increasing proportion of workers in the United States were giving up their work at a set age while at the same time the length of life was increasing. In the past, retirement from work was the prerogative of the well-to-do or was forced on

---

*In 1900, 68% of all men 65 and over were in the labor force, in 1967, 27% were in the labor force. Data for 1900 from Table 4, Slavick and Wolfbein, 1960. Data for 1967 from Table A-2, *Manpower Report of the President*, 1968.

**Frédéric Le Play was an early sociologist who considered the social aspects of work particularly in relation to the family (1855).

those too sick to work. Now, it was becoming widespread among all segments of the population, working men as well as their employers. At this stage in his thinking, Havighurst became convinced that, first, work has different meanings for different persons; and that, second, retirement brings or will bring "a loss of certain satisfactions and thus create a void in a person's life which he will seek somehow to fill" (Friedmann & Havighurst, 1954, p. 6). Individual good adjustment in retirement, then, is dependent on the person's finding activities in retirement which offer satisfactions to replace those which he received from work.

It should be pointed out that this theory of adjustment to retirement based on the substitution process was developed by Havighurst a score of years ago. Havighurst himself would not necessarily advocate the theory at the present time. The theory, however, had and continues to have considerable influence on sociological research in retirement.

The theory of adjustment in retirement developed by Havighurst and outlined by him and his associate Friedmann in *The Meaning of Work and Retirement* was social-psychological in nature. The theory presumes that:

1. Giving up work will involve a sense of loss on the part of the individual.
2. The focus of this sense of loss will differ from person to person.
3. For a satisfactory adjustment in retirement it is necessary that the individual make some substitution for what he has lost in work.
4. This substitution involves replacing one set of activities by another.

The theory outlined by Havighurst and Friedman is primarily an activity theory. If one set of activities, that is, work, is removed from the person, then another set of activities, "meaningful" leisure, is to be substituted. In elaborating their theory, Havighurst and Friedmann posited a principle of equivalence of work and play in which they argued that many of the values of play can be achieved through work and many of those of work, through play. Basically the substitution theory of adjustment states that for good adjustment in retirement an individual must substitute for work other activities which will give him the satisfaction of work. Havighurst and Friedmann recognized that in stressing activity in their theory they might simply be reflecting their own middle-class backgrounds. They spoke of guarding against the bias of over-enthusiasm "which might lead us to underestimate the iron necessity of work for the overwhelming majority of men in our society—a need which is not as yet alleviated by the average retirement pension . . . . But having accepted the fact that men do and must work for gain we are then inquiring into the conse-quences of having spent a major portion of one's adult life in the activity which society defines as a job" (p. 185-186).

The substitution theory raises certain pertinent research questions. First among these is: What are the meanings of work? Using this theory, it is not possible to study adjustment in retirement without setting up some typology of the meanings of work. Other questions are: How do these meanings of work differ among various persons, and do they vary by sex, by age, by occupation, or by other characteristics? In addition: How can one substitute the meanings of leisure for the meanings of work? And finally: How are the meanings of work related to adjustment in retirement? Implicit in this last question is another problem which has influenced research in aging since the late 1930's: What is a good measure of adjustment?

The research which resulted from the use of the substitution theory tended to be studies of the meaning of work. Havighurst began his use of the substitution theory by seeking to identify the meanings of work for various occupational groups. Studies of the meaning of work were made among samples of steel workers, coal miners, skilled craftsmen, sales people, and physicians. The primary meaning of work for steel workers turned out to be money; for craftsmen and sales people, activity; for coal miners, routine and association with their fellows; and for physicians, service. (See Table 1.)

The Havighurst and Friedmann studies were frankly exploratory. While the samples studied were carefully selected from specific occupational groups, the questionnaires used in each study were not the same. In some occupational groups there was a significant amount of non-response to the questions. The age categories studied varied from group to group. Friedmann and Havighurst recognized that these technical weaknesses might affect their findings and their interpretation of the data, but they were unable to estimate the extent of such bias. In any case, they were more concerned with developing hypotheses for further study than in refining their techniques.

An attempt to apply the substitution theory in a national probability sample of older people was made by Shanas (1962). In a 1957 study of persons 65 and over, retired men were asked to list the things they missed about not working, and employed men to indicate what they would miss when they stopped working. Then the respondents were asked to select the single item that they missed or would miss most. Half of all men, both among the employed and the retired, indicated income from the job, money, as most important. About three of every ten retired men and four of every ten working men said that something other than money was most important to them. (See Table 2.)

Income was mentioned much more often in the 1957 national sample study of the elderly than in the Havighurst-Friedmann research. Some explanation of the marked variation in findings between the two studies is needed. The differences seem to have

TABLE 1*

Comparison[a] of five occupational groups on the meaning of work

| Meaning | Steelworkers | Coal-Miners | Percentage Distribution | | | |
			Skilled Craftsmen	Sales People	Physicians
Total	100	100	100	100	100
Money	28	18	11	0	0
Routine	28	19	15	21	15
Self-respect, respect of others	16	18	24	23	20
Association	15	19	20	20	19
Activity	13	11	30	26	15
Service		16	[b]	10	32
Number of Respondents	128	153	208	74	39

*Adapted from Table 26 from Friedmann and Havighurst (1954).
[a]Results are in relative percentages assuming each person to have given a single response.
[b]Not covered in interview.

TABLE 2*
Major item missed in retirement, and major item likely to be missed in
retirement, retired and employed men, aged 65 and over

| | Percentage Distribution | |
Major Item	Retired	Employed
Total	100	100
Money	50	48
Other items[a]	32	40
Nothing	10	3
No answer	8	10
Number of respondents	468	324

*Adapted from Tables 41 and 43 from Shanas, 1962.
[a]Includes people on the job, feeling of being useful, respect of others, routine,
new things on the job.

been the result of three factors: the occupational make-up of the
samples, the age of the subjects, and the question format. The
bulk of older American workers are blue-collar or service workers.
Because a probability sample was used in the Shanas study, these
formed the majority of its respondents. Only three of the groups
studied by Havighurst and Friedmann were blue-collar workers
according to the Census classifications, and members of one of
these, the skilled craftsmen, were in highly élite occupations.

All respondents in the national survey were aged 65 and over.
The Havighurst and Friedmann respondents included many persons
who were not yet 65. A group aged 55-64 were included in the
steel worker study; half of the coal miner respondents were
between the ages of 50-60; and the salespersons ranged in age
from 55-71.

Finally, a standard question format was employed in the Shanas
study, but various questionnaires, designs, and interviewing techniques were used in the different occupational studies summarized
by Friedmann and Havighurst. Furthermore, "the interviews
reported in the Friedmann-Havighurst book did not ask for the

primary meaning of work, but rather for the *meanings* of work. (Only skilled craftsmen were asked to rank the meanings.) Thus the respondent was probably cued to state non-financial meanings as well as financial meanings, and he often talked at greater length about the non-monetary meanings because there was more to be said and explained about them" (Robert J. Havighurst, personal communication).

The 1957 national study raised new questions about the substitution theory. Was money the major meaning of work for most American men? Were the other meanings of work reported by Friedmann and Havighurst irrelevant for most American workers? In 1962, the same question used in 1957 was again employed in a national sample study of persons aged 65 and over. The findings from this question are reported in Table 3. Here the answers to the question are tabulated by the employment status and occupation of the respondent. (See Table 3.) Two major findings emerge, one relating to the role of money in the meaning of work, and the other, the differing non-economic meanings of work for different occupational groups. Retired men in the United States, irrespective of occupational group, are most likely to miss "money" when they retire. When occupational differences are considered, however, blue-collar workers, whether retired or employed, are more likely than white-collar or agricultural workers to report that money is the thing they miss most about their jobs or would miss most if they gave up working.

The non-economic meanings of work differ from occupation to occupation. Among the non-economic meanings of work, "the people at work" was most significant to white-collar workers; the work itself to agricultural workers; and both "the people at work" and the work itself to blue-collar workers. Interestingly enough, a significant number of persons, as many as 9% of all retired men, said they missed "nothing" about their jobs. White-collar and professional workers—those with the highest retirement incomes—

TABLE 3*

Major item missed in retirement and major item likely to be missed in retirement, retired and employed men, aged 65 and over, by social class

Percentage Distribution

Major Item	White Collar		Blue Collar and Service Workers		Agricultural Workers		All	
	Retired	Employed	Retired	Employed	Retired	Employed	Retired	Employed
Total	100	100	100	100	100	100	100	100
Money	35	25	51	52	37	32	45	38
Nothing	13	3	8	2	7	1	9	2
People at work	26	20	16	14	3	—	16	13
Feeling useful	7	25	6	11	16	21	8	19
Things happening around one	4	6	2	4	5	4	3	4
Work itself	14	20	16	13	31	39	18	21
Other items	1	2	1	3	—	1	1	2
Number of respondents	167	122	408	134	115	71	690	327

*Adapted from Table XI-8 and XI-14 from Shanas et al., 1968.

are more likely than other workers to miss "nothing" about their work.

While research using the substitution theory has concentrated on the meaning of work, money is mentioned so often by older men as the major item they miss or are likely to miss in retirement that it raises some question about the relevance of the substitution theory of adjustment to retirement within the present framework of American society. Two things operate to limit the non-economic meanings of work for retired men in the United States viewed as a whole: the large proportion of blue-collar workers among the retired, and the widespread phenomenon of unplanned or "disorderly" careers. The majority of retired men in this country are lower-class and lower middle-class blue-collar workers. Indeed, there are more blue-collar workers among the men now retired than there are white-collar and agricultural workers added together. The blue-collar worker has relatively little control of his work and little job satisfaction (Blauner, 1960). There is evidence that among some lower and middle-class workers retirement from the job is favorably anticipated (Dubin, 1963). An industrial worker who chose to retire at age 62 vividly expresses this point of view when he says:

> I had intended to talk just about social security benefits and the fact that they are frozen, but if the committee would permit me, I would like to digress just a bit to cover some of the remarks I heard here prior.
> One thing that really disturbed me was a remark made here a short time ago by one of the witnesses that factory workers, do they really know whether they want to retire or not? Another remark that quite shook me up was the fact that maybe some of these people love their work. Now I could understand a person in a chosen profession, and most of the witnesses have been professional people—I could understand them having a love for their work but I think

that the gentlemen on the platform understand as I do, that working in a factory, which includes about 95% of the people on social security, is not a matter of choice. When you go into a factory, it is a matter of assignment. They say, 'Do this,' and you are assigned to a machine and that is what you do and you repeat it over and over and over, the same routine little operation, there is no diversification and absolutely no opportunity for persons for knowledge or exchange or anything else—you just stand there all day long, day after day, year after year for a lifetime. And then somebody asks you, 'Do you really want to retire?'

To me having put a life-time in the Ford plants, which I think personally are probably as good as any plants to work in and possibly better than some that I know, it actually alarms me that anybody working in one of those factories, if you have ever been in one, could question a person's desirability to retire.

Now I think it would be a wonderful thing if the factory jobs could be arranged in such a way as to have some diversification, then the work would be something a person would want to continue, but unfortunately they are not. I would say this. As regards to early retirement—practically every person working in a factory today wants to retire. The only deterrent to people retiring from factories is whether they are going to get a pension on which they will be able to live and support their wife or other dependents in the mode or manner in which they have become accustomed. That is the only deterrent.

So when the Big Three came along with $400 a month, I immediately retired. There was no question in my mind of whether I wanted to retire or not. It was only a question of having enough to retire on, live in some semblance of dignity, and not become a burden on your family or a burden on the community. That's the big thing with a person retiring from a factory [*Retirement and the Individual*, 1967, pp. 517-518].

In addition to having only limited job satisfaction, many industrial workers have no reasonable and planned movement through their work life. A strong attachment to the job usually implies that the worker has had an orderly career in which job follows job, each bringing increasing responsibilities and satisfaction. Wilensky (1961), in a study of the "middle mass," points out that men who have had such an orderly work history have more friends than other men, and that these friends tend to overlap work contacts. It is the men who have had orderly careers who might be expected to find non-economic meanings in work. Yet only 40% of the men in Wilensky's study of "middle mass" men had orderly careers. The rest had careers that were at best borderline; at worst, broken by unemployment, job shifts, and various repetitive and destructive career starts.

The findings from national sample studies indicate that, irrespective of its basic assumptions, the relevance of the substitution theory seems limited within contemporary American society. In part this limitation flows from the high proportion of blue-collar workers among the retired and the high proportion of men without orderly careers. Further, there seems to be a changing American "ethos" in which rest and leisure-time activities are beginning to be valued in and of themselves. The question may be raised whether, if Americans had adequate retirement incomes, their adjustment in retirement would be maximized. Present data do not enable us to answer this question, but two interesting research findings should be mentioned.

The first comes from a study made by economists, the second from a report of the Social Security Administration. Katona and Morgan (1967), in a national sample study, found that a large proportion of American men plan to retire early, that is, before the age of 65. The major item that influences early retirement, according to these investigators, is the expected level of income. In other words, if men can assume a certain level of future income, they will choose to retire rather than to continue at work. In analyzing the Social Security Administration Study of a national sample of retired men, Palmore (1964) reports the obvious pleasure which some men get in retirement. He says: "There seem to be more and more men who are well enough to work and who might get some kind of job if they were interested, but they prefer the leisure of retirement" (p. 7).

While the data are still too sparse to demonstrate conclusively a changing American attitude toward work, it may be that for an increasing number of men the job is only a source of income and that these men have their real interests in leisure-time activities.

To this point, we have outlined a theory of adjustment to retirement which is based on a process of substitution. We have indicated the presuppositions of this theory, given some examples of research inspired by this theory, and finally raised some questions about the relevance of the theory within the structural framework of contemporary American society. We turn now to another approach to the study of adjustment to retirement—the accommodation theory.

ADJUSTMENT TO RETIREMENT—THE ACCOMMODATION PROCESS

Accommodation, not substitution, would seem to be the key process in adjustment to retirement. The accommodation theory grows out of a consideration of the differences between the factors which influence retirement and the factors which are influenced by retirement. The factors which influence retirement are partly individual and partly social. In general, the exact time when a person retires is a complex intermix of demographic factors: his sex and his age; social-psychological factors: his self-conception and his perception of his health; and of social structural factors: his occupation, his financial status, the general level of employment opportunities in the society, and the

availability of retirement benefits (Slavick & Wolfbein, 1960).
The factors which are influenced by retirement, however, are
different in nature from those which influence retirement. The
factors influenced by retirement are primarily individual and
social-psychological. Retirement usually entails lessened opportunity for social contacts or social involvement, and a cessation of
important social roles (Streib & Orbach, 1967). Some persons will
seek new social roles. Others will accept the reduced involvement,
either because they have never been greatly involved in the first
place, or because they welcome the lessening demands upon them.
Still other persons will continue to hold on to as much of the
work role as possible (Havighurst, 1968b; Reichard, Livson, &
Peterson, 1968).

Retirement means a change in the scheduling of activities and
the daily pattern of work and leisure. For some persons this may
affect the whole pattern of behavior. As an extreme example, the
man who worked a night shift may have serious problems in
accommodating to daytime hours. Retirement affects the state of
health of the individual, both physical and mental. Stressful
activities related to the job are removed. New stresses may be
introduced in their turn. Physical health may improve in retirement, or, because of changes in habits, it may deteriorate.
Retirement curtails the income the individual received from work.
Lessened income may result in profound changes in level of living
so that the necessities of earlier years may become the luxuries of
retirement.

All these changes in self-conception, patterns of leisure, physical
function, and level of living are taking place along a temporal
dimension. They are occurring at different rates and at different
instances in time. At any given time, one area of change may be
more important to the individual than another. "Retirement," as
has been stated, is used to describe an event, a process, and a life
stage. While retirement, the event, has a specific time referrent,

retirement as a process has a wide variety of time referrents.

Figure 1 shows the factors which influence the event of retirement and the factors which are influenced by retirement. Adjustment to retirement cannot be considered as a function of the factors which influence retirement: age, or earlier occupation, or earlier health status, or even self-conception before retirement. Nothing can turn the clock backward and make the old man young. In the same way, occupation cannot be replaced by leisure. The two are different in kind. Health may improve as well as deteriorate in retirement. And even conception of self may be adapted, trimmed, and accommodated to the new retirement situation. In interpreting Figure 1 one may say that retirement, the event, marks a turning point within the life span. Viewing retirement as process, however, means that the person who experiences retirement undergoes a period of change in which the self seeks to adapt to a new social role, to a new rhythm of activity, to a new body awareness, and often to a different level of living. Adjustment in retirement then is dependent on the individual's accommodation to these life changes.

The social-psychological changes involved in accommodating to retirement may in their turn influence social structure. For example, if enough people feel that they have problems in retirement, be these economic problems or feelings of rejection by the larger society, they may unite and bring pressure on society to meet their needs. New communities grow up to serve the retired, new patterns of education and leisure are offered for their consideration. The factors influenced by retirement, as these are presented in Figure 1, may indeed change the social structure which influences retirement.*

It is against the background of the interaction between the

---

*I am indebted to Gordon F. Streib for pointing out the circularity of the retirement process.

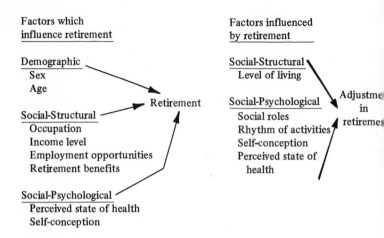

FIGURE 1. The accommodation process in adjustment in retirement.

individual and the social structure that the accommodation theory can be best understood. The accommodation theory states that adjustment to retirement is a process which begins when retirement is first considered by the individual and which abates when the individual has achieved a new distribution of his energies in non-work roles and new modes of behavior (see Rosow, 1963). The accommodation theory, like the substitution theory, is social-psychological in nature.

The theory presumes:

1. That the factors which influence retirement (that is, the giving up of work) are different from the factors influenced by retirement.

2. That adjustment to retirement is dependent not upon the causes of retirement but upon the nature of the life changes resulting from this event.

3. That adjustment to retirement may vary at different times within the retirement period as social structural and social psychological constraints on the individual vary.

The term "accommodation" is no longer widely used in contemporary sociology. George Simmel, however, used "accommodation" to describe the balance which is achieved after conflict. In many instances accommodation is the result of compromise, withdrawal, and renunciation (1903). As the term is used in the "accommodation" theory of retirement, it is somewhat similar to what Havighurst now calls "adaptation." In a recent paper, Havighurst, after reviewing his earlier work, points out that the individual at every age is continually adapting to the conditions of life. This is as true in youth as in old age. Havighurst says: "In all segments of the life-span, growing older means an adaptation to: (a) change in the structure and function of the human body, and (b) changes in the social environment. The adaptation process is ruled, more or less actively and autonomously, by the ego or personality. What we call personal adjustment, measured in various ways and called by such names as *Life Satisfaction* is a product of the adaptation process" (1968a, p. 69).

The writer prefers to use the term "accommodation" rather than "adaptation" since the theory as outlined sees the individual as being in a state of change and unrest. If the retired person has a good deal of physical energy and a concept of himself as an active person, he invests much of this energy in working out new roles and activities for himself in retirement. If he has less energy or a concept of himself as a passive person, he may accommodate to retirement by simply doing less. The same person may have reached a state of accommodation at one period of time, and then have to achieve a new accommodation as new social structural constraints appear or old ones vanish.

Adjustment to retirement, then, is a continuing on-going process of accommodation. If adjustment to retirement is considered in this way, then certain research questions become important. First among them must be: What is a good criterion of adjustment in retirement, or, what criterion of adjustment in retirement will enable us to state that an individual is in an optimum state of accommodation? There are other pertinent research questions: What changes occur in social constraints and in social-psychological areas as work is abandoned? What social roles are lost, which are replaced? How does self-conception change in retirement? What different allocations are made of time? How does health, both actual and perceived, change with retirement? Is there any temporal order to these changes? Are some more important for adjustment than others? Answers to the research questions suggested here would yield the data necessary to convert Figure 1 to an operational model.

At this time there is no research which explicitly tests the accommodation theory of adjustment to retirement.* There is a considerable literature which deals with the measurement of adjustment in old age; there have been some studies of morale in retirement, a topic related to our overall interest; and one major effort has been made to measure adjustment in retirement by investigating whether retired men want to return to work. We shall here treat briefly the measurement of adjustment, make some mention of the Cornell research, the most important study of morale in retirement, and give the findings from a recent national study in which men were asked whether they wanted to return to work.

A variety of measures of adjustment of the aged have been developed by scholars operating with different preconceptions and interested in different aspects of adjustment. The whole area of adjustment studies has been critically reviewed by Rosow who indicates the presuppositions, strengths, and weaknesses of the various instruments (1963). Rosow divides all measures of adjustment in old age, however identified, into three categories: those

---

*It may be that the theory cannot be tested. It should be possible, however, to test a series of propositions derived from the theory which deal with the consequences of retirement.

involving role content and changes, those which are measures of morale, and those which are measures of personality. Some measures of adjustment involve more than one of these areas and are in a sense additive since measures of personality are usually combined with measures of activity.

Rosow argues that "good" adjustment represents maximum continuity and minimum discontinuity of life patterns between two periods in the life of the individual. However, changes which eliminate previous negative aspects of life or add new and positive features must be viewed as contributing to "good" adjustment, and stable patterns which introduce frustration or dissatisfactions must be viewed as contributing to "poor" adjustment (1963). Then any measure of adjustment in retirement using this paradigm must compare the individual after retirement with his own state of behavior before retirement.

The Rosow design would measure adjustment through time. Therefore it seems a relevant measure to use with the accommodation theory. Some consideration is now being given to a longitudinal study which would concentrate on changes in the individual as these occur during the several years before and after retirement.

As Rosow indicated in his review paper, measures of morale can also be used to determine adjustment in retirement. In cross-sectional studies, however, there is no way of knowing what the morale of a person was like before he retired. Probably the best attempt to use morale as a measure of adjustment in retirement is that reported by Streib and his associates at Cornell University (Streib & Thompson, 1958). The Cornell research was longitudinal in design rather than cross-sectional; that is, a group of men were investigated both before and after retirement. Comparisons were made of the pre- and post-retirement status of the retired. Also, the status of those men in the cohort who retired was compared with that of those who continued to work. In a 1956 paper on the "Morale of the Retired" Streib stated: "Occupational retirement is a situation which does not operate in isolation," and argued that work status, health, and socio-economic status must be considered together in their determination of the morale of the aged. Streib developed a measure of morale which included goal-centeredness, satisfaction, and reaction to adversity. Using this measure and analyzing his sample by work status, health, and income level, Streib found that persons who were retired but who had good health and high income had higher morale than their working peers with poor health and low income.

The Cornell study stressed the need for controlling a variety of factors in studying retirement, and for longitudinal research in this area. Unfortunately, the important guidelines developed in this study have not received the attention they deserve, and most recent research on retirement continues to be cross-sectional and thus dependent on retrospective reports of what life was like before the person retired.*

In a 1962 study, Shanas endeavored to measure retirement equilibrium by asking retired men whether they wanted a job. It was felt that the use of this question would avoid the element of fantasy that might be associated with retrospective reports while at the same time the answers to the question would give some clue as to the state of accommodation of men in retirement. Men who did not want a job would be presumed to have accommodated to the loss of work. Shanas reasoned that retired men who wanted to return to work would be those who had been in retirement a relatively short time, those who were financially in much worse straits than they had been as workers, and those who were in good health.

The findings indicated that a higher proportion of men who had been retired for less than three years (33%) compared to those

---

*A longitudinal study influenced by Streib and Thompson is reported from Britain (Moran & Doran, 1966).

who had been retired three years or more (19%) wanted to return to work.* This might be expected since the recently retired men were on the average younger and in better health than men retired for longer periods.

Shanas used an index of functional incapacity to measure health status. When all retired men were classified by their incapacity scores, 27% of those with no incapacity compared to 11% of those with marked incapacity said they wanted to return to work (Table 4). Interestingly enough, among the retired men with no incapacity, 29% or almost three of every ten said their health was too poor for them to work. While these men had no impairment in their ability to function physically as retired men, they apparently were unable to cope with the stresses of a job.

All respondents were asked to compare their present financial status with their status at the age of 60. A higher proportion of men whose status had worsened (31%) compared with those whose status was similar or better than it had been (18%) said that they wanted a job (Table 5). The men who want a job after they retire, then, differ from other retired men in the length of time they

TABLE 4
Desire for job by retired men, aged 65 and over, by incapacity scores

| Desire for Job | Percentage Distribution | | |
	Score 0	Score 1-2	Score 3 and over
Total	100	100	100
Wants work	27	22	11
Does not want work	44	25	8
Health too poor	29	53	81
Number of respondents	460	173	102

*Unpublished data from a national survey of old people supported first by the National Institute of Mental Health, M 5630, and then by the Community Health Services Branch of the Public Health Service, CH00054. Published data from Shanas et al., 1968.

TABLE 5
Desire for job by retired men, aged 65 and over, by comparison of
financial status now with age 60

| | Percentage Distribution | |
Desire for Job	Status Same or Better	Status Worse
Total	100	100
Wants work	18	31
Does not want work	46	20
Health too poor	36	49
Number of respondents	375	324

have been in retirement, in the state of their health, and in economic status. In analyzing these and other data on the attitudes of the retired Shanas says: "These would-be workers are usually recently retired men in good health who feel that they can still do 'a day's work' if they had the opportunity. The longer the time men are retired, the less likely they are to want to return to work. This disinterest in work cannot be attributed to lessening strength associated with advanced age. Rather, there seems to be a critical turning point, at which a man ceases to think of himself as a potential worker and instead accepts his role as one who is retired" (Shanas et al., 1968, p. 345).

Unfortunately, the Shanas materials do not include data dealing with the self-conception of these retired men. It may be that the men who wanted to return to work had a conception of themselves as active persons which was threatened by their retired status. On the other hand, the importance of length of time in retirement in determining those who want to return to work must not be underestimated. In keeping with the accommodation theory, self-conception too may change in retirement.

In this section we have outlined a theory of retirement which is based on a process of accommodation. We have indicated the presuppositions of this theory and given some consideration to past research which bears on the theory. We have also suggested some of the research questions which might be investigated using this theory.

CONCLUSION

While retirement is a major event in the lives of persons in industrial society, studies of retirement as a social process, not purely an economic event, are relatively few. The term "retirement" is used widely to describe an event, a process, and a life stage without much attempt being made to distinguish between them.

In this paper we have considered two processes which may operate in adjustment to retirement—substitution and accommodation. The presuppositions which underlie each of these approaches and the kinds of research associated with them have been presented. In addition we have indicated future research which might derive from the use of the accommodation theory.

The substitution theory is a life-stage theory in which a set of post-retirement activities is presumed to substitute for a set of pre-retirement activities, and in which the measurement of adjustment must be how well post-retirement activities fulfill the same needs as pre-retirement activities.

The accommodation theory views adjustment in retirement as a process in which the individual after retirement achieves a new distribution of his energies in new roles and new modes of behavior. Adjustment in retirement may vary within the retirement period as social and individual circumstances vary.

CARL EISDORFER, PH.D., M.D.

Dr. Eisdorfer obtained his graduate degrees in psychology from New York University and his medical degree from Duke University where he is now Director of the Behavioral Science Program in the School of Medicine. In addition, he is Professor of Medical Psychology, Professor of Psychiatry, and Director of Duke University's Center for the Study of Aging and Human Development. For the 1969-70 academic year, Dr. Eisdorfer was Visiting Professor of Psychiatry at the University of California Medical Center in San Francisco and Visiting Professor of Architecture in the School of Environmental Design at the University of California in Berkeley.

Dr. Eisdorfer, whose research interests and publications cover the developmental spectrum and range from changes in learning and cognition to psychophysiological processes, is also involved in the study and practice of community psychology and psychiatry. He is President-Elect (1971) of the Gerontological Society and Past President (1969-70) of Division 20 (Maturity and Old Age) of the American Psychological Association. During leisure hours, Dr. Eisdorfer is a skin-diver and a photographer.

9: ADAPTATION TO LOSS OF WORK

CARL EISDORFER

Work—as an activity in its own right, as a system for obtaining a variety of rewards to fill more or less essential needs, and as a basis for establishing major parameters of one's style of life including the status and number of roles played—would appear to be crucial in determining personal adjustment. Then loss of work must precipitate a new phase of adaptation.

Given an open market, older workers hold a vulnerable position in the labor force. Kreps (1963) demonstrates that they tend to be among the first to be fired during times of economic hardship and the last to be hired. Whether or not aged persons are employed is a function of the labor supply and the economic condition at a given point in time: in periods of high employment and scarce labor supply, older persons work; when labor is abundant, they are not hired or retained. In view of increases in individual work productivity, Kreps predicts that in the immediate future a decreased labor force will be needed. This should lead to greater unemployment of the aged and the heightened probability of retirement from the labor force at an earlier age. In addition to these economic facts and predictions, there are projections of population growth which indicate an increase in the number and proportion of persons aged 65 and over in the near future.

Such information about the population and the labor force lends urgency to the need to analyze retirement in terms of its implications for human adaptation. This chapter first identifies and discusses variables which appear to have major significance for response to loss of work and which consequently may be relevant to the design of investigations into retirement as an adaptational process. It then describes three models of psychological reactivity, each one of which might seem to organize the relevant variables into a coherent hypothetical framework for analysis of retirement.

RELEVANT VARIABLES

The pattern of preprogramming termination of job at a particular age, although related in a general way to deficits found in the aged, seems to have developed independently of any empirically derived understanding of the effects of age. The work-related problems found among the aged can only be said to interact with advancing years. As a consequence of the paucity of accurate information, retirement has been associated with several sets of conjectures. These assumptions, as summarized by Kent (1965), include the construct that there are predictable, negative effects upon aged persons who retire, and that such effects may be seen in physical or social deterioration or both in the immediate post-retirement period. In view of the complexity and scope of the issues involved, it seems appropriate to discuss the relationships of retirement with health, social interactions, work status, finances, feelings of self-worth, and emotional pathology.

Health

The relationship between retirement and health or physical pathology is complex. The work of Thompson and Streib (1958) suggests that poor health frequently leads to retirement, particularly among "blue collar" workers, and that there may be a post-retirement improvement in health in many individuals. For many years, however, it has been conjectured that retirement and its attendant interpersonal difficulties led to a poorer level of health.

Ellison (1968), in fact, proposes that the sick role may be adopted as an alternative to the retired role. He suggests that while retirement is identified with hopelessness and helplessness, the expectation for the sick is improvement and return to health. In addition, the sick role is more consistent with the dependency status in which some retirees perceive themselves. Thus, the worker may turn to sickness as a way of legitimately exempting himself from social responsibilities.

As Martin and Doran (1966) have pointed out, however, the evidence concerning the relationship between health and retirement is equivocal at best. Their survey data on men over the age of 55 show a steadily increasing incidence of illness requiring medical intervention, which drops from 50% to 30% immediately after retirement. All of the evidence, they feel, points to a drop in illness with retirement.

A confounding issue in these investigations is the measurement of health as reflected in the relationship between self-health ratings and other indexes of health. It has been reported that, despite chronic illness, a great majority of the aged do not identify themselves as seriously limited (Suchman, Streib, & Phillips, 1958). In a report to the National Institute of Health task force on aging and retirement, Ostfeld (1968) suggested that his sample of older persons in an urban area had considerably greater physical impairment than they recognized or reported. His subjects, all welfare recipients, were examined by physicians, and more than half were found to have symptoms reflecting moderate to severe illness. Yet a significant proportion of this group of physically ill individuals had accepted their symptoms as the limitations of normal old age. Most of Ostfeld's subjects, in fact, had not sought medical help for their ailments. It is not surprising, then, that in the sample of community volunteers who visited the Duke Center for two days of examination, about a third of the aged significantly misjudged their physical condition (Busse, 1967).

In assessing the relevance of failure to recognize poor health, it should be recognized that self-perception of health may be less accurate during a static period, when the individual is at rest, than it is during a period when the individual is involved in sustained physical activity such as work. The early or milder forms of many chronic diseases are rarely observable until the victim exerts himself. Cardiovascular illness and emphysema, which are common disorders among the aged, may manifest themselves initially only as shortness of breath upon exertion. This complaint is subjectively interpretable as being out of condition due to lack of exercise or "old age creeping up," and the individual may report that he is physically fit for his age.

In a similar vein, the positive value of retirement to individuals with subtle and minor physical problems may not readily be identified, despite the relevance of poor health as an etiologic factor. The findings of Ryser and Sheldon (1969) on 500 aged retirees in Massachusetts do, in fact, indicate that while over 10% indicated poorer health post-retirement, nearly one-quarter of the sample reported improved health. Overall, 85% of the subjects (ages 60 to 70) indicated good or very good health, although 32% indicated some limitations imposed by the state of their health. Reported visits to physicians was the only objective criterion of health reported in this study. It is impressive that, despite their reports of good health, 40% had made more than routine visits to a doctor.

In his discussion of these issues, Eisdorfer (1968) identified the pitfalls of using self-estimate of health as a criterion for making judgments about the physical status of subjects. Health, particularly as it involves the problems of functional capacity (Lawton,

1968) and the separation of "illness" from age, needs to be better delineated. The remarkably high proportion of older persons suffering from chronic diseases makes this variable an essential one in attempts to study any behavioral function among the aged.

Interpersonal Relations

Cumming and Henry (1961) stress the adaptive function of progressive social withdrawal in their disengagement concept. Remarkably little is known, however, about the relationship of subclinical or poorly identified illness to this process. Withdrawal from social situations, as described in the context of disengagement theory, implies an active movement away from interpersonal contacts by the aging individual. In reality, of course, there is an important admixture of involuntary withdrawal. The amputation of extensive as well as intensive social interactions through death, retirement, or removal from home and neighborhood may cause a pattern of multiple crises resulting in personality changes which we have yet to understand fully. In their investigation, Cumming and Henry focused primarily upon the extent of interpersonal involvements, and gave scant attention to the intensity of relationships. The possibility that a limited number of very intense relationships may act as a buffer against loss of extensive role relationships of a more superficial kind should not be overlooked.

It is reasonable to assume that retirement results in a decrease in the number of automatic social contacts. In their observations regarding their own person-to-person contacts during the first few years after retirement, Pressey and Pressey (1966) imply that in order for the aged retiree to sustain a high number of contacts, he is required to "work at it" by appropriately restructuring his environment.

Rosow (1967) observed that social homogeneity as well as residential proximity is important in forming and sustaining friendships, and that the social contacts of the manual worker may be relatively more vulnerable to changes in his immediate neighborhood than are those of the middle-class or upper-class individual. It seems probable, too, that the neighborhoods surrounding the residences of manual workers are more vulnerable to change, adding to the impact of loss of job-related contacts. In this regard, workers in our lower socioeconomic classes may have more difficulties. If there is a differential life expectancy related to income level, then the aged poor may stand a relatively greater chance of losing their friends through death.

The impact of loss of any intensive relationship, such as that with a spouse or life-long friend, is difficult to assess in the absence of information concerning other contacts, and the life style and mobility of the aged retiree. Such interpersonal losses, however, should constitute an important focus for study in attempting to understand the difficulties of aging individuals. It may be helpful to contrast this stage of life and its attendant losses with the events of youth, which typically involve increasing numbers of interpersonal contacts as well as greater mastery over the environment.

Perhaps the greatest problem presented by retirement is the loss of automatic, job-defined roles. The ex-president of a corporation or former government official has some status without his previous power, but too often he may prefer to fall back upon his self-perceived old status rather than redefine his relationship to others.

Interpersonal relationships, then, represent a second crucial area of concern for the retiree and for the investigator hoping to assess adaptation to loss of work. There may be quite significant differences between the loss of certain types of job-related relationships, those relationships seen as transcending the employment status, and those with varying degrees of interpersonal intensity. Simple quantitative analyses of number of contacts, group memberships, and the like may reveal little about adaptation, in the absence of knowledge about the intensity and perceived desirability of such relationships.

Work Status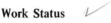

Simpson, Back, and McKinney (1966) have indicated that response to loss of work is in part a function of the kind of work performed prior to retirement. They propose that upper-status workers (for example, executives and professionals) have the highest degree of job satisfaction. This includes feelings of job autonomy, recognition of performance, and receipt of higher wages. Middle-status workers, by definition, have less autonomy. They are usually identified with the results of their work to a lesser degree, and they vary significantly in the extent to which they share values with other workers. The workers in such middle-status jobs report some job satisfaction. Semi-skilled work seems to involve the least job satisfaction and is associated with limited development of skills and low work autonomy. It involves some norms related to the work situation, but few occupational norms.

In view of these differences, lower status workers would seem to have less to lose upon retirement in terms of job-related satisfaction. Simpson, Back, and McKinney do, in fact, report that upper white-collar retirees were most likely to be involved with retirement concerns prior to retirement, semi-skilled retirees were least likely to be so involved, and middle-status retirees were in their customary intermediate position. It is important to note, however, that following their retirement, the sample of upper-status retirees experienced the greatest loss of involvement, the middle-status the least, and the semi-skilled an intermediate amount. The survey data from this panel of subjects suggests that while the upper-status retirees did experience a loss of self-esteem from retirement, the extent of their loss was less than among retirees of lower status.

It seems clear, too, that while the upper-status retirees lost a larger percentage of specifically work-related interests, overall they lost fewer interests. Reduction in income appeared to be a more important influence than the intensity of involvement with job deprivation among the semi-skilled retirees, while work involvement was as influential as income in predicting the effects of job deprivation among middle-status workers. Orderliness of work history, even apart from job status, seems to reduce the likelihood that pre-retirement involvement will be lost. A pattern of status and orderliness seems to emerge as inversely related to feelings of job deprivation and directly related to morale.

Among the middle-status retirees, involvement in a variety of activities is as important as a high ratio of pre- to post-retirement income in lessening job deprivation. In contrast, among the lower-status workers, the post-retirement changes seem intimately related to the sharp drop in income which accompanies their exit from work. These data are similar to the results obtained by Thompson, Streib, and Kosa (1960), and support the hypothesis that the effects of job deprivation differ by economic strata as well as by the variety of other variables which operate in the work situation.

Among those factors which have not been well studied in the social-psychological research on retirement is the relative work success of the middle-class worker, and the impact of his success upon his subsequent retirement. In this regard, the work of Berkey and Stoebner (1968) is of some interest in focusing on a select population, that is, the career army officer. A retirement syndrome, according to Berkey and Stoebner, is found in a number of officers facing retirement and includes anxiety, depression, and somatic complaints.

Among the field grade officers described by Berkey and

Stoebner, an embittered, hostile, and depressed attitude was initially observed at about two years prior to retirement. To a very real extent, the retirement of this group results from their failure to be promoted (to the rank of full colonel). Despite past military achievements which they frequently mention in conversation, these officers seem very bitter about their military experience.

Several variants make this particular sample different from other pre-retirees. One major difference is that to many of these individuals the military career had become a way of life, involving an intricate set of adaptive patterns which shaped most of their daily activity during on or off duty hours. Secondly, the retirement of this group was usually at a much younger age, during their 40's. Third, promotion would have carried with it the opportunity for extended service. Thus, being "passed over" for the last time led to an enforced retirement which could be perceived as failure.

Unfortunately, Berkey and Stoebner give no data on the relative risk of such a syndrome. Their description does provide support for the contention that the worker who feels that he has not achieved a suitable level of success may be quite vulnerable to negative effects of retirement. For such individuals, retirement signals the termination of their efforts at upward movement, and therefore confronts them with their own failure. For the field officers who failed to achieve the rank of colonel or above, as well as for the middle-status worker who was work oriented but never reached the higher levels of executive autonomy and status, retirement must appear as an insurmountable barrier to long-term goals of success. This is probably less true of the semi-skilled worker who sees the job more in terms of income, or the higher-status worker who has many non-work-related pursuits and, indeed, has achieved many of his goals.

A variety of issues related to work status, then, lend themselves to the investigation of personal adaptation to retirement. Not only could socioeconomic status and the relative importance of job-related income be better understood, particularly in real dollar terms, but also self-perception of success-failure might well be explored. This can be studied, not only directly at the time of retirement, but perhaps also in the middle years when it becomes clear to the individual what the probability for his self-fulfillment on the job is to be. A withdrawal or heightened involvement with the job, many years pre-retirement, on the part of a middle-management executive may be an important factor in appreciating his response to anticipated retirement.

Finances

It may be useful to note that the aged must live at income levels approximately half those of younger workers (Rosow, 1967; Brotman, 1967a). Thus, data describing the social contacts and interaction patterns of the aged might well be reexamined in terms of the economics of social participation. Membership dues for clubs, church contributions, and travel costs may impose limitations on participation because of the marginal or submarginal income of the retiree. Even visits to the family may involve economic hardship for the aged individual with a low income, since transportation costs and gifts for grandchildren are among the hidden expenses which make such visits relatively costly. The oft-voiced contention that retirees do not need money because their children are grown is a disturbing misconception. The potential cyclic effects of social withdrawal, secondary to economic privation, can be significant. The aged person who may have constricted his activities involuntarily is no longer considered a prospective participant in the social unit, and therefore contacts with him are reduced. The aged individual counters what he may perceive as a new rejection by further increasing his active withdrawal (disengagement?).

From the studies of Thompson and Streib (1958), it has been suggested that aged blue-collar employees do not look negatively upon retirement and that, in fact, they may look forward to giving up full-time employment with positive feelings, particularly when retirement income is adequate and when there is a health-related difficulty. Ash (1966) has reported that for blue-collar workers in Great Britain, the closer an employee is to the age of retirement, the more likely he is to say that he does not want to retire. However, a particularly interesting aspect of this study is that, in contrast to a similar survey performed a decade before, 10% more of the employees were accepting of their imminent retirement. At the time of the second study (1966), fewer felt it to be the worst thing that could happen to a person. This seems also to be reflected in the finding that while a decade before more than half (56%) viewed retirement relatively passively, only 20% so regarded it in 1966. The number who regarded retirement as a reward went from 30% to 45% in ten years. The employees of the prior decade were more likely to see retirement as based on physical disability, while the employees of 1966 were more likely to regard it as a reward for services rendered. This shift on the part of the retiree in the direction of a more positive attitude toward retirement is an important development.

The worker's attitude that his retirement income was earned through his own efforts and was not merely a charitable act by the government may be a significant variable in determining his acceptance of retirement. It is reasonable to assume that income should be viewed not only in terms of its direct effect on purchasing power but also in terms of the attitude of the receiver. While financial status is related to self-worth, identification of income as charity is perhaps not as supportive to the integrity of the ego as the same income perceived as earnings. This may be another example of the need to feel autonomous and the master of one's own fate. Retirement income as deferred wages earned through work, and not as a "hand-out," implies independence and adds to self-esteem.

Ash's data indicate, too, that positive attitudes and better adjustment in retirement are both related to the extent to which the employee anticipates and makes plans for this major change in his activity pattern. Thus, of those employees 60 years of age and older who had made retirement plans, 81% wanted to retire. Of those who had made no retirement plans, only 38% expressed an interest in retirement. In the follow-up of persons retired more than three years, previous planning appeared to make a striking difference. Among those who had made plans for retirement, only 8% expressed the feeling of having nothing to do, in contrast to 22% of the group that had made no plans.

In interpreting such results, the selective bias of the subjects becomes a central issue. While a positive relationship was found between planning for retirement and favorable attitude toward retirement, it may only demonstrate that persons with favorable attitudes toward an event are more likely to think about and to provide for that event. The value of pre-retirement planning and counseling, while widely heralded, needs to be the subject of investigation, particularly with regard to the client's age and the period in employment history when such planning is most meaningful. It would hardly be surprising to discover that pre-retirement counseling initiated with a group of sixty-year-old workers who have denied their impending retirement, and who have insufficient time remaining at work to plan effectively even for their financial needs, might result in more negative than positive effects.

The notion that money is important to adaptation could hardly be ranked as a major insight. Despite the obvious character of this relationship, there has been relatively little investigation into adjustment to poverty or near poverty, and perhaps even less into the effects of replacement of income. Combined economic, social, and psychological studies are sorely needed for understanding this critical problem.

Psychopathology

Individuals over the age of 54 are more vulnerable to a variety of psychological disorders than are younger adults (Kramer, Taube, & Starr, 1968). The relationship between this heightened prevalence of disability and the retirement process remains an unanswered question. The work of Johnson (1958) is typical of the literature on this subject. It gives several examples of a "retirement syndrome" characterized by depressive affect, somatic complaints, social withdrawal, and similar symptoms, and then relates these difficulties to unresolved neurotic conflicts centering about the work experience, as well as to difficulties in the formation of interpersonal ties with spouse, family, and friends after retirement. Normative or epidemiologic data are conspicuous by their absence.

MODELS FOR ADAPTATION

The variables described above are obviously not to be considered a definitive listing of factors involved in work loss or retirement. Rather, they represent broad categories which may be identified with individual adaptation to work and which therefore require elucidation in investigating adaptation to retirement.

In an effort to organize significant variables into some coherent structures for the design of research studies, three models of adjustment are described below. Each model has achieved a certain degree of acceptance for its ability to describe and predict individual adaptation to the environment. The crisis model is concerned with man's ability to respond effectively to rather short-lived traumatic events in life and the consequences of certain responses. In the second model, reinforcement and maturational principles are used to derive an approach to retirement based upon the lifelong pattern of learning and goal setting. The final model incorporates the additional component of all success-failure experiences on the part of the individual. In it, retirement serves as only one aspect of a pattern of significant negative events which re-shape the personal motivational style and influence subsequent behavior.

A Crisis Model

On the face of it, retirement would appear to be an emotionally hazardous situation. According to Klein and Lindemann (1961), "any sudden alteration in the field of social forces within which the individual exists, such that his expectation of himself and his relationship with others undergo change" (p. 284), carries with it a potential for serious disturbance in the individual. Major events identifiable as emotionally hazardous include the loss of a significant relationship, and rapid changes in social status, with consequent changes in role relationships and social mobility.

According to this model of adaptation, the individual is typically in a state of relative equilibrium with his interpersonal environment. On occasions this balance is upset, and a person finds that he is unable to maintain an appropriate relationship with his world through previously successful behavior. At such times he may undergo a serious, often protracted, emotional upset which is labeled a crisis. The crisis situation becomes a focus for maximal expenditure of energy and problem solving. A successful solution appears to bring greater feelings of mastery over the environment and increased maturity in coping with other interpersonal problems. Failure often brings the reverse.

Caplan (1964) describes the subjective state of the individual in a crisis as one of "upset." This feeling is frequently associated with anxiety, fear, or guilt, depending upon the specifics of the situation. The person feels helpless in the face of an overwhelming problem. Tension may build in four stages: (1) a rise in tension from the problem situation which elicits usual problem-solving behavior; (2) failure to overcome the ongoing difficulty which is associated with increased tension and feelings of upset; (3) a major mobilization of effort to solve the problem or alter its impact by seeking novel solutions, redefining the difficulty, or shifting goals; (4) failure to solve the problem, to define alternative modes of coping with it, or to resign oneself to the new situation, resulting in serious disorganization of the personality, often with dramatic consequence.

Retirement, with its loss of control over crucial situational and life-style variables in the face of diminished personal resources, could readily predispose an individual to crisis. It is important that this model be understood as (1) a psychosocial rather than biological event system and (2) not necessarily an age-related phenomenon. A shift in social climate as well as changes in health care might so alter the status of the elderly that the experiences now occurring to an individual in his sixth or seventh decade might be postponed until the eighth or ninth decade. The model is an interesting one and carries with it the possibility of intervention and help. It should be noted that a state of crisis in the terms of this model is not the same as psychopathology. The model suggests an emotional disequilibrium and period of heightened risk from which the individual may emerge with an increased sense of maturity and ability to cope with the daily stresses in his life. Alternatively, he may be left with feelings of defeat and injury which have long-term consequences. The absence of any appropriate epidemiologic information forces us to conclude that the extent and severity of such hypothetical intrapersonal crises must remain speculative.

A Reinforcement Model

Crisis theory is oriented toward an understanding of the acute response to a sudden change in life style. The long-term effects of retirement after several decades of work may present a separate problem. Work fills a multiplicity of functions. The positive response to gainful employment as opposed to subsidized support, and the achievement orientation of the large middle-class segment of our society, reflect well institutionalized ethics in Western culture. It is also clear that there is not simply one work ethic but rather many patterns which involve social and cultural subgroups. If viewed in this context it seems probable that work fills specific needs for the socialization of individuals, and that differences among individuals may be aggravated or diminished with increasing age.

The examination of potential reinforcers for work may be a useful area for investigation and hypothesis formation. It might be well to explore the continuity of reinforcement through the life span and the changes immediately before and after retirement. For the child, school achievements and "paying" jobs such as baby sitting, newspaper delivery, or special household chores earn parental approval and positive reinforcement. There are, however, class and family distinctions, and these may well be predictive of later attitudes. During one's mature work experience, such obvious reinforcers as income and the products it buys, job recognition, autonomy or the meeting of dependency needs, group identification and morale, personal investment with the product or the employer, and relations with the union or specific work ethics, all interact with the reward pattern established in the earlier years. Clearly, then, scientific interest in the work history of adults should include a focus upon childhood experiences and upon the resolution of work-related conflicts (such as dependence-independence) within the early family which may be seen in alternate forms in later life.

Reward systems vary among individuals and social classes. As greater income is earned, the reinforcement value of the products it buys may be diminished or altered. Thus, it could be predicted that for the higher income levels, take-home pay becomes progressively less relevant as the primary reinforcement for work, while autonomy, recognition, and social power tend to dominate. In contrast, for the individual in the lower socioeconomic classes, salary should represent a major proportion of job satisfaction. To the extent that this is true, the reduction in income neccesitated by retirement should have a greater impact on the life satisfaction of the lower socioeconomic class than on that of the upper class. This is, in fact, consistent with much of the data discussed earlier. Decreased income may not be the crucial issue for the upper-status worker. His satisfaction in retirement might be better related to the number of non-work interests he has developed and is able to transpose to his new situation.

A primary concern in successful adaptation to retirement should be the new environment of the retiree. Much research has focused upon pre-retirement status and reaction to retirement. More information is needed about the limitations imposed upon the individual during retirement. It may be easier to determine *from* what the worker is retiring than to determine *to* what he will retire. This approach would involve identifying factors in work that are related to post-work adjustment. If we employed this orientation and determined, for example, that the social aspect of work is important for some persons, we could predict that the impact of job loss will relate to the relative changes in other social reinforcers (for example, whether friends are still available off the job, or whether death has claimed one's closest interpersonal allies).

Potential aversive reinforcements also exist in the work situation, and in many instances previously positive reinforcements lose their value. Positive involvement with the end products of work probably varies as a direct function of the amount of discernible individual effort contributed. As the product of his work requires diminished personal involvement and there is less individual craftsmanship, the work product may effectively cease to be an object of reward to the worker. Similarly, identification may shift from employer and factory unit to the union, and the job setting may shift in its value. Union-management friction and the adversary approach to wages and benefits have doubtless resulted in some ambivalence toward employers.

Clearly, too, much leisure time is becoming available to significant segments of the working population, who also have the finances to enjoy such leisure. It follows that with changes in the culture, attitudes will shift. Thus, as leisure becomes increasingly more acceptable and more income is invested in leisure activities, the worker will find that the time spent away from the job is more enjoyable than time spent at work. At present, the leisure of the wealthy and worker's holidays seem to be of more value in the eyes of the public than is leisure associated with retirement (Rosow, 1967). It is reasonable to suppose, however, that with improved retirement income, an increasing retired population, and further de-emphasis on the human element in production, there will be more acceptance of shorter work weeks, blue-collar sabbatical leaves, and early retirement. One might also predict that heightened leisure spending, reflecting as it does time invested in non-work activities as well as the investment of funds in major items such as boats, sports equipment, and camping gear, signals a shift from a work to a non-work orientation. This in turn may lead to the increased willingness of the worker to retire, all else being equal. For professionals and certain subprofessional service roles, work-related satisfactions may remain high.

A Motivational Style Model

In attempting to understand orientation to work and retirement, over and above the obvious reinforcers associated with work, it may be useful to employ the concept of cognitive dissonance (Festinger, 1962). When the motives for working and not working are in conflict, we may note that a relatively unpleasant or undesirable task can become valuable or pleasant when it is accepted as part of a shift in personal perception. Thus, if the unpleasantness of work increases and conflicts with the work ethic, dissonance theory would propose that we resolve the dilemma by emphasizing other aspects of the job that presumably have value for us. Work promotes good health, is often more enjoyable than it is thought to be, has the virtue of helping others, can contribute important products to society, and has other assets which make it desirable. When the pressures for retirement are marked despite a strong work ethic, there is little dissonance since the retiree has little choice and no cognitive conflict to resolve. If the pressures for retirement are less severe but work is still seen as a good thing, dissonance will be generated and the resolution in favor of retirement may involve adopting a "sour grapes" attitude toward work on the part of the retiree.

Motivation is, of course, central to the learning and reinforcement model. Apart from such basic needs as food, protection, and the like, certain overriding motivational styles may have special relevance for the aged. As indicated earlier, the "need achievement" motive has been proposed as a significant aspect of Western culture. Aging and its attendant personal losses and failures may be characterized by new motivational patterns, perhaps in conflict with the old ones, but probably coexisting with them. In any situation characterized by repeated failures in attempting to achieve new goals or to retain mastery over old ones, a shift in strategy (and goals) may be predictable. Fear of failure and conservation of energy may emerge as motivational styles in order to protect the ego integrity of the individual. In turn, fear of failure or conservation of energy would be the basis for behavioral constriction.

The withholding of responses and its detrimental effects upon learning and performance (Canestrari, 1963; Eisdorfer, Axelrod, & Wilkie, 1963) as well as a much more conservative risk-taking strategy (Wallach & Kogan, 1961) reflect this tendency on the part of the aged to be more sensitive to failure. Such response constriction or inhibition, coupled with motivating forces designed to conserve energy or protect the organism from failure (defensive-adaptive rather than manipulative-adaptive), would further compromise outgoing social interaction. The resultant changes in day-to-day behavior may be quite significant.

In this context, withdrawal from a competitive work situation may be salutary for some aged individuals. The reduction in need achievement reinforcement and the ascendance of fear of failure may lead to overtly constricted and even apathetic-appearing behavior. However, from the subjective point of view, the individual may be much more at ease. The disturbing feature of this model is that similar consequences, that is, behavioral inhibition, may occur in workers who are prematurely forced into a defensive posture by the culture. In this event, depression rather than personal comfort is the probable concomitant.

This model brings with it a possible intervention approach toward minimizing or moderating behavioral withdrawal. Maintenance of social power and the provision of appropriate rewards do much to sustain a heightened achievement orientation. It may be appropriate to observe, too, that this model is not particularly age linked but rather is based upon subjective interpretation of feedback from the environment.

Man is not only a social being interacting with the pressures of his environment, but also a biologic organism with a shifting level of physical and mental resources. These resources vary from individual to individual, but the very young and very old are more likely to have diminished capacity (reserves) in relation to the demands of daily activity. Infants have limited reserves because of poorly integrated central nervous systems and metabolisms oriented toward internal growth and development; the aged, as a result of cellular losses and pathophysiologic changes in the body. With diminished reserves and capacity, conservation of energy as a motivating force may play an important adaptive function, and the desire for minimal activity may be a dominant theme.

Certainly alternatives to full retirement are possible. Societal needs for service may enable the older worker to retire (or reorient) from producing products to reinvest his energies in providing services. Needs and capacities, however, will vary from individual to individual. Ability to remain flexible and in relative control is a function of many variables. Changes in interpersonal relationships, the requirements of new routines, and the surrender of old patterns of behavior are imposed late in the life span. This interplay of forces, in relation to the adaptational history of the individual as seen subjectively and objectively (Williams & Wirths, 1965), is significant, and clearly it is a researchable issue. We have a great deal to learn in understanding the strengths that have enabled most persons to adapt to retirement.

DAVID GUTMANN, PH.D.

Dr. Gutmann received his training in clinical psychology with the Committee on Human Development of the University of Chicago, at the University of Illinois Medical School, and at Michael Reese Hospital. After receiving the doctoral degree, Dr. Gutmann practiced and taught clinical psychology at Harvard Medical School and at the University of Michigan, where he is currently a Professor of Psychology.

Since 1964, with the support of a Career Development Award from the National Institute of Child Health and Human Development, Dr. Gutmann has been carrying out comparative studies of aging psychology in preliterate societies: among the traditional Navajo, the Lowland and Highland Maya of Mexico, and the Druze tribesmen of the Golan and Galilean highlands. Final stages of the preparation of the manuscript for his chapter were carried out in a remote field station on the Golan Heights.

Dr. Gutmann's current researches are aimed at isolating psychological features of the aging process which are intrinsic and universal, and at developing field-work methods based on principles of clinical psychology. He is particularly interested in comparing urban and traditional milieux as settings for ego development, and in extending the study of the human ego as a psychosocial phenomenon.

10: EGO PSYCHOLOGICAL
AND DEVELOPMENTAL APPROACHES
TO THE "RETIREMENT CRISES" IN MEN

DAVID GUTMANN

THE EGO INTERFACES

In this chapter the crisis of retirement is considered from the perspective of psychoanalytic ego psychology. At the outset, it should be made clear that there are currently two major—and contrasting—ego psychological modes, each developed by different theorists, at different periods, and referring to different data sources. This presentation will delineate these lines of thought, indicate their origins in observation and experiment, and consider their utility for various kinds of problems, particularly those having to do with retirement.

In addition, data and tentative findings will be presented which bear upon a developmental theory of male crisis and crisis resolution in later life. Again, both the crisis and the possible outcomes will be discussed from the pertinent ego psychological perspectives.

The Ego-Id Interface

Psychoanalytic ego psychologists have studied two distinct domains of ego transactions—that between the ego and internal sources of stimulation (ego-id interface) and that between the ego and external sources of stimulation (ego-milieu interface). In the first case, the problems studied arise out of the relationship between the ego and the impulse life: the interaction between impulse and ego defense, the consequences for the personality of defensive failure, and the tactics—such as sublimation, displacement, and counter-cathexis—whereby energies sexual and aggressive in origin are neutralized and put at the disposal of the ego. Typically, the metaphors for discussing this ego-id interface are derived from the study of energy systems: We think in terms of mobile forces, and the structures which block, channel, amplify, and convert such forces.

The Ego-Milieu Interface

Thus—though Gill (1963) points out that this is an oversimplified view*—the id-ego interface is conceived of as the demarcation between free psychic energy, seeking discharge, and relatively fixed psychic structures. Because the ego originally developes out of the id, and because its energies derive ultimately from the id, the ego is also considered to stand—like the id—in potential opposition to the outer world. Thus, according to the id-psychologists, the id-ego struggle is to some degree replicated on the ego-milieu interface.

But this "energetic" view of ego-milieu relationships does not help us understand the data of the ego-milieu interface. On that interface we are not impressed by the opposition of energy and structure. Though the structures differ, both the ego and its milieu are structured realms. Nor do we find on that interface a necessary

---

*Gill points out that the id is not without structure, and that ego defenses indirectly gratify and express the very impulses that they guard against. Thus, the ego does not have exclusive possession of structure, and the id does not have exclusive domain over un-neutralized energies. A clear-cut boundary cannot be drawn between these sectors.

opposition between energized internal motives and external constraints. The motives that we find in the ego often have counterparts in external customs and values. Indeed, however we look at the normal "non-clinical" ego, we find more evidence of transaction than of conflict with the external world.

"Ego" and "community" are, after all, the joint products of an intertwining process of human evolution, and it should not surprise us that between the "normal" ego and its usual environments we find the kind of structural fit that exists between organism and ecology. We find ego and community to be transitive, interwoven domains, metaphors and extensions of each other, rather than opposed systems. That is, systems dynamic within the ego are at the same time the internal extension and the internal re-phrasing of external systems and models.

The ego's vital identifications—which give pattern and organization to its efforts at both defense and growth—maintain as internal dialogues what were once crucial external interactions between the self and significant others. Forms of language, thought, and imagery—the endowment of the community to the individual—are as vital to the self-regulatory systems of the ego as they are to interpersonal communication. The ego's discovery of its own equivalence, its *identity* with certain communal perspectives, provides the basis for self-recognition, for continuity of self, and for adult efforts at defense and self-regulation. Attempts, such as those by Rapaport, (1960) to explain this evident isomorphism between ego and psychosocial ecology exclusively in energy terms, or exclusively in terms of conflict and conflict resolution can be brilliant, but they are also forced and contrived.

In order to understand the ego-milieu interface in its own terms, it was first necessary to see the instincts as something more than quanta of free energy. The instincts had to be understood as inborn potentials for relatedness and transaction, which only produced peremptory, highly "energized" activity when their relevant objects or their usual expressive pathways were lacking. Steam will not explode a boiler if it has an engine to drive.

Psychologists were guided towards this revision by anthropological and sociological observations of normal populations, by experimental and developmental research, and by the work of ethologists. For example, the work of Tinbergen (1953) indicated that the instinctive reactions of animals to normal habitat conditions are marvelously coordinated to those features of milieu that bear on individual and species survival. It is only in states of extreme deprivation that animal behavior takes on the imperious and monolithic quality that supposedly typifies impulsive and "instinctual" behavior in man. Such findings pointed to those adaptive, "transitive" features of instinctually guided action that are overlooked by classical psychoanalytic theory, which emphasizes instead the disruptive and unmodulated quality of such behavior. These findings also led to notions of built-in organism-environment reciprocity as the structural basis of the human ego. Thus Hartmann (1958) proposed that the individual is from birth pre-adapted to an "average expectable environment" and that this adaptation is biologically guaranteed, not the happy outcome of compromises among contending instinctual pressures.

Along these lines, Erikson (1959) develops Hartmann's notion, implicitly rejects the idea of necessary individual-societal conflict, and instead proposes that individuals—like the organisms studied by ethologists—have a guaranteed potential for coordination with the species milieu. In the human case, this is some version of community. This potential is revealed through successive stages of ego development as the individual ego coordinates itself, with varying results, to increasingly complex and abstract versions of community—from the infant-mother (or infant-breast) dyad, to a society which embraces the living and the dead, the economic, supernatural, and institutional orders.

Erikson develops this view in his epigenetic theory. He proposes a continuum of ego stages, of normative developmental crisis points, persisting long past the adolescent apex of sexual maturation. Experiences at each stage can have profound consequences for future personality growth or retardation. Indeed, *Ego-Integrity*—the last potential in the Eriksonian sequence—can only unfold towards the end of life, at the point when the individual must come to terms with his unalterable past.

The implication is that new interactional modes continue to mature through life, and that a complete life span is required if the full spectrum of potentials is to emerge. In this view, the psychic themes of later life might be based on emerging ego potentials that have an urgency relatively independent of infantile needs. For Erikson, the adult ego not only reacts to the environment with a pre-ordained, fixed repertoire of resources. It seeks out the problems that it needs to solve, so as to turn emergent age-graded potentials into new executive capacities.

In the Eriksonian view, ego autonomy is—paradoxically—founded in individual-communal mutuality and interdependence; and the community's recognition, definition, and disposition of emergent capacities determine whether or not they will become part of the ego's repertoire of resources. Thus, given average endowment and facilitating milieux, wisdom in older men may be as predictable as smiling in infants.

To sum up, we are here dealing with two models of ego functioning, each of which treats motivation, growth, and pathology in different ways, and each of which locates the epicenter of personality at a different "point," one on the ego-id interface, the other on the ego-milieu interface. In the first model the ego develops out of the id and is centered mainly around the id, either to struggle against it or collaborate with it. The second model proposes an ego that seeks for mutuality and alignment with external agents. It is organized to collaborate with successive versions of community, and to achieve autonomy through such collaboration.

The Utility of the Ego Models

It is clear that the two contrasting models of ego process help to generate and account for different orders of data. The ego-id conceptions were developed from psychotherapy with clinical populations. They propose an organism in crisis, at odds with the environment and divided within itself. Overt behavior is symptomatic and stereotyped, a forced compromise between severe internal pressures. The model is a hungry, driven organism, even though the deprivation may be self-imposed, and the organism starves in the midst of plenty. The ego-id conceptions are thus very useful for understanding neurotic symptoms, the products of internal conflict between sharply differentiated, equipotent needs. The id-centered conceptions are definitely less useful for understanding the social, expressive, and creative activity of an individual who is not in a state of neurotic emergency.

While each model is presumably most relevant to a separate clinical or normal population, both models may also be relevant to distinct, age-graded states of the same individual. Even the most "normal" individuals go through periods of crisis: those which are developmental in origin, and are imposed from within; and those which are triggered by personal and social catastrophe, and are imposed from without. Whatever the source of the crisis, the individual has lost, or has not yet developed, adequate routes for drive discharge. Blocked impulses can build up, and monolithic defenses can be deployed against them. The psyche is at least temporarily organized in terms of conflict, and can be understood from ego-id perspectives.

The ego-milieu model is most useful for understanding the periods which follow crisis resolution. These are periods of relative inner quiescence. New personality structures integrate the previously conflicting elements, and the individual is free to seek out milieux which ratify his solutions and allow for the further development of emergent ego executive functions.

Accordingly, when we study the ego-milieu interface, our analytic approach takes account of those systems, social and personal, that there manifest themselves to each other. Our methods are neither exclusively depth-psychological nor exclusively sociological, but "psycho-sociological." In order to understand and predict behavior that is both socially and personally qualified, we study both the objective patterning and the subjective implication of the individual's corporate life. We study the kinds of roles that he seeks out, the kinds of interactions and institutions in which he typically enlists himself; and we study the behavioral and attitudinal requirements set for him by the institutions, formal and informal, which own his allegiance. Taking a more subjective tack within this framework, we also study the *present* effects of *past* institutional and communal affiliations: the subject's recollections of those institutions and people that played important roles in his early socialization. Such studies can tell a good deal about how the crisis-free individual will think and behave in norm-governed settings.

AGING AND THE EGO INTERFACES

Turning now to the latter part of the life cycle, we can tentatively isolate crisis, resolution, and post-resolution phases; and we can discuss the nature of normative crisis, options for crisis resolution, and the adaptive possibilities of the various possible outcomes from the pertinent ego perspectives. My investigations of urban American, Mexican Indian, American Indian, and Levantine Peasant groups suggest that most normal men, regardless of sociocultural origin, go through an internal crisis of relatively long duration, beginning in the 40's, peaking around the middle 50's and coming to some resolution in the early or middle 60's. The content and precursors of this crisis will be discussed mainly from ego-id perspectives.

The masculine crisis of middle age can be resolved in a variety of directions, each representing a different arrangement of the ego. The typology of orientations available to the ego as models for crisis resolution will be presented in the next section. Each of these so-called mastery orientations can lead to adequate or inadequate individual adaptation, depending on the psychosocial setting in which it is exercised. Accordingly, after the typology has been presented and the middle-age crisis has been discussed, each major ego state will be briefly considered as a possible design for masculine life in the pre- and post-retirement years. That is, we will look at the mastery types in relation to the "average expectable environments" of American men in their 60's, and speculate on the problems and possibilities that each orientation might generate for its adherents. Ego-milieu perspectives will guide this discussion of the interplay between the various ego orientations and the standard contingencies—such as retirement—of later life.

THE MASTERY TYPOLOGY

The studies which led to initial formulation of the typology were undertaken as part of the Kansas City Studies of Adult Life, of the Committee on Human Development, University of Chicago. The research, described in greater detail elsewhere (Neugarten & Gutmann, 1958; Gutmann, 1964), involved a sample of 145 mentally and physically fit white males, 40 to 70 years in age, all residents of the Kansas City area. The data consisted of Thematic Apperception Test (TAT) stories given in response to selected stimulus cards. Three major types and five component sub-types emerged from the TAT analysis, each presumably representing a special form of relatedness towards the world, and each representing a distinct solution to the ego's task of maintaining internal and external mastery.

The age by type distribution of Kansas City men is shown in Table 1. Younger men (aged 40-54) tend significantly towards active mastery, while older men (aged 55-71) favor passive or magical mastery.* Thus, the types significantly discriminate age groups, suggesting the possibility that the mastery typology defines a continuum of ego states through which men move as they age. Cross-cultural tests of this "developmental" hypothesis will be presented in a later section. Meanwhile, each mastery type will be briefly discussed in terms of (A) the salient motives and relational modes that it expresses, (B) the life issues and "psycho-social ecologies" relevant to these potentials, and (C) the coping or defensive styles that result from the interplay between motives, executive potentials, and environments.

Active Mastery

Motivational issues

The active (or alloplastic) mastery style seems to have as its motivational foundation strivings towards autonomy, competence, and control. The active mastery individual works within or collaborates with external action systems in order to maximize his effect on them, in order to bring some part of them under his control. He is wary of having his actions and choices limited by others, and he is therefore mistrustful of any dependent wishes in himself that would lead him to trade compliance for security.

---

*Other investigators—Shaw and Henry (1965); Rosen and Neugarten (1960); Shukin and Neugarten (1964); and Hays (1952)—particularly those who have studied the covert and implicit aspects of personality in middle and later life, tend to report similar results. Confirmatory clinical observations have also been made by psychiatrists—Meerloo (1955), Zinberg and Kaufman (1963), and Berezin (1963). All the above stress the aging individual's withdrawal from active engagement with the world in favor of more "cerebral," introversive, and self-centered positions.

TABLE 1
Distribution of the Kansas City male sample by major age periods
and by mastery orientations

Mastery Style	40-49	50-59	60-71	
Active				
Promethean-competitive	7[a]	8	3	
	}17	}26	}12	
Productive-autonomous	10	18	9	
Passive				
Emphasized receptivity	8	20	12	
	} 8	}26	}23	
Anxious constriction	0	6	11	
Magical	4	15	14	145
	29	67	49	

[a]This distribution of the mastery cell subtotals is significantly different from
chance ($\chi^2 = 17.417; DF = 8; p < .02$).

Turned inward, these strivings for control and for effect make fo
vulnerability to *shame*. The active mastery individual strives also
against unruly inner tendencies which do not match his own
picture of what he should be. He wants his will to be registered in
the world, and he also needs to be master in his own interna
house.

These various dispositions cumulate to what might be called an
"active-productive" orientation. Like all men, the active mastery
individual desires emotional and physical security, but he is
happiest when he can supply these needs through his own
capacities, and when he is a source of security to others. Thus, he
is most comfortable with resources—be they a business, a flock, or
a cornfield—that he has created for himself and for his dependent
through his own competence and disciplined effort.

Environments

The active mastery individual views the world as a setting for action and movement. He is interested in properties of objects which make them available for management and control. He is interested in boundaries and barriers, so as to circumvent them, test himself against them, or use them. He is interested in the ways in which social and political systems distribute power and leverage, and he is interested in training those personal capacities that fit him for successful competition. He is not much interested in nuances of feeling and conception, either in himself or in others. His sensitivity is turned outwards, to the kinds of behavior that can be measured, predicted, and counteracted; and he is not much concerned with the ideational or emotional counterparts of such behavior.

Ego defenses

The active mastery individual's coping style and defensive strategies are fitted to manage the kind of internal and external experience that he creates for himself by virtue of his competitive and productive orientation towards the world. His major ego defenses include reaction formation and externalization. He is reaction-formed against the dependent tendencies that could interfere with his social and physical mobility, and his combative prowess. His natural tendency towards outer world vigilance leads him to impute responsibility for his thoughts, actions, and feelings to exciting and challenging external events and agents. As a result, such men also tend to refer potentially troubling inner conflicts to the outer world. Active mastery men do not ruminate much over inner problems; rather they look for outer agents who represent, or can be held responsible for, what they dislike and fear in themselves. They legislate their inner problems into collective enterprises—for example, realistic fights against political corruption, intruding enemies, or some refractory segment of external nature.

Sub-types

The active mastery orientation includes *Promethean competitive* and *productive-autonomous* sub-types. These may be found together within some active mastery individuals, or they may in other cases discriminate between men of this orientation. The first sub-type emphasizes combat and competition; strength and prestige are trophies won from an enemy. The second sub-type emphasizes self-reliance and autonomy, enacted through vigorous and productive effort. In productive autonomy there is less emphasis on external enemies and challenges, more emphasis on living up to high internal standards. One competes, in effect, against oneself.

Passive Mastery

Motivational issues

The passive (autoplastic) mastery individual also needs to control the sources of his pleasure and security. But the passive mastery individual does not feel effective enough to create, by himself, his own emotional and physical logistic base. From his standpoint, strong, independent and capricious external agents control what he needs. Accordingly, the passive mastery individual guarantees his security and wins the good regard of the powers-that-be by regulating the one terrain amenable to his control—himself. He can only influence others indirectly, through what he does to himself. He shapes himself to fit the expectations of others; he demonstrates mildness rather than challenge; and he tries to expunge those tendencies that might lead him into dangerous conflict with the provident authorities. He does not, in the Promethean fashion of the active mastery men, try to *wrest* power from the gods; rather he participates passively in external power by identifying with and complying with those who control it. Humility and accommodation are the keynotes of this stage.

Environments

The passive mastery individual ultimately feels that the world eludes his control: It is not responsive to his action or his will. His world tends to be closed, bounded by prohibitions he cannot revoke and dangers he cannot survive. This is not a setting for vigorous action towards increased life space; in his world one moves mainly to discover the limitations on movement and to justify staying put.

Ego defenses

The active mastery individual uses his energy to bring some sector of the world under his control. The passive mastery individual—acting in the name of some external perspective that has moral authority—turns his effort at control against himself. If the active mastery individual is vulnerable to shame stimulated by his covert passive wishes, then the passive mastery individual is vulnerable to guilt that is stimulated by his covert anger.

Accordingly, the ego defenses of the passive mastery group are of the obsessive-compulsive and intellectualizing sort. They lead to caution, to respect for the rules, and to the substitution of fantasy and rumination for direct action. And, when the passive mastery individuals find themselves in situations where the rules—being various and changing—are hard to follow, they tend to seek out placid settings that fit their defensive propensity for order and predictability. If the passive mastery individuals display any aggression, it is not through large action but through this kind of quietly stubborn retrenchment. They can only attack the authorities and their rules by caricaturing the obedience that they require.

Sub-types

Passive mastery also includes two sub-types: autoplastic autonomy and emphasized receptivity. Again, these may coexist within some passive mastery individuals, while they differentiate between others.

In *autoplastic autonomy* the emphasis is on maintaining the sense of effectiveness, of security, and of autonomy through constriction of life space. These men may want to be central in some scheme of things, but they do not want to risk the failures and the wounds to self-esteem possibly attendant on such striving. Experience has taught them that the larger world takes little account of them, that it is full of possibilities they cannot enjoy, that its rules are hard to follow, and that the future will not be much better. In response, the autoplastic autonomy person maintains the illusion of centrality and control through restriction of life space. He retrenches, draws back into those familiar, limited terrains that reflect his schedule and are responsive to his will. This is the "tend your own garden" style, and the passively autonomous person convinces himself that nothing worthwhile exists beyond the precincts of his garden. The productive style moves inward towards the cultivation, in a redundant world, of pleasant thoughts, pleasant sensations, and predictable experiences.

Syntonic receptivity individuals are concerned with tangible supplies of food and love. They relate to the world in terms of getting and giving, though they are much more apt to give after their own wants have been taken care of. These men play down conflict between others and deny their own aggression. They try to maintain the illusion that they exist in the best of all possible worlds, where all needs and purposes are compatible. They are senior "flower children."

Magical Mastery

Motivational issues

The preceding orientations are centered around aggressive motives which are to be expressed (in active mastery) or controlled (in passive mastery). But for magical (omniplastic) mastery individuals, the major motives group around the receptive theme. In this they are like the syntonic receptivity men, although they lack their capacity for delay of gratification and for identification with the gratification of others. In the other styles, instrumental actions—either against the world, the self, or both— intervene between impulse and gratification. In this group, the wish and its execution are not boundaried from each other, but tend to be part of a syncretic unity, such that the wish itself tends to be experienced as the only necessary precondition for its own fulfillment.*

---

*Slater (1964) used psychoanalytic libido theory to construct a conception of ego processes in later life. He argued that the conservation of psychic energy could lead to two mutually exclusive outcomes: priority of boundaries over objects, and priority of objects over boundaries. In the first case, libido is withdrawn from objects and concentrated in maintaining rigid self-boundaries; in the second case, libido is dispersed into objects but withdrawn from self-boundaries. The first leads to disengagement and self-absorption; the second, to undifferentiated warmth, denial, mystical states, and eccentric behavior. It seems clear that Slater is describing, in a more parsimonious and systematic fashion, the states that I refer to as passive (boundaries-over-objects) and magical (objects-over-boundaries) mastery.

Environments

When the illusion of mastery is attained through nullification of boundaries, the world tends to become—especially at times of arousal and ambiguity—an extension of that aroused self and a theater whose elements play out roles in the psycho-drama of the self. Thus, objects in the "magical" world lack fixed, standard meanings but can vary with hungers and fears that they arouse and appease. The object can represent the promise of pleasure or it can become a picture of the subject's reactive disgust at such pleasures; and the object can waver between these extremes, depending on the relative strength at any moment of the contending forces. Thus, the world is seen in simplistic and extreme terms. The world is full of potential providers (who can never provide enough) and potential predators. Vulnerability is the keynote of the relationships to the world.

Ego defenses

Where men of the other orientations manage threat through instrumental action, receptive men handle threat in a way which mingles magic and passivity. Instead of changing the environment, they change their perception of it and confuse their revised perception with the realities. Accordingly, the magical mastery ego defenses are those which accompany and require weak ego boundaries: denial and projection. Denial substitutes for instrumental action against environmental threats, and projection substitutes for instrumental action against the self.

In denial, potentially dangerous external events are seen as innocuous or benign; and in projection, threatening personal motives are imputed to the world and registered as an externally based attack against the self. Realistically, these magical defenses are maladaptive: calculated ignorance is a dangerous luxury. But viewed from the magical mastery perspective, these defenses preserve the vital illusion that all good properties and agents are bonded to the self, and that all malignant agents are outside it. The consequent sense of rightness and goodness justifies further demands against the world.

The Mastery Types and Other Measures

These ego states are not mutually exclusive. The same individual can display them all in different contexts or at different times. They are presented as exclusive states for heuristic purposes, to highlight differences. The typology does have an empirical basis. Men sorted into these types on the basis of their TAT performance were also discriminated by interviewer's ratings of overt behavior and affect; by performance on the "Draw-A-Person" test; by the "Life Satisfaction" measure, a validated scale devised by Neugarten and associates (1961); and by other independent measures derived from interview and observational data provided by these same subjects (Gutmann, 1964; Williams & Wirths, 1965). In general, the prediction was that the active mastery men would achieve high ratings on these measures, that the passive mastery men would achieve lower ratings, and that the magical mastery men would receive the lowest. In the main, these predictions were confirmed.* Accordingly, while they may coexist within persons, each mastery orientation seemingly refers to a distinct psychic organization that combines, across individuals, a fairly standard body of interrelated motives, conceptions, attitudes, and behaviors.

---

*Along the same line Clark (1967) found that the self-conceptions of normal San Francisco subjects, aged 60 and over, were consistent with passive mastery criteria, as predicted for this age group.

CROSS-CULTURAL STUDIES OF THE MASTERY TYPOLOGY

Thus far, the hypothesis considered here—that men age psychologically along a continuum delineated by the active, the passive, and the magical mastery orientations—has been tested in four groups of traditionally oriented, preliterate agriculturalists: the Lowland and Highland Maya of Mexico, the Western Navajo of Arizona, and the Druze tribesmen of Israel. Child-rearing practices, age-grading systems, economic systems, and value orientations vary greatly across these sites; but in all cases older people are respected, have an advisory role towards the young, and tend to amass political and ceremonial power.

The prediction was that the age distribution of mastery orientations would be replicated in societies that differ greatly from the urban United States in terms of the variables that presumably influence personality development. If such a prediction were borne out, we could with some confidence equate the mastery orientations with the divisions of the life cycle. Mastery orientations that distribute more predictably by age than by culture can be regarded as bench-marks of the individual human life cycle, and not as cultural styles that differentiate age cohorts within societies.

Collection and Analysis of Cross-Cultural Data

TAT and interview data were collected from representative Indian and Druze* men, mainly in the 35-75 age-range. Thus far, the TAT analysis has been concentrated on those cards which were used without modification. These include the "rope climber"**

---

*The Six Days' War of Israel interfered with the transcription of our Druze data tapes, so that the analysis of individual Druze protocols has not yet begun. Impressions of this group will be reported, but not formal findings.

**The Rope-climber card suggests to many respondents in any culture a vigorous, muscular, and possibly nude figure who could be going up or down a rope.

and "heterosexual"* cards of the standard Murray TAT set (used in Kansas City, and at all Indian sites); and the Desert Scene** (used only at Indian sites).

As with the Kansas City data, the approach to the cross-cultural data has been exploratory and inductive. The goal has been to make themes which are implicit in data, and relevant to the ego mastery conceptions, explicit and comparable. All stories generated by each card were analyzed separately, one culture at a time. Active mastery stories were those in which issues were recognized by the respondent, active stances were proposed, and vigorous action led to good consequences. Passive mastery stories were those in which hero figures were seen as ineffectual, overwhelmed by external force, or receptive *vis à vis* some external provider. Magical mastery stories were those in which major stimulus features, particularly those suggestive of conflict and trouble, were distorted or ignored.*** For each card thus analyzed, the prediction has been that the age by mastery type distributions would discriminate older from younger men, at any site, along the lines first noted in the Kansas City data.

Results of Cross-Cultural Studies

Figure 1 contains 11 displays, each of which presents the age distributions of mastery orientations elicited by one card, from

---

*The "Heterosexual Conflict" card depicts a young man turned away from a young woman who reaches towards him.

**This card portrays a desert, gullied in the foreground, empty of people, but transected by a trail and barb-wire fences.

***Thus, in regard to the Rope Climber card, active mastery stories are those—regardless of cultural origin—in which the hero climbs vigorously for either a competitive or productive purpose. Passive mastery stories can be those in which the hero is constrained or menaced by outer forces (he does what is expected of him; he flees from a fire). Passive mastery stories are also those in which the hero indulges himself playfully, or accepts food and shelter. Magical mastery stories are those in which the hero is seen to be lying down instead of climbing, or the rope is seen as food.

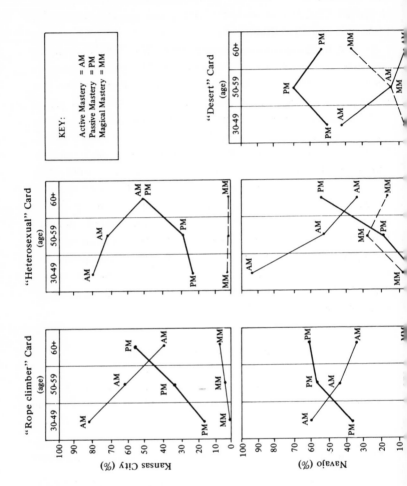

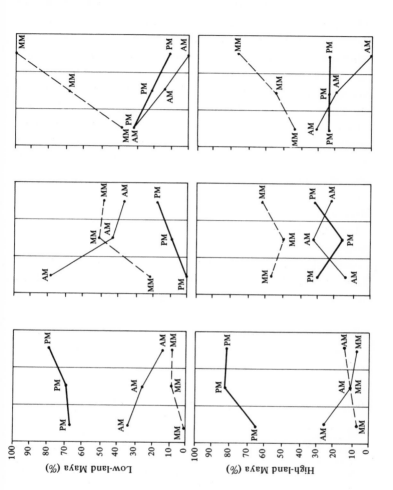

one cultural sample. This figure enables us to make various inter-card, inter-culture, and inter-generational comparisons, most of which support the conclusion that the thematic criteria for the various mastery orientations give rise to categories which discriminate age groups in standard fashion across cards within cultures, and across cultures within cards. While the relative rankings among the mastery orientations can vary by card and by culture, these effects tend to be constant; and there is an age effect which appears to be independent both of cards and of cultures.* As predicted, and with few exceptions, active mastery declines with age, while the percentage of passive and magical mastery stories increases with age, according to the sequence, Active → Passive or Magical Mastery.

The age and culture distributions of standardized data are consistent, though the original stories differ as to manifest content. This consistency suggests that the mastery orientations have trans-cultural distribution; and that while cultures can amplify or retard particular mastery orientations, their sequence is fixed according to an intrinsic schedule that is independent of culture.**

The finding of an age effect in the trans-cultural distribution of mastery orientations permits us to assume that they define a continuum along which men move as they age, in this and other societies. Each culture "specializes" in some particular sector of the continuum. For example, Maya seem to move from passive

---

*These positive results constitute a validation of the original judgments concerning the degree of activity or passivity registered in particular story themes. Also validated is the *a priori* assumption—often contested by anthropologists—that personality data from other cultures can be analyzed from a conceptual framework not indigenous to those cultures.

**These TAT findings are also borne out in the Rorschach and interview data gathered at the same sites. Rorschach imagery and interview themes from the American and Mexican Indian societies distribute by age in line with predictions derived from the Kansas City findings. A more complete account of the analysis and findings from the cross-cultural data is in preparation.

middle age to magical old age, while urban Americans mainly move from active middle age to passive old age. However, in all cases the movement is in the same direction.

This review of the cross-cultural findings supports the contention that the various mastery stages delineate sectors of the individual life cycle. Accordingly, we can now speculate as to the age-graded influences that move individual men along the continuum. The focus will be on American men, and particularly on the shift from active to passive mastery. We will also consider the crises that these shifts might entail, and the fate of the bearers of the various mastery orientations in later life, particularly when they come to the point of retirement.

THE CRISIS OF MIDDLE LIFE

As Figure 1 suggests, the distinctive mastery orientation of our society, in contrast to the three Indian groups, is active mastery. Though this orientation falls off with age, active mastery is well represented even among older Americans, being more common among this cohort than it is among younger Maya. The importance of this orientation in the American psyche is clear. Therefore we must assume that powerful forces are required to shift those American men who make the active-passive transition towards the more passive orbit. Indeed, the causes and consequences of this shift are probably drastic enough to bring about at least a temporary crisis for the ego.*

---

*Our American and Indian data suggest that the shift from active to passive and magical stances is most pronounced in the mid-fifties; and we would accordingly expect indications of psychic unease at about this time, of the sort that would accompany a crisis. Some confirmatory evidence comes from Peck (1956), who reports an "adjustment dip" in the fifties; and from Kaplan (1956), whose tables of age-specific suicide rates show a marked increase during the period 55-64.

The Closing of the Future

Interviews with American, Indian, and Druze 50-year-olds give some indications that this middle-age crisis can be sharply felt by achievement-oriented men in any culture; that it is especially poignant for urban American men; and that it is at least partly brought on by a profound change in the individual's conception of his future. Men in this age cohort seem to recognize that their fantasies in regard to achievement—whether these involve increase in land, flocks, or professional standing—no longer predict the future. In these terms, their future will be *at best* no better than the present. There is, in effect, a "loss of the future," and with it perhaps some final loss of illusions about oneself. If we are not extended in the future, then we have to take ourselves as we *now* are, with all our present limitations. The loss of the future also implies that there is no contract with the universe. Virtue, hard work, and delay of gratification do not predict future bliss, but only more of the same. Both executives and preliterate peasants report this realization, each in terms of his particular achievement motifs.

While this realization seems to be universal, it does not in all cases have the same effect. Some "premature" passive mastery men may even welcome the loss of strength and the closing off of the future. Because of it, they can with some honor abandon the rat race. But whether they are liberated or devastated by this recognition, middle-aged men come to believe—perhaps correctly in urban societies, perhaps wrongly in traditional societies—that they will not develop capacities beyond those that they already possess; and that their future will not be shaped by their wish or by their will. The result is either a relieved "letting go" or an inner crisis stimulated by the covert, shame-provoking wish to "let go," to finally take it easy.*

Thus, the loss of the future has important consequences for the management of inner life, particularly in its sensuous and receptive aspects. These consequences have to do with what may be standard intra-psychic relationships between achievement-oriented fantasies, the ego defenses and the appetites—that is, between aspects of the ego and the id. Therefore they will be reviewed from the ego-id viewpoint.

Ego-Id Relationships and the Middle-Age Crisis

The active mastery style implies a boundaried universe, but active mastery is also founded on fairly rigidly maintained internal boundaries against receptive wishes, diffuse sensuality, and tender feelings. Ferenczi explained the Co-ordination of Inner Boundaries and active mastery when he wrote (1938) on the phases of libidinal management that accompany development. He stated that normal development involves giving up one's dependence on the instrumentality of the parents and coming to rely on personal resources. We prepare for instrumentality by forging our bodies and minds into tools and weapons. As part of this process we

---

*While crisis issues may be fairly standard across individuals and cultures, crisis manifestations may vary greatly. Denial of passive wishes may be expressed through hyperactivity, belligerence, or promiscuity. Ego defenses may move in a paranoid direction, such that the young are seen as exemplars of denied passive wishes and are condemned as "lazy" or "soft." External agents may be held responsible for the passive wishes that they stimulate: thus, wives may be accused of being domineering, enforcing passivity on their husbands; or bosses may be accused of being autocratic, demanding submission from subordinates. The defenses mainly involve an externalization of inner conflicts into external circumstances. For example, psychosomatic illness during this period may serve to externalize responsibility for passive demands: "It is not I who ask for help, but my body."

renounce the polymorphous eroticism of our body and bind the erotic capacity within the genitals. Thus, Ferenczi states: "If there were no such separation of pleasure activities, the eye would be absorbed in erotic looking, the mouth would be exclusively employed as an oral-erotic instrument, instead of being employed in necessary self-preservative activities . . ." (Slater, 1964, p. 36).

The energy required to maintain the necessary internal and external boundaries is gained through an implicit "contract" with the id. In effect, we tell ourselves that we are delaying rather than renouncing pleasure, and that what we give up now will be returned ten-fold in the future. Thus, the system of ego controls in men is structured in large part around the commitment to a meaningful, engrossing, and rewarding future. When reduced virility, health, and achievement (and the prospect of death) devalue this commitment to the future, the "contract" with the id is in effect not honored. As a consequence, there is less ego rationale for maintaining those costly inner controls and boundaries against diffuse sensuality on which the active mastery stance is based, and the denied polymorphous erotic strivings again press their claims. Passive mastery, especially in its syntonic receptivity phrasing, represents the ego state that results when the diffuse strivings toward oral, tactile, and affectional supplies have reestablished their primacy in the erotic life. Some of the possible "somatic" and social consequences of these shifts are discussed below.

Post-Crisis Receptivity: Cross-Cultural Evidence

A standard sequence of interview questions asked at all sites concerned the sources of contentment, the sources of discontent, and the remedies for discontent. Table 2 shows the distribution by age, culture, and thematic category of

TABLE 2

Age and thematic distribution:[a] Traditional Navajo and
Highland Maya responses to question:
"How do you restore contentment?"

Age	1. Reliance on Instrumental Action	2. Reliance on "Omnipotent" Figures	3. Reliance on Oral (and Other) Supplies
30-49	Highland Maya 8 $\Big\}13^b$ Navajo 5	2 $\Big\}3$ 1	1 $\Big\}3$ 2
50-96[c]	Highland Maya 5 $\Big\}11$ Navajo 6	5 $\Big\}15$ 10	7 $\Big\}19$ 12

[a]Highland Maya, N = 28; Navajo, N = 36; Total, N = 64.
[b]χ^2 (of cell totals) = 11.066. $DF = 2, P < .005$.
[c]6 Navajo, 2 Highland Maya S's aged 80 and over; 2 Highland Maya under 35.

Traditional Navajo and Highland Maya responses to the question: "When you are unhappy, how do you restore contentment?" This table indicates that younger men regard productive work as the remedy for most trouble, but older men across these two dissimilar cultures look for help to powerful allies (village authorities, saints, doctors) or to suppliers of food, drink, and friendly attention.* This table illustrates the readiness of older

*Responses to the question, "What makes you happy?" pattern similarly by age and theme. For example, the younger Highland Maya and the young Navajo equate contentment with productive work. They are happy when they acquire livestock, bring new cornfields under cultivation, or find lucrative wage work. Older men are most likely to define happiness in passive-receptive terms: They are made happy by visits from relatives, by their accustomed food, pleasant music, the sight of a flourishing vegetable garden, or a pretty view.

men to shift the burden of instrumentality to the shoulders of powerful natural and supernatural authorities, and to become the recipients of their provision.

Increased orality seems to be one of the psychosexual consequences of this age-graded tendency to rely on the active mastery of others. In order to test the hypothesis that oral interests increase in later life, the Navajo interview and projective data were coded for orality. All mentions of eating or of food preparation, purchase, or production were assigned weights which reflected the intensity of oral need presumably expressed. The orality scores are presently being checked for reliability, but the first estimates differentiate older from younger Navajo, and in the predicted direction. More interesting in regard to the hypothesized instrumentality of younger men is the finding that the highest proportion of young men's orality scores derive from mentions of trade and production of food, while the highest proportion of old men's scores derive from mentions of eating and pleasure in food.*

The hypothesis that the erotic life takes on a more diffuse or "distributive" form, once personal instrumentality is relinquished, is further borne out by trans-cultural data which indicate that older men are interested in the pleasure function of the eye, as opposed to younger men who are more interested in this organ's instrumental function.** This age-trend towards "ocular" supplies

---

*This is not an original finding: Simmons (1945) in his important work on primitive aging devotes his first chapter to the thesis that food has a special and universal importance for old people. This thesis is illustrated with examples from over 30 groups, widely varied as to ecological, ethnic, and sociocultural circumstances. Across this cultural range, Simmons claims, older men have typically used their prestige to ensure the choicest foods for themselves by making them taboo for younger men.

**According to psychological theory, the oral and scotophilic drives are intrinsically linked. Therefore it is not accidental that both should move to psychic prominence at about the same rate in later life. For example, the psychoanalyst Otto Fenichel (1945) explicitly links scotophilia with oral eroticism: "The eye may represent pregenital erogenous zones symbolically.

emerges with particular vividness when we consider the age distribution of all "rope climber" TAT stories that mention visual activity—all those stories in which the hero is either "looking" or "looked-at." The response categories and the distribution of stories by age, by culture, and by these categories are shown in Table 3. Younger U.S. and Indian men usually suggest that the rope climber's visual activity is instrumental: The hero checks progress towards some goal. For older men, "looking" *is in itself the goal*: The hero climbs to see something beautiful or to get a better view.† (A few older—and no younger—Kansas City men see the rope climber as a sexual voyeur.)

To summarize, I am proposing that the "loss of the future" rather than retirement itself is the paradigm crisis of later life; that it may constitute a narcissistic wound which, along with the other disappointments and decrements of later life, leads to a reduction of those inner controls on which active mastery is based, and to at least a partial reinstatement of the sensory and erotic modalities that had once been relinquished in the service of active mastery. Following this change in priorities, from production to reception, the trans-cultural data indicate that, once again, "the eye is absorbed in erotic looking, the mouth . . . is employed as an erotic instrument . . ."

As a sense organ, it may express oral-incorporative and oral-sadistic longings in particular" (p. 227). "Such 'oral' use of the eyes represents the regression of visual perceptions to the incorporation aims that were once connected with early perception in general" (ibid., p. 491).

†Following these leads, those Navajo Rorschach responses which made specific reference to beautiful objects, colors, and landscapes, and to animal or human visual activity, were noted, and the mean percentage of such responses was computed for the youngest (25-49) and the oldest (60 and over) Navajo groups. The difference between these means was significant at the .05 level.

TABLE 3
Distribution by age, thematic category, and culture[a] of
watchfulness responses (rope climber card)

		35-54	55-95
1. Hero watched (attentively or admiringly)	Kansas City Navajo Lowland Maya Highland Maya	17 4 } 25[b] – 4	10 6 } 20 – 4
2. Hero is watchful for productive, task-centered reasons	Kansas City Navajo Lowland Maya Highland Maya	5 6 } 15 – 4	2 11 } 18 4 1
3. Hero is watchful of audience response to his performance	Kansas City Navajo Lowland Maya Highland Maya	3 – } 4 – 1	8 – } 8 – –
4. Climbing and unmotivated watchfulness are hero's only activity	United States Navajo Lowland Maya Highland Maya	6 – } 13 3 4	1 2 } 7 1 3
5. Emphasized (erotized) watchfulness: increased visual input is hero's chief goal	United States Navajo Lowland Maya Highland Maya	1 2 } 7 4 –	5 7 } 26 11 3
TOTAL		65	79 143

[a]Kansas City, N = 58; Navajo, N = 38; Lowland Maya, N = 23; Highland Maya, N = 24.
[b]$\chi^2 = 13.473$ (for cell totals), $DF = 4$, $P < .01$.

THE RETIREMENT CRISIS

The period of crisis and shift reviewed here results in the primacy of passive over active mastery, and in the increased importance of magical mastery. However, while passive and magical mastery both gain adherents, and while active mastery loses adherents, all three orientations are represented in the "post-crisis" American male population (Table 1).

Regarding this older cohort, we are no longer concerned with an intrinsic crisis, a product of the general species condition, but with an *imposed* or extrinsic crisis, brought on by the cultural practice of retirement. The contention here is that the impact of retirement, including its very status as a crisis, is mediated by the mastery orientation of the retiree. At this point, we consider the relations between stabilized ego orientations and the external work milieu; and we consider the ego's reactions to more or less arbitrary disruptions of such relationships.

Accordingly, we will now refer to the ego-milieu perspective for insights into the meaning of work and retirement for the representatives of various mastery orientations. The ideas which follow are not findings but hypotheses. They are presented to illustrate further ego-psychological thinking and to indicate some possible directions for empirical research. They are conjectures based on intensive interviewing and observation with a variety of populations.

Work, Retirement, and Active Mastery

Table 1 indicates that, within the active mastery category, the Promethean-competitive and productive autonomous sub-orientations are about equally represented among younger active mastery men, but that the latter style achieves a 3-to-1 lead among Kansas City men aged 60 or over. Accordingly, we will concentrate on the meanings of work and retirement for the senior productive-autonomous men, keeping in mind that they are probably hold-outs against strong internal and perhaps external pressures towards passive-receptivity.

Generally speaking, active mastery men are likely to rate themselves in terms of their effect on external systems. Such men feel amplified and enlarged by what they do *to* larger systems, not by what they get *from* them. Work is for them the medium through which they relate to and affect larger systems, and it is the standard by which they estimate their personal effectiveness. Wage or salary is another standard by which they measure their effect and value. Work also validates the counterdependent defenses: Through work, active mastery men assure themselves that they are in charge of the sources of their own security, and that they consume only what they have first produced.

Retirement probably has its most drastic effect on active mastery men. Retirement deprives them of their effectant relationship to larger systems of action. Hence, it deprives them of psychic extension or stature, and they would experience this deprivation as a loss of self-respect. Loss of salary could also deprive them of tangible measuring rods for estimating their worth. More generally, retirement deprives these men of intimate contact with those larger action systems into which they could otherwise externalize the possibly intense active-passive conflicts of this stage.

Older active mastery men in traditional, religiously oriented societies find congenial social settings waiting for them when work becomes too hard. These may replace work settings as "projective ecologies." That is, the sacred, supernatural order, and the way of life that is built around it, seem to provide the traditional older man with an ecology that both accommodates and requires his passive mastery postures. Therefore these do not come into conflict, as they emerge, with his responsible and even autocratic secular position.

In the traditional Druze society, for example, the old man does not have to disengage from society in order to live out the resigned, receptive parts of himself. Rather, as these emerge he deflects them—*via* the prayerful role—towards Allah, even as he continues to dominate his sons. Furthermore, the traditional older man's propitiatory, humble stance towards the gods draws their good influences towards him, and into the community that he represents to the gods. His passive-receptivity fits him for a valued social role. Thus, dependent leanings may, in the traditional society, become the cornerstone of the older man's elevated social status, and the basis of new ego executive capacities.*

For the typical older active mastery man in U.S. society, "projective ecologies" are successively reduced as aging proceeds, and replacements are not usually provided. Retirement finally leaves active mastery men with little to contend against besides their own nature. These determinedly independent men are then likely to be faced with the recognition of their own passive wishes. Enforced domesticity following retirement and constant contact with their wives may also increase the threat from denied passive temptations. For active mastery men, retirement sets off a crisis, and it deprives them of their usual routes for handling crisis.

Work, Retirement, and Passive Mastery

The autoplastic autonomy and syntonic receptivity sub-types are about equally represented in the oldest passive mastery cohort. Work is problematic for both these sub-groups, though for different reasons. Both probably benefit from retirement, though in different ways.

It is abrasive contact with others, and the resultant loss of control and order, that make work problematic for the autoplastic

---

*Traditional societies have learned how to use those men who are tough enough to survive independent old age; but it is only in a few professional sub-cultures—law, medicine, politics, and academia—that Americans are likely to avail themselves of the special virtues, the special integration of realism, sensitivity, and selflessness that autonomous old men are capable of developing.

autonomous men. Some of these men have protected territories of file-rooms, workshops, or crop-land. For others of this orientation, work entails unavoidable meetings with intrusive employers, clients, and fellow workers. On the positive side, work provides this group with an armature of order and schedule around which to organize both the working and the private life. Furthermore, these men can use work priorities to rationalize their demands for order and privacy. Finally, for autoplastic autonomy men, salary or wage perhaps has the special meaning of reward for virtue, and the sense of virtue grows with the size of the bank account.

Retirement has a variety of positive and negative meanings for this group. Following retirement they are less abraded by an uncaring, inconsiderate world, but they miss the sense of order and predictability that the work schedule brought to their life. They may also miss the sense of moral order that comes from doing a job to the satisfaction of internal or external authorities or both.

Syntonic receptive men would value the wage, the external schedule, and the companionship provided by work and work settings; but the work itself would be seen as an imposition, a demand on limited resources. By the same token, these receptive men might see retirement as a liberation, particularly if social agencies took over the function of supplying funds, direction, and even companionship. Some of these needs for direction and sociability are probably supplied by the wife (often known as "mom"), assuming that she does not resent the constant presence of her often demanding husband in the home. By the same token, properly managed retirement could free these men to seek out and construct the kinds of secure, kin-centered communities that they require.

Work, Retirement, and Magical Mastery

In its later life phrasing, magical mastery in "normal" men is probably an elaboration and extension of syntonic receptivity.

That is, where the syntonic receptivity men combine a passive-receptive orientation with a fairly intact ego process, the older magical mastery men combine receptive yearnings with a rather primitive ego organization, featuring the diffuse ego boundaries and archaic defensive strategies described earlier. Accordingly, their orientation towards work is probably as negative as that of the syntonic receptivity group, while their arbitrariness would make them less valuable as workers. Though this group would probably welcome retirement, the consequent loss of reality demands and guidelines could accelerate their slide into senile decompensation.

In sum, it appears that older active mastery men might do best in milieux which provide disguised outlets for their covert passive strivings. Autoplastic autonomy men probably require protected enclaves where, on a limited scale, they can run their lives to suit themselves. Men of the receptive orientation might flourish in extended, multi-generational family groups; and magical mastery men would at least be kept on the rails by imposed structure. Thus, what is optimal for one type may even be contra-indicated for the other. Where the receptive men need tangible assurances of love and supply, the active mastery men would probably be threatened by any such clear offer of external support. By the same token, the receptive men would reject the authoritative roles that the active mastery men require.

U.S. SOCIETY AND POST-RETIREMENT ADJUSTMENT

This review of men's possible post-retirement requirements suggests that U.S. society is not particularly supportive of any of the mastery orientations of later life. Viewed broadly, the society supplies neither the age-status system nor the traditional patriarchal orientation most supportive of active mastery. Rapid demographic and physical changes tend to undermine the ecological stability required by autoplastic autonomy. Family dispersion makes it much harder for syntonic receptivity types to get the emotional supports that they need. Retirement deprives magical mastery men of necessary reality structuring.

By and large, post-retirement prospects appear brightest for the autoplastic autonomy types. U.S. cultural values tend to support this orientation and, given sufficient income, such people can wall off relatively private enclaves and tend satisfying gardens within them. Senior citizens' clubs, retirement communities, and special activity programs are also helping to create enclaves where elderly people of the autonomous persuasion can associate with their own kind and deplore together the immorality of the young.

The post-retirement years may indeed be the "golden years" for the psychologically autonomous, financially independent aged. Post-retirement programs will probably have to deal mainly with casualties and potential casualties from the productive autonomy, syntonic receptivity, and magical mastery cohorts.

Post-Retirement Casualties

In this last section we are more concerned with post-retirement casualties than successes. We are concerned with those men for whom retirement provokes an authentic and continuing crisis. Because they do not bend even under the implacable coercion of aging, the active mastery group may generate the most tragic and least "treatable" group of aging casualties in our society. During the post-retirement years, after they have been deprived of opportunities for expansive action, the active mastery men are most likely to be in conflict with the dependent yearning side of themselves. Satisfaction of this group's dependency needs—unless these are disguised by psychosomatic illness—can cause them intense shame. By the same token, complete denial of their dependency needs may lead to increased (unconscious) receptive demands and to increased inner conflict.* Failures from this group may turn to their own version of magical mastery, solving conflicts through illusory means. Alcohol can convey a temporary sense of power while satisfying unconscious receptive demands. Paranoid distortions can run interference for megalomanic ideas, involving a febrile sense of energy and mission. Suicide may express final despair when the magical palliatives fail.

Failures within the syntonic receptivity group may also fall back on magical mastery (as was already pointed out) and rely on blatant denial of troubling realities. They too might use alcohol to support this shaky denial. Depression and apathy (but probably not suicide) would reflect the receptive person's drastic reaction to the breakdown of denial.

As for magical mastery men, the lack of a daily job would leave them with much unclarity in their lives. At times of emotional arousal these men might start to see in ambiguous events their own frightened, excited reaction to such events. Their behavior at such times could become so erratic as to require hospitalization.

Some Remedial Possibilities

Older active mastery men, like spirited and adventurous adolescents, are the misfits of an industrialized mass society. It is not easy to see how their psychic lot would be greatly improved in the post-retirement years without a fundamental shift in the structure of society. However, while this is bound to be a troubled group, they also have important ego resources. At least some individuals among them can be helped by sensitive therapists and counsellors. Post-retirement active mastery casualties might benefit from

---

*Clark (1967) studied value orientations in samples of mentally ill and normal individuals aged 60 and over. The mentally ill were characterized by values—ambition, competitiveness, counter-dependency—which bespoke a strong and unrelinquished active mastery orientation.

short-term intensive treatment, managed by "patriarchal" older therapists who would reassure them they had earned the right to relax, and that some slacking off was not the same as total capitulation. Specially trained job counsellors might help them find their way to meaningful work, for example, as sub-professionals in community development projects. They could also be steered to the products of the "active leisure" technology and become consumers of the new compact, efficient trailer and camping equipment.

As for the receptive group, their financial outlook improves over the years as welfare coverage increases, but their emotional supports are probably falling off as society becomes more mobile and dispersed. Retirement communities will help the more affluent, but the disadvantaged of this group may eventually have to be subsidized in low-cost communities, perhaps organized around church affiliation. Both receptive and magical individuals would probably be fairly responsive to remedial social programs, though neither cohort would seek them out. Services would have to be brought rather forcefully to the attention of these passive individuals.

RESEARCH DIRECTIONS

These diagnoses and remedies are not asserted with any great confidence. There are no doubt other psychological patterns, other individual-societal fits, other crises, and other versions of remedy besides those outlined here. What these might be is a matter for further and better empirical research. But I would insist that researchers look for, and social agencies must plan for, the variety of psychological "species" in the aging population. Social workers are apt to define their target populations in terms of the agency services available for them. But ego psychology—whether "id-centered" or "ego-centered"—teaches us that we must go to the populations involved and ask them to spell out their various and often conflicting definitions of adjustment, crisis, remedy, and social service. The typological approach that has been sketched here gives some idea of the conceptions that could inform such a study, and it attempts to predict some of the stances towards work and retirement such a study might uncover. In this endeavor, the various perspectives of ego psychology do not provide *a priori* answers. They do suggest where and how we might look for fruitful answers to some problems of later life.

MARJORIE FISKE LOWENTHAL

Marjorie Fiske Lowenthal is director of the interdisciplinary Adult Development Research and Training Program, Langley Porter Institute, and Professor of Social Psychology in Residence, University of California School of Medicine, San Francisco. Previously she taught and conducted research on the Berkeley campus of the University of California, and prior to that was Associate Director of Columbia University's Bureau of Applied Social Research. In the immediate post-war years, she was Deputy Director of the Voice of America's research division.

In addition to frequent publications in professional journals, Mrs. Lowenthal's work includes *Aging and Mental Disorder in San Francisco* (1967), *Lives in Distress* (1964), *Book Selection and Censorship* (1959), and co-authorship of *The Focused Interview* (1948), *Mass Persuasion* (1946) and *Crisis and Intervention* (1970). Mrs. Lowenthal is a Fellow of the American Sociological Association, the American Psychological Association, and the Gerontological Society.

Her current interests, as the chapter in this volume suggests, are socio-psychological aspects of transitions in the adult life span. Problems and concepts which she is exploring in this connection include cumulative stress, idiosyncratic transitional stages, and the dynamics of change in perceptions of the social system and in the quality of close interpersonal relationships, from a life-cycle perspective.

11: SOME POTENTIALITIES OF A LIFE-CYCLE APPROACH TO THE STUDY OF RETIREMENT

MARJORIE FISKE LOWENTHAL*

This chapter develops the thesis that the manner in which retirement is experienced generally repeats processes of adaptation to change developed at earlier stages of the life span. This thesis rests on certain broad definitions of the concepts "adaptation" and "change." For purposes of this discussion, "adjustment of the life style" is what is meant by adaptation, "life style" being viewed as a configuration comprising (a) conscious aims, and (b) day-to-day and week-to-week patterns of behavior. Change is defined as new events or alterations in conditions in the personal or social systems. In this chapter, further, the emphasis will be on perceived change, though the assumption throughout is that such perceptions are often influenced by needs or aims of which the individual is not necessarily conscious. Types of change include what might be called normative transitions such as marriage or retirement, and idiosyncratic transitions such as major occupational shifts, telling insights or revelations, or the shock of physical incapacity or major illness.

The first part of the paper elaborates on these concepts and

*Betsy Robinson contributed valuable research assistance in the preparation of the final version of this chapter.

suggests ways of making them operational for research purposes. A tentative life-style typology is then proposed and explored for its implications for the study of retirement.

PREMISES AND DEFINITIONS

A promising avenue to the study of adult development is through the image of the self and the image of the social system immediately relevant to the self and, especially, the nature and degree of articulation between these two sets of imageries. Both concepts can be examined within the framework of (a) the individual's purposes and (b) his behavioral style. Purposes consist of commitments, aspirations, and values which influence decisions. Behavioral style refers to the general pattern of activities, best seen through the uses of time, and cognitions and affects relating to these activities. In addition, there are certain conditions influencing his purposes and behavior, such as acts of nature (influencing his health, for example), economic and political unrest, and wars, which the individual views as beyond his self and his immediate social system, and, most importantly, beyond his control.

There may be modal congruities and incongruities both within and between these two domains (purpose and behavior) during the adult life span. Changes within each domain and in the relationship between them may be developmental (inherent) or circumstantial (imposed by external circumstances), or both. One promising way to assess the comparative importance of these two possibilities is to analyze the extent to which changes within and between the two domains take place in the presence and in the absence of normative transitional events (such as first job, first child, retirement).

The individual's awareness of poor fit between these two

domains is apparently more stressful at some periods than others. Alterations in his time sense, which conceivably could come about as a result of either common transitional occurrences (the point where he feels that his life is half over, for example, or the menopause, children leaving home, retirement) or idiosyncratic circumstances (such as career changes, divorce, serious illness), are major intervening factors between the perception of such incongruity and the degree of experienced stress.

Related Concepts

Several substantive themes weave through this framework. One is *role theory*, and it must already be apparent that the focus on transitions, or continuities and discontinuities in the adult life span, includes role increments and decrements, though there are some kinds of transitions not specifically related to role change. For example, there may be internally or externally precipitated insights involving a change in self-image or in time perspective. An illustration of the former is provided by Mrs. T., who reports as a major turning point in her life a period when she was closely involved with a small social group of Americans abroad, during which she "grew up," becoming "a person in my own right—I don't think my husband liked that."*

Reference group theory, as well as the idea of referent individuals (Hyman, 1960), which we believe should also include the former self, provides important frames of reference for exploring the individual's perceptions of the viable segments of his social system, as does *attitude theory*, particularly that segment of

---

*Illustrative material is drawn from a collection of about 100 detailed life histories, half of them from elderly subjects studied at four points in time for another purpose (NIMH Grant No. MH-09145), half from exploratory interviews conducted in connection with a new study of continuities and discontinuities in the adult life span (NICHD Grant No. HD-03051).

it concerned with the relation between attitudes (and values) and behavior. In effect it might be said that the theoretical framework suggested in this paper is in itself an attempt to focus on a limited segment of the problem of the relation between attitudes and behavior, the underlying premise being that this complex represents "personality in process" or, from a slightly different perspective, adaptation in the broadest sense of the word.

From a more limited viewpoint, insofar as the individual's perceptions of the nature and influence of his reference groups, referent individuals, and societal norms relate to age-grading and related phenomena, this framework also provides for a phenomenological approach to the study of *socialization* for the various stages of adult life, though in the case of old age it might better be called, in our society, socialization to a non-stage.

Obviously implicit in this framework too is an interpretation of *personality theory*. As mentioned above, one way in which personality-in-process can be studied is by examining the changing content of, and the relation between, aims and behavior. This interpretation stems in part from the work, among others, of Gordon Allport (1937, 1961), Henry Murray (1962), and Clyde Kluckhohn (1962).

It has also been said that at least as important for the study of adult development as reference group theory would be a "*reference time theory*," or a theory bearing on the relevance of a changing time perspective to changes in life aims and behavioral style. Although there is increasing interest in perceptions of time, in both the social and psychological sciences (Moore, 1963; Kastenbaum, 1965), as there is in the not unrelated problem of conceptions of death, we are still far from having a theory. This writer is convinced that time perspective will prove to be vital for the study of socio-psychological change in adult life.

Finally, *stress theory* is not unrelated to this approach. The concept of cumulative stress has already proved to be of considerable explanatory value in analyzing the factors associated with mental health and illness in adult life (Langner & Michael, 1963; Lowenthal, Berkman, and associates, 1967). Time dimensions as explicated in experimental work on stress (Janis, 1958; Lazarus, Opton, & Averill, 1968) may prove to be supported in longitudinal community studies of adults (Neugarten, 1968). Similarities in the findings of these two very different research approaches hold promise for the results of a much needed rapprochement between field and laboratory research methods.

STRESS AS BREECH BETWEEN GOALS AND BEHAVIOR

At some point in middle age men and women appear to sense incongruity between what they believed they wanted in life and how they are actually living.* To reduce this tension, there seem to be two alternatives: to reinterpret goals in order to maintain the accustomed behavioral style, or to reorient behavior to fit the aims. This kind of mid-life crisis, which has been observed by psychoanalysts as well as poets and novelists, has been called the decision to stagnate or grow (Pearce and Newton, 1963). The mid-life period appears to be crucial for later adaptation to retirement, or to the physical insults of aging, when non-volitional events and change often *demand* reorientation of goals to fit a feasible behavioral style.

Imbalance within the Behavioral or Purposive Domain

The sense of imbalance *between* aims and behavior may in fact result in the growth of awareness of conflict *within* one

---

*Such incongruence apparently has significance on several levels. Public opinion researchers working from a cross-national perspective report, for example, that the individual's perception of incongruity between his country's stated aims and goals influences his morale to a notable extent (Crespi, 1966).

or both domains. This feeling of unease can most readily be subsumed under the general headings of instrumental and expressive.* The striving for balance may be of two types, one having a life-span perspective and the other a more immediate one. The latter would be illustrated by the mother whose children are branching out on their own and who begins to plan for a closer relation with her husband before or after his retirement. The former is illustrated by an erstwhile hard-driving army officer who consciously works at a life-span balance by spending his retirement years growing roses; and a younger man, in our empty-nest sample, who has become an enthusiastic grandfather, as though to make up for what he experienced as (unavoidable) neglect of his children when they were small.

For the very young, however, at least for the middle and upper middle class young of today, the pull seems to be not so much toward balancing the instrumental and the expressive in their aims and in their behavior, but toward making a choice between them. Thus we have a high school senior who nostalgically looks back on his third-grade year and wistfully ahead to retirement because in those periods there was and will be, he feels, no conflict between his need for achievement and his need for "play." A newlywed wife works very hard in a bank in order that she and her husband, who has already dropped out of graduate school in anticipation of this trip, can take a year off "to find and be themselves," implying that they find it difficult to balance instrumental and expressive needs.

---

*As our analytic work continues, it may become necessary to develop typologies within each of these rubrics. Under instrumental, for example, we have thus far isolated three types (of which more later): the excessively instrumental; instrumental/other directed; and effectant (White, 1961), where the satisfaction is in doing for its own sake. Under the rubric, expressive belongs a category which we might call receptive/nurturant, suggesting a reciprocity in interpersonal relations not explicit in the term expressive.

This is very different from the way today's middle-aged, middle-class men and women recollect their plans and choices when they were 18 or 23. For persons now, say, in their mid-fifties, men and often women had to find jobs as quickly as possible in order to survive. For men now in their mid-forties, World War II and the draft did not pose problems of choice or decision making. For both men and women, the expressive act of falling in love usually carried with it instrumental goals as well, those centering around marriage as an institution, such as occupations and establishing a home. It may be that the sense of a conflict between these instrumental and expressive aims comes about when the individual believes he can make a choice, that he has options. Today's adolescents are aware of more options than were their parents at the same age. This may also be one of the difficulties with which retirement confronts some people, at least those who do not have to expend all their resources on sheer survival. Unlike today's young, today's retirees are not accustomed to coping with alternatives in the uses of their time.

In any event, relying on retrospective reports of today's middle-aged, there does in fact appear to be a qualitative difference between the generations—*within* the middle class. The parent generation does not feel they had an either/or choice to make in youth—when ready to work they felt lucky if they could find a job—any job. Nor were there, for most of them, value conflicts about the draft for World War II. In mid-life, their aims seem to be to establish or maintain balance between the instrumental and expressive elements of their lives. Their children feel they have to make an either/or choice between these elements. Such a dichotomy, however, does not exist for the working-class young, who closely resemble in their plans and decisions the retrospective images the middle-class middle-aged have of themselves at 18 or 23, as having no alternatives but to find a job (or fight the war) and eventually establish a home and family.*

A Note on Generational Differences

Perhaps this is a good point to digress on these seeming similarities and differences between generations, in terms of the potential explanatory importance of historical factors (depression and World War II compared with affluence and Vietnam, for example), and in terms of the parental role models provided for each. One might speculate that in the United States the parents of today's middle aged, middle class resembled the parents of today's blue-collar youth in respect to role models, with the father consistently fulfilling the instrumental (and perhaps authoritarian) role and the mother the receptive/nurturant role. But at the time when today's middle-aged, middle-class people themselves became parents, say in the 1940's, they had been, through formal education as well as in their absorption of the mass media, heavily exposed not only to a more permissive attitude toward child rearing, but also to a far less rigid notion of male and female roles as parents. Fathers were expected to care for and play with children, and mothers often were employed. That ambiguity or interchangeability of parental roles may have a significant bearing on the conflicted stance of their children is suggested by the recent work of Westley and Epstein (1969).

Such generational differences are difficult to document with hard data, and the suggestions above merely illustrate the complexity of the endeavor to sketch out a developmental approach to the problem of retirement. In looking at the retired

---

*This observation clearly does not apply to the young black militant segment of our society, for whom rebellion or revolution offers yet another option.

cohort of today we are largely looking at parents of those now middle aged, the grandparents of the 18-year-olds. While we find the instrumental/expressive model a useful way of looking at the purposive and behavioral domains at all stages of the adult life span, we must at the same time bear in mind that some of our observations such as the either/or stance of the young, the efforts to strike a balance in mid-life, and an effort at a kind of life-span balance among the grandparents may not be developmental but imposed, the results of sociocultural-historical change.

AN EXAMPLE OF A LIFE-CYCLE MODEL

With this reservation, and it is a serious one, I should like now to pick up the thread of a life-cycle approach to the study of retirement. To recapitulate, the underlying premises are that the process of adaptation to external and internal change involves adjustment within and between the purposive and behavioral domains, and that a characteristic patterning of this process may be established quite early in life (and may in itself be a significant expression of personality). Diagram I is a schematic view of this approach. We have further suggested that normative and idiosyncratic transitional events may heighten the individual's consciousness of this process. The content dimensions of instrumental and expressive (among others) within goal/behavior domains provide a convenient point of departure for elaborating on a life-cycle approach to the study of retirement.*

As will be noted in Diagram I, though changes within and between the two primary domains may well comprise adaptation

---

*In "Intentionality: Toward a Framework for the Study of Adaptation in Adulthood," *Aging and Human Development* (in press), these concepts are operationalized, and many hypotheses suggested here are substantiated.

DIAGRAM 1. Domains for analysis of life-stage adaptation

A. *Pre-transition Phase*

(1) Situational factors	(2) Perceptual characteristics	(3) Goal-behavior constellations	(4) Adaptation
cumulative and recent stress continuous and discontinuous social networks, e.g.:: roles, social scope, group affiliations, and dyadic relationships	stress perceptions social perceptions (interpersonal, reference groups, social issues) self-concept life-course perspective perceptions of pending transitions	values and specific aspirations values and motivated behavior specific aspirations and motivated behavior	morale psychological resources and deficits physical health status

Intervening circumstance: incremental or decremental transition; or no transition

B. *Post-transition Phase*

(1) Change in situational factors	(2) Change in perceptual characteristics	(3) Change in goal-behavior constellations	(4) Change in adaptation
(dimensions as listed above)	(dimensions as listed above, with last item perception of recent transition)	(dimensions as listed above)	(dimensions as above)

in the most global sense, a secondary domain of more conventional measures of "adjustment" has been added, to explore the
relation between life style at successive stages and various of the
usual indicators. It may be, for example, that a life style reflecting
disharmony between goals and behavior is less related to the
traditional indicators of adaptation in youth than in mid-life, and
perhaps more closely related in mid-life than in old age.

The two other major domains of the framework represented by
Diagram I consist of social and intrapersonal "givens" (1), and
certain perceptual and cognitive characteristics of the individual (2)
which serve as predisposing or intervening factors in the adjustments
made in the goal/behavior constellations (3).

Diagram II shows an approach to an analysis of the content
dimensions of the purposive and behavioral domains as shown in
Diagram I. Here both aims and behavior are classified in the
dimensions of instrumentality and expressivity. On the basis of
some preliminary analysis of elderly subjects, it seemed advisable
to add a third category, namely the self-protective, since we have
found people among whom aims or behavior (or both) seem
primarily directed toward the avoidance of the assertion of self in
either the pursuit of instrumental aims or the expression (and
reception) of human love and warmth. (Psychiatrists would
probably call these schizoid personalities.) This illustrative correlation of aims and behavior yields a typology of nine (at this point
very arbitrarily labeled) life styles.

DIAGRAM II. Goal/behavior constellations

Purposive Domain	Behavioral Domain		
	Instrumental	Expressive	Self-protective
Instrumental	obsessively instru-mental	autonomous or effectant	cautious
Expressive	instrumental/other-directed	receptive/ nurturant	dependent
Self-protective	conformist	manipulative	self-protective

Analytic Potentials

One analytic use of such models would be to compare people in mid-life with those in the transitional stage of retirement, or better still to study the same group at both stages. In the mid-life stage, for example, one could take both working men and working women and categorize their goals and their behavior in terms of the extent to which they are primarily related to work activities, to non-work activities, to both, or to neither. We would expect working people whose aims are primarily related to non-work activities or qualities to perceive retirement as a time of fulfillment. For example, Mrs. M. is a working mother with expressive aims, who works to help educate her two sons, to contribute toward a week-end retreat for the family, and to save money for post-retirement travel with her husband, and she anticipates that period with great pleasure.

The obsessively instrumental executive whose aims and leisure, as well as his work hours, are directed toward the achievement of power, money, success, or prestige will have difficulty in perceiving and planning for the possibility of retirement. He may be incapable of altering either his goals or his behavioral style, and he may become physically ill or clinically depressed if forced to retire. (These are the people, largely middle or upper middle class, from whom the concept of a retirement crisis has been derived.) Similarly, the person for whom work has provided a protection against intimate relations with others would find retirement traumatic if he became highly exposed to the needs or demands of close others.

Those whose aims find expression in both work and non-work activities are usually (though not always) persons whose goals are both instrumental and expressive. They may pursue the former in work and the latter in non-work, in which case they may have problems with retirement, or they may pursue both types of aims in work as well as non-work activities, in which case we would not expect them to find retirement unduly disruptive.

The resolution of the mid-life crisis, when it is experienced, is crucial not only for the life style of late middle age, but for the anticipation of and transition into retirement and the establishment of a life style viable for the retirement period. Diagram II suggests a schema for examining life styles in both periods, and therefore the changes between them. For example, the woman with expressive goals who has satisfied her nurturant needs mainly in relation to her children may, at the empty-nest stage, transfer her nurturant focus to her husband. Or she may (as many do) become more instrumental in her aims in which case, unless she finds an outlet of her own, she may seek to manipulate her husband, goading him to higher occupational achievements at precisely the time when at least some men begin to take more interest in interpersonal relationships. While these opposing tendencies in husband and wife may be tolerable during the man's work-life, such a couple will almost certainly have more problems at retirement than a couple wherein the wife redirected her receptive/nurturant behavior to her husband. In other words, where a person stands at pre-retirement in the typology of Diagram II suggests the options theoretically open to him for the retirement stage.

Before concluding with one or two other examples of how the model proposed here may be applied, I should like to point out that for the writer the process of coding, from detailed interviews, the purposive and behavioral domains in terms of content and structural dimensions, and in relation to each other, has provided a very convincing basis for deducing unconscious (or at least unstated) aims. For example, the middle-aged civil servant who, apparently as a result of the interviews, decided to take exams for a better job was, prior to that decision, planning for unusually early retirement. (He also is entitled to an army pension.) In his current state of vigor, and in the complete absence of retirement plans, his original alternative seemed to the analyst rather like succumbing to a death wish.

Typological Uses of the Model

The typologies suggested above, supplemented by information from the other domains of Diagram I, may prove to have predictive as well as heuristic uses. To illustrate the former, out of the purposive/behavioral configuration we extract—for example, for the post midlife crisis phase—five lifestyles from the nine suggested in Diagram II. These can be described in terms of perceptions of self and social systems, and predictions can be made in relation to the perceptions of and adaptation to retirement. (See Diagram III.)

Life styles in relation to retirement

As the studies of life styles (Reichard et al., 1962; Williams & Wirths, 1965), and of adult personality (Havighurst, 1964; Neugarten and associates, 1964; Gutmann, 1967), as well as developmental research (Cumming and Henry, 1961; Cumming, 1964) suggest, adult humanity, even in one culture, cannot readily be reduced to a few "types"—perhaps less readily than is true for children or adolescents. But for a start let us consider a few prototypes:

1. *The obsessively instrumental style.* David Gutmann described people who have evolved this life style, in personality terms, as counter-dependent. In the language of child psychology, they would probably be called over-achievers. Alvin Goldfarb (1965) might refer to this style as one of "masked dependency." Whatever its psychodynamics or etiology, to the observer this style appears directed toward instrumental ends and its people appear work-driven to the exclusion of all else and often to the point of exhaustion. The self-made successful businessman is perhaps the most conspicuous example, but the compulsive housewife, the

determinedly sacrificial mother, and the indefatigable do-gooder probably belong here too. Recreation, play, or leisure—if they occur at all—will be pursued with the same driven quality, often ostensibly directed to the same instrumental ends as work, or interpreted as a means of renewing strength for work. Manipulation of people, objects, nature, or even animals is a characteristic of this style.

2. The instrumental/other-directed style. This has long been the culturally prescribed masculine life style in American society, and the personality type might best be described in Riesman's term "other-directed" (Riesman, 1950). People do not adopt this style in order to suppress their dependency needs; rather, their other-directedness reflects a mode of meeting these needs, and in our society the principal way to be accepted (particularly for a male) is to pursue instrumental ends. In a non-instrumental culture, such other-directed people might develop quite different life styles. In our culture, these are the men, and sometimes the women, who may work as hard as the obsessively instrumental, but their life styles tend to be more complex and to include relationships, qualities, and activities that are ends in themselves. Work is not a drug or an escape but a means—to peer acknowledgment, comfort, success, security.

3. The receptive/nurturant style. This life style has been, except for the Feminist movement, the culturally prescribed one for women in our society. (Masked dependency among women seemingly adopting this life style may result in an extreme form of "momism," in which case they would be more appropriately included under the obsessively instrumental.) Even in our culture, certain occupations permit men to adopt this life style (e.g., teaching). It is often characterized by networks of close personal relationships, and some men in our culture may combine this style with a non-obsessive instrumental style, or move from the latter to the former as they grow older (Neugarten and Gutmann, 1964).

DIAGRAM III. Lifestyles in relation to retirement

Life Style	Characteristic Perceptions of Self-system (as Manifest in Conscious Goals)	Characteristic Perceptions of Social Networks (as Related to Conscious Goals and Behavioral Style)	Perceptions of Retirement	Adaptation to Retirement
1. Obsessively instrumental	Clearly formulated; intolerance for ambiguity or conflict; inflexible; reorientation difficult or impossible	Symbolic; people and systems seen in relation to own goals only; manipulative; no true intimacy	Little planning: comes as traumatic event; does not become a phase	Possibly clinical depression, suicide if substitute channels for pursuing conscious goals not available
2. Instrumental/ other-directed	Clear; awareness of conflict; some capacity for reorientation or resolution	Realistic, though often viewed mainly in relation to own goal system; some capacity for empathy or reciprocity	Varied—depends on extent to which the goal system focused on occupational role	Low morale; temporary if substitutions found or if goal system is flexible enough for resolution

3. Receptive/nurturant	Goals often formulated in terms of social roles and relationships; flexible, awareness of conflict	Realistic, with stress on intimacy and reciprocity; aware of needs and goals of others	Varied—depends on compatibility of work life with goals and if incompatible, on extent to which work roles were supplemented	If work incompatible but supplemented, retirement may improve life satisfaction (morale); if work compatible, temporary low morale followed by substitution (or reorientation if necessary)
4. Autonomous or effectant	Clear, varied, often with stress on growth or self-expression; flexible (if truly autonomous); awareness of conflict	May resemble second or third above	May choose life style where retirement is optional; for others, retirement likely to be viewed as one of many life transitions—anticipated, planned for, becomes phase of life	Possibly temporary low morale—adaptation less dependent on social context than is true for above two groups
5. Self-protective	Described in terms of conventional, stereotyped roles or in terms of staying out of trouble	Symbolic, remote, people and systems seen in terms of stress, threat, or source of anxiety	If work served as way of avoiding close relationships, retirement may be viewed as a threat; if work required sustained interaction with others, retirement may be a relief	Little change so long as detachment from others and "independence" can be maintained

4. *The autonomous style.* This style is probably characteristic of what David Gutmann refers to as autoplastic persons. Riesman (1954) uses the term autonomous, but seems to imply self-generativity in the creative sense. I would agree, if we could broaden the concept of creative so that it includes not only artists and intellectuals and the like, but relatively simple and uneducated people with a capacity to assimilate, interpret, and grow through their life experiences. For some, their occupation may reflect autonomy (artists, independent professionals, independent farmers); for others, the work role may primarily provide the basis for autonomy in other spheres. Eventually, perhaps, this style should be subdivided so that the autonomous/creative are separated from those whom we have called effectants.

5. *The self-protective.* This style is adopted by persons with as powerful dependency needs as those of the obsessively instrumental style. They are also fully as obsessive, but the style does not counter the dependency, as is the case with the obsessive achievers; rather, it denies it, using the word in the analytic sense. This style appears to have been adopted to protect the individual not only from dependence on others, but from responsibility for others. Among men, occupations such as sailor, logger, longshoreman, traveling salesman may offer such protection. Among some women, any occupation may itself reflect avoidance of the receptive/nurturant life style. This style may appear autonomous because of its extreme detachment; these individuals have in fact always been "disengaged," and retirement and widowhood may provide sanction for their preferred style. Both men and women in this life style may be denying sexuality as well as dependency needs.

The underlying needs of the obsessively instrumental and of the self-protective may be similar. The style they evolve to satisfy these needs is no doubt in large part dependent on such characteristics as sex, class, energy level, and intelligence. These two styles, plus the autonomous, all may superficially resemble Riesman's inner-directed type, but the obsessively instrumental and the self-protective are driven by neurotic needs. To continue with Riesman's terms, the autonomous would be the truly inner-directed, while the instrumental/other-directed and the receptive nurturant are both other-directed, the latter, however, most often in an intimate interpersonal sense. Both of these latter groups also will harbor varying degrees of autonomy.

Perceived goals and their social contexts in relation to adaptation to retirement

Life styles described earlier as *obsessively instrumental* encompass a wide variety of conscious goals. In discussing their aims, people who have adopted this style often stress the amount of hard work, energy, and self-abnegation involved, and though their words ring out with overtones of the Protestant Ethic, the listener is left with the distinct impression that only constant striving can assuage their fear (or guilt?) and only extreme fatigue can prevent them from facing deep-seated dissatisfaction (or overwhelming depression). They are articulate about their aspirations, exaggerate their achievements, and minimize their failures. At the same time—regardless of goal success—their accomplishments provide little satisfaction and, once achieved, a goal must be replaced by another so that they can remain driven. *Substitute* goals are feasible, but goal *reorientation** in any transitional phase is difficult if not impossible.

As is true for people adopting a self-protective life style, others in their social world tend to be more symbolic than real—but while the self-protectors fear people and avoid them, the obsessively instrumental manipulate them. Unlike the self-protectors, they

---

*These terms are inadequate, but no better ones occur to me at the moment. Let us say for now that goal *substitution* involves the replacement of a goal with its psychic equivalent. Goal *reorientation* is conceptually close to the idea of *resolution,* and may involve dropping one goal and adopting another which meets different psychic needs, such as giving up an achievement-oriented goal and substituting an expressive one such as nurturance, intimacy, or focusing on existential experience.

may be gregarious, even excessively so. Like the self-protectors, they have no capacity for empathy, reciprocity, intimacy, or responsibility in the sense of concern for another's needs or development. Often strong believers in self-determination, they rarely acknowledge that others have been involved in the evolution, achievement—or frustration—of their goals.

For men in this life style, retirement is a greater trauma than it is for any other group. For obsessive housewives, the husband's retirement (which may interfere with her sphere of instrumentality) may be traumatic. For both, physical illness or incapacity involving close dependence on others is also exceptionally threatening. A belief in self-determination reinforces the rigidity of the goal structure, and the accompanying tendency to self-blame makes them relatively impervious to the mitigating influence of therapy or a close personal relationship. Substitution is the modus operandi of this group on retirement. If substitution becomes impossible or appears to them to be impossible, they may become clinically depressed, even suicidal (though they would rarely permit themselves the luxury of ranking low on a morale measure). Or they may suffer a physical illness.

The *instrumental/other-directed* life style is also conducive to conscious goal formulation though, unlike those adopting an obsessive style, people who adopt it often are aware of goal conflict as well as a capacity for reorientation (as contrasted with substitution). These reorientations may occur before retirement, as with Kornhauser's (1965) workers who change their definition of success as time goes on, or with Jacques' 37-year-olds who reorient their goals (Jacques, 1965).

To the extent that their major goals involve an occupation, and this is usually the case with men in this group, work gratifications include personal relationships, and work dissatisfactions include "not enough time for family and friends." There is at least some empathy with others and often a potential capacity for, if not the actuality of, close personal relationships. The acquisition of a girl friend, fiancee, or wife may be reported as a period of greatest personal growth.

Their views of reference groups and referent others (parents, spouse, friends, colleagues, heroes, or models) are often related to their work goals and achievements. They appear to be realistic in their appraisals of how others (or the more remote social context) have helped or hindered them in formulating or achieving their aspirations. They can be appreciative of others, though more for their material help than for their personal qualities, and at the same time are more likely than their obsessive counterparts to attribute some of their successes and failures to circumstance, fate, or luck.

How retirement is anticipated, experienced, and adapted to by persons following this life style depends in part on the extent to which their occupation gratified their needs for peer acceptance and approval.* When work has been compatible and few supplemental sources of satisfaction have been developed, retirement may be a crisis for this instrumental/other-directed group. But unlike the obsessively instrumental, after a transitional period, possibly accompanied by low morale or non-clinical depression, they usually settle more or less comfortably into retirement as a phase of life. Being other-directed, they stand to benefit most from organized pre-retirement planning, and may contribute to the development of norms and roles for the retirement stage of life.

Their solutions may be substitutions, or more rarely, reorientation or resolutions. Or there may be a trend from substitution in

---

*In other words, this life style would be further elaborated and will eventually no doubt include several subtypes. Donald Spence has suggested two dimensions for such a typology: compatibility of occupation with personal needs, and extent to which non-occupational modes for satisfying these needs have been developed.

the 60's and early 70's to reorientation or resolution in the late 70's or 80's. A substitution would consist of retaining a goal of, say, instrumentality but changing the means. (The retired executive applies his skills in the leadership of voluntary organizations, for example.) A resolution would consist of a more marked goal reorientation, from instrumentality, say, to nurturance of an intimate relationship or simple enjoyment of "freedom," which is an expression often used by persons anticipating or experiencing retirement. (The latter concept requires considerably more exploration—freedom for what? Existential experience?) Reorientation will be harder for this group than substitution because it often involves an unaccustomed shift to "inner-directedness." If, after the retirement adjustment has taken place, physical weakness or illness should make the substitution solution impractical, those unable to make this shift may become clinically depressed as do some obsessives upon (or in anticipation of) retirement.

\ The goals of people in the *receptive/nurturant* life style (and at least until late life these tend to be women, though by no means exclusively so) are likely to be vague, and on the surface, stereotyped. They speak of aims such as being a "good mother," "good wife," or "good teacher." Further discussion usually uncovers considerable preoccupation with the quality of depth of interpersonal relationships and includes acknowledgment of the need for love as well as satisfaction in providing it.

√ Some obsessive women may appear to have such goals. How they differ from the receptive/nurturant may become dramatically clear during the empty-nest phase. They will not let their children go or, if they do, they will react with the same desperation as their male counterparts on retirement. The receptive/nurturant woman will replace her objects or find other ways of achieving her goals if her social context permits. (She may renew concern with the needs and welfare of her husband, or possibly take up a job, paid or not, involving children.) Similarly, if she has been a working woman, retirement will not be a permanent crisis. For some, it may be a relief, for while the receptive/nurturant life style is compatible with some occupations, other occupations may create role conflict.

/Intimacy is probably the overarching need or goal for the receptive/nurturant, and they may be quite creative or ingenious in the way they go about meeting this need at various transitional stages. If the social context (such as a poor marital relationship) thwarts this style of life, the morale of people in it may be low. They are unlikely to become clinically depressed or suicidal, however, because knowing their capacity for developing close relationships, they will retain hope that they will be able to do so again. That some men appear to "develop" into this life style may be less the result of developmental change than of the relaxing of social pressures for instrumental performance at retirement.

Riesman (1954), Maslow (1954), Barron (1963), and others have described the *autonomous* individual in our culture. In discussing their goals they are likely to be highly articulate and highly motivated. Most characteristic of this life style is the complexity of aspirations: qualities of being, depths of interpersonal relationship, growth and self-expression through "instrumentality" or creativity, and often a concern with spiritual and moral qualities.

Their perceptions of the social context—and of their relation to it—vary considerably. There is the proverbial genius who uses or ignores people, and there are other autonomous people who resemble the receptive/nurturant, in that creative and close reciprocal relations with others appear among their main goals. The latter differ from the receptive/nurturant, however, in that their social concerns also extend to a less personalized humanity, their motivational wellsprings appear to be independent of close relationships with others, and they are more resourceful in developing reorientations or resolutions. (Eleanor Roosevelt may be the prototype, though she clearly attained an autonomous phase after a long period more aptly characterized by the receptive/nurturant style.) The autonomous person often has a sense of mission, and an awareness of human, sometimes cosmic, drama. More than persons in any other life style, he has a flexible time sense and may be a "natural" psychologist of adult development.

Many people who have evolved an autonomous life style will not experience retirement as a crisis because they have chosen work (e.g., art, writing, other self-employed professions) in which the retirement decision is theirs. For others, retirement will at first be a transitional phase—and they may not be immune to temporary depression until their goals have been reappraised and reoriented. Many apparently autonomous people, including the highly creative, prove not to be so in later life—and Hemingway may be the prototype. In fact, as we begin to study changes in individual life styles up to and beyond retirement, we may find it necessary to add a "psuedo-autonomous" category to our typology. And, as has already been suggested, this type should probably be further subdivided into autonomous/creative and autonomous/effectant.

The conscious goals of people in the *self-protective* life style are expressed in very stereotyped, conventional terms. They will speak of being a good worker, a good citizen, a good wife or mother, and, unlike the receptive/nurturant, no attempt at probing will provoke much in the way of elaboration. Asked what they have been most satisfied with thus far, they stress staying out of trouble, avoiding arguments, surviving illness. Often, their lives do not appear to have been as stressful as those in other styles, but along with the emphasis on avoidance or survival of "pain," is a singular flatness in regard to goals or aspirations. Neither qualities of being nor doing, nor relations with other people appear to be valued. Fearing aggression as they fear everything else, these are threatened and anxious people for whom life in any phase and almost any circumstance has been such a struggle that the traumata of aging, including retirement, may be a relatively minor link in a chain of insults.

They are as lacking in autonomy as the obsessive achievers, and their view of social norms and expectations is limited to conventions and specifically excludes the challenges of the achieving culture hero. The viable social system consists of "they"—plus, often, some rather impersonal other (doctor, lawyer, social worker) to call on in a crisis. Earlier social systems revolving around work or family are recalled in terms of problems, strains, or interpersonal conflicts. They often profess to be proud of their "independence" in old age, but this type of independence seems to have as its main goal a continuation of the avoidance of others who might make demands for affection, responsibility, reciprocity. These are the hypochondriacs, the food faddists, the flitters from one to another evangelical fringe group, and perhaps the compulsive television fans, not only of later life but of earlier life as well.

So long as it involves no radical change in dwelling, standard of living, or physical status, for non-working women who follow this life style, neither the empty-nest phase nor widowhood may be a serious crisis. If her husband makes new demands on her, his retirement may be. For working men or women, retirement may be viewed with both relief and anxiety, relief if the work has involved close proximity to others, anxiety if retirement thrusts them into day-long contact with family members. Otherwise, work seems readily replaceable by the routines of self-maintenance, and casual work contacts by equally casual encounters in shops, on tours, or in other organized groups. Since the goal remains, as it has been, survival in a hostile world, the major problem may come if and when physical frailty requires dependency on a caretaking other. Such intimate contact may provoke anxieties insupportable except through paranoid projections.

The schematic presentation in Diagram III summarizes the

foregoing. Eventually, it should be extended to include characteristic modes of coping with transitions, as implicit in Diagram I. It is very clear that, though we know little about the developmental aspects of the personal system, our knowledge of how the social system is perceived at successive life stages is even sparser. Missing from Diagram I, too, is the actual social system as it influences the individual, which is of course not necessarily identical with his perceptions of it. Each life style also appears to represent a manner of coping with dependency needs. These needs are presumably antecedent to the life style and are, therefore, not presented in the diagram. They may be briefly summarized as two forms of denial (obsessively instrumental, self-protective); two fairly clear-cut styles of acceptance (receptive/nurturant, autonomous); and one where such needs may be only dimly perceived, but with no necessity for denial (instrumental/other-directed).

An example of an heuristic use of the model suggested here is shown in Diagram IV. Using content dimensions of both domains similar to those just illustrated, it becomes clear that the approach lends itself to a variety of perspectives such as intrapersonal, interpersonal, and attitudinal. (The labels for each "box" are meant to be suggestive only.) The diagonal from upper left to lower right represents consistency between the purposive domain and behavior. One obvious question which could be answered by this schema is whether there is a trend toward consistency with advancing stages of the life span and, if so, in which domain the adjustments are made. This model should also be useful in tracing the influence of a prior life style on the evolution of an altered life style in the presence or absence of transitional events (or of major sociopolitical events).

Let us take, for example, the young newlywed who is working hard both at her job and at home so that she and her husband may take several months off to travel. Her current life style, in broad terms, is expressive in the purposive domain and instrumental in the behavioral style. In terms of the additional categories of Diagram IV, she might be described as idealistic in the intrapersonal sphere (she and her husband will find themselves during this year off), as altruistic in the interpersonal sphere (she does it for him), as potentially socialistic in the sociopolitical sphere (at the moment she seems to have little concern in this area), and potentially an activist, though it would probably take strong encroachments on her personal life to stimulate her into sociopolitical activity. Assuming that the young couple does indeed take their year off, it is conceivable that this idiosyncratic event will influence her life style: for example, she may miss the material comforts provided by her job, and perhaps shift her goals from expressive to instrumental. From an interpersonal perspective, she would then begin to appear obsessive, and in her relations with others, manipulative. Or, to take a more normative transitional event, she might become pregnant, retaining her expressive goals and adopting a behavioral style more compatible with them. Thus from an intrapersonal perspective, since both goals and behavior would be expressive, she would fall into the integrated category, while in the interpersonal sphere she would be in the nurturant category. One might also see her settling for liberal political views and advocating arbitration rather than social change.

To conclude with an illustration more closely related to the subject matter of this volume, we might speculate about the middle-aged man for whom being interviewed may have provided an idiosyncratic transition, resulting in a shift in his goals from avoidance of stress to more effectant objectives, in this case a job more in keeping with his abilities. Assuming that his behavioral style remains more or less expressive, this would put him in the autonomous category from an intrapersonal perspective and in a leadership capacity from an interpersonal perspective. In retirement one would expect him to find alternative roles in the

DIAGRAM IV

Four perspectives on the relation between purposive domain and behavioral style

Purposive Domain	Behavioral Style		
	Instrumental and/or Effectant	Expressive	Avoidance of Stress
I. Intrapersonal			
Instrumental and/or effectant	obsessive	autonomous/creative	passive
	idealistic	integrated	cautious
Expressive			
Avoidance of stress (or seeking of ease, comfort)	substitutive	receptive	self-protective
II. Interpersonal			
Instrumental and/or effectant	manipulative (encroaching)	leadership	seductive
	altruistic	nurturant	withdrawn
Expressive			
Avoidance of stress (or seeking of ease, comfort)	other-directed (accommodating)	dependent	isolated

III. Sociopolitical-attitudinal			
Instrumental and/or effectant	revolutionary	non-conformist, rebellious	conformist
Expressive	socialist	liberal/democratic	retreatist
Avoidance of stress (or seeking of ease, comfort)	right-wing ext.	conservative	alienated
IV. Sociopolitical–behavior			
Instrumental and/or effectant	agitator/dictator	innovator	follower
Expressive	activist	arbitrator	reactive
Avoidance of stress (or seeking of ease, comfort)	worker	contributor	inactive

community or in the extended family which would sustain him in these categories. If, on the other hand, he fails to achieve this more complex and responsible position, we would expect him to maintain his present life style as long as he works: substitutive in the intrapersonal sphere, accomodating in the interpersonal, and probably politically conservative. Forced to retire from his unsatisfying job, we might then expect him (since he would have a modest pension) to adapt his behavioral style to his stress-avoiding goals. He would therefore, in the intrapersonal sphere, move into the self-protective category, in the interpersonal, to isolation. It would be in keeping with this pattern for him also to become politically alienated, indifferent, and inactive.

EDWARD L. BORTZ, M.D.

When this chapter was written, Dr. Bortz was the Senior Consultant in Medicine at the Lankenau Hospital in Philadelphia, Pennsylvania. He was a graduate of Harvard University where he received the Baccalaureate of Arts and Doctor of Medicine degrees. Dr. Bortz served his internship at the Lankenau Hospital and did graduate work in pathology in Vienna and Berlin. He was Associate Professor of Medicine at the Jefferson Medical College and the Graduate School of Medicine of the University of Pennsylvania.

For a number of years Dr. Bortz had been engaged in studying the problems of aging in the Research Division of the Lankenau Hospital. In 1961 he was a Consultant to the White House Conference on Aging. Following his retirement from the University of Pennsylvania, Dr. Bortz followed the advice he gives in his chapter: He began a new career as consultant to the Lankenau Hospital on research on aging.

Dr. Bortz served as President of the American Medical Association from 1947 to 1948, and as President of the American Geriatric Society from 1959 to 1960. He has received a number of citations and honorary degrees. His publications include *Creative Aging* (1963) and *Diabetes Control* (1951). His next book, *Man in Transition,* is scheduled for publication. Dr. Bortz' avocation was classical and neo-modern music. His death occurred during publication of this book.

12: BEYOND RETIREMENT

EDWARD L. BORTZ

ROOTS OF CREATIVITY

Living is a series of continuing, ongoing changes. It is possible to chart the major events as experiences which are followed by a variety of consequences. These are feedback mechanisms with a reciprocal relationship; the preceding status, equipped with the genetic pattern and environmental stimuli, exercises a dominant but not conclusive influence on the next phase. Biologically, the initiation of life is a creative process; it is a productive accomplishment. Nature is lavish in supply of materials but exceedingly precision-guided as the fertilized ovum starts the elaborate construction that finally attains great beauty and charm, the adult human body. This is of course partly a dream, with yet a generous element of possibility.

Biologically, each cell and each organ system within the body is goal-directed; that is, it is created (elaborated) for a definite function, for the part it is destined to play in the body as a whole. There is power, symmetry, rhythm, harmony, and design in the mature product. The young couple create their offspring. The urge to create is a biological compulsion. Once the new unit appears, the various factors which influence the child, the youth, the grown-up, lend direction to subsequent experiences.

Experimentally, it is easy to increase or curtail the length of life of an animal. Likewise, with humans, it has been noted that, "Nature experiments, we but observe." By observation, comparison, and investigation of controlled situations with lower animals, science has acquired a huge mass of information which is of the greatest importance to the human race. Unfortunately, most of these data are encased in libraries used by a relatively small number of students. Suffice to comment, knowledge is doubling every ten years (Millis, 1967).

The need for more research in the complex field of human behavior is widely recognized. Thus, the analysis of the original (genetic) endowment and behavior in early months is pertinent. From the earliest stages of body (and personality) growth, certain factors—such as energy supply (nutrition), activity (work), latency (rest and leisure), and motivation (goal direction, with achievement, fulfillment, involvement)—are dominant. They might be designated as Health Essentials. Each has received experimental study and, while still in the early stages of elucidation, may be classified as an area of productive promise for social science.

These factors are operative in every period of the life span. Their priorities vary according to the age of the individual. For example, in early life, nutrition, exercise, rest, and motivation mold a healthy vehicle for life's later challenges. There is an ascending complexity and introduction of new elements (for example, sexual awakening at puberty) as growth to the summit years proceeds. The warm thrill of marriage, new birth, and social engagement coincide with the work-period years, as maturity of parents evolves.

Beyond menopause, which is most dramatic in women but in exceptional cases may influence the male, continued maturation depends on a number of variables. While body growth attains full adult status between twenty-five and thirty years of age, intelligence, training, social expansion, and increased productivity may continue into the eight and ninth decades.

Retirement is a custom established soon after the turn of the century as a means to shed the older worker in favor of the younger generation looking for advancement. Seventy years ago, this may have been a pleasant practice which relieved a relatively small number of old men from any routine demands as they passed the time, in rural privacy, until their days were no more. The industrial and scientific revolution of the twentieth century changed that. One may doubt that retirement was ever more desirable than activity in the mainstream of life. Youth has ever striven to displace his elders, so the unsolved problem may always have existed, albeit intensified by the industrial and scientific revolutions, the population explosion, and urbanization. In either view, it is apparent that the forces which created the highly competitive industrial society have given rise to numerous unsolved problems of immediate importance to modern man. In truth, there are murmurings of dehumanization, and of downgrading of the individual in our affluent, overly plush society.

The Initial Thrust

To recapitulate: activity, renewal (rest, leisure), and motivation are basic phenomena elaborated by nature to sustain the individual. When any decrement appears—as when inactivity takes the place of activity (work)—unless compensatory means are brought into play, shrinkage of the individual becomes possible. The newborn infant turns outward to his surroundings and is stimulated by the increasing variety of objects which capture his attention (Schachtel, 1959). He is outgoing, with an active searching for satisfaction. Among his earliest satisfactions is that of enjoying the exercise of his growing body in discovery and exploration. Extension is health-producing, withdrawal is enervating—in the child, as well as in the mature individual at the summit of the years. Man's search for meaning and method needs this yearning for growth.

To clarify the consequences of the meaning of retirement and its impact on behavior in the later years, it is necessary to regard retirement as but one episode in the total life span, placed in the context of earlier experiences and later sequelae. Its impact on the individual as a gain or loss is readily accessible to study. Retirement, as the opening door to new areas for exploration and adventure, is, in a way, the confirmation of man's sovereign potential. It leads to the next stage in development. This is dependent on preservation of the initial thrust for continued growth. Schachtel (1959) terms this the "allocentric mode of perception," and considers it the most important step in the development of perception in the growing child. At any point along life's timetable, as perception is heightened, maturation is fostered. The whole field of perception, sensory and extrasensory, is uncharted territory but most exciting in its promise for extending human frontiers.

Emergence by Decades

People are living longer (Brotman, 1967). Man's longevity potential is approximately 110 to 115, "as judged by the authenticated records of the longest-lived people" (Comfort, 1956). Then, before the advent of the twenty-first century, the hundred-year life span may be a commonplace. The quality of living in later decades, therefore, must be a challenge of first concern to society. An hypothetical timetable for living ten decades offers a panorama of individual emergence from one period to the next. The various major events on this timetable are birth, adolescence, marriage, career (first and second), retirement, recession, and completion.

The life span can be divided into trimesters of thirty years, with the tenth decade, from ninety to a hundred, a time of rich enjoyment and recall of a fruitful life for many. The first trimester, from one to thirty years, is the time of greatest cytological growth and preparation for the second trimester, from thirty to sixty, when the establishment of a new family and engagement in the first career take place. Beyond sixty is for many the flowering period of rich maturity; the second career beckons (Bortz, 1963).

The forceful impact of the scientific and cultural revolution is producing more efficient methods in education, the professions, industry, and labor. The daily lives of all citizens are in a continuing state of flux. New goals and our system of values are up for review. Old traditions are being discarded while their replacements are yet to be identified. The tragic waste in resources of mature citizens, the result of indifference on the part of the major segments of society, is a national disgrace. Medicare and society must make some real advances if the extending years of life are to be times of rich enjoyment rather than of vegetative, rejected existence.

This is a large problem which will require the team effort of biologists, sociologists, anthropologists, medical and paramedical personnel for research in the fascinating field of human growth and development; no one discipline is qualified to encompass the entire scope. This is the holistic approach which includes the episodic data already collected by the various special study sections.

A surprising amount of practical knowledge is available that can even now be applied in the construction of a timetable for a healthy, century life span. The necessity for adaptation and adjustment at various critical episodes in our journey down life's pathway will be most dramatic at certain times—adolescence, marriage, the opening of the second career, and retirement.

The Biological Timetable

What is the impact of retirement on the biological timetable of the human body? Is it stimulating, depressing, or neutral? As one of the principal events in the life scale, retirement is a transition episode which can best be understood when it is seen in context. Living processes follow a definite harmonious rhythm of advance. Growth to optimum function is inherent in the human body (Proceedings of the First Ontario Conference on Aging, 1957).

While physical growth is completed around twenty-seven years of age, intellectual growth and emotional enrichment may continue far into the higher years. Accumulating evidence suggests that activity of all the body components to the stretch point favors smooth and enjoyable function of all parts. This is a key factor in assessing the practice of retirement. When full physical vitality has been reached, conditioning can maintain satisfactory function into later decades. This has been demonstrated in training experiments. Conditioning should bring a sense of well-being. Pacing oneself wisely is lifesaving in the productive forties, fifties, and sixties. It is a conserving feature, protecting against the early stroke or coronary occlusion. Too often, brilliant leaders in community affairs, professional activities, and social functions drop from an accumulated exhaustion which the individual refuses to admit.

Likewise, the heavy industries, especially those requiring repetitive movements, are enervating to the extent that frequent breaks are necessary. Automation and labor-saving equipment have now been developed so that, in the future, exercise breaks will replace coffee breaks. To laboring men, retirement poses different sequelae than those met in the work life of white-collar employees. As retirement has many facets, determined mostly by the nature of the first job (career), the way of life beyond retirement is a profitable topic for assessment.

Experiences, memories, and plans for the later years are determinants of life's future adventures. The average citizen today is "young" longer than any previous workers. The human machine, with its remarkable in-built recharge mechanism, has a potential of one hundred healthy, useful years. The zenith years, therefore, offer a fabulous opportunity for investigation and experiment. The biological component is under study in many laboratories to discover the conditions that threaten life. The various diseases are known. Three-quarters of all premature deaths (below one hundred years) are the result of premature breakdown of the heart and blood vessels to the brain and other parts of the body. Cancer will be conquered in the next two decades; other diseases are being examined by experts. It is becoming more difficult to die!

Differential Aging

It is well known that long-lived ancestors, macrobiotes, are more likely to produce offspring capable to extended years. According to Cowdry (1947), the possible life span of various organ systems is different from that of the body itself. He cites Friedenwald who estimates the possible life span of the eyes as at least 120 to 130 years if the body could last that long. The outer layer of the skin, the epidermis, may have a span of life exceeding that of the eye.

Cowdry maintains that there are reservoirs of cells that never age and die except by accident. These cells are found in the bone marrow and in the epidermis. The life of each individual cell begins with the division of the cell preceeding it and extends to the time when it, in turn, divides giving rise to two new cells. Cowdry designates these as vegetative cells since they live a primitive kind of life and serve only to maintain the resevoir and provide new cells. The epidermis continues to form new cells as long as the body itself lives. The older cells are worn off at the surface.

The degree of aging of some cells depends upon the activity of others. There is a rare disease which occurs in youth, Progeria. The youngster shows the appearance of an aged man with the wrinkled skin, baldness, and creaking joints. Cowdry suggests this may be due to a pituitary gland deficiency.

It has been noted that senile changes in the skin many be retarded or even reversed by the secretions of the gonads. The role of the sex glands has been undergoing studies for many years. In women following menopause the ovaries may shrink to mere fibrous threads. Administration of ovarian extracts will increase the size of the shrunken uterus, improve the texture of the senile vaginal tissues, improve skin tone, and alter the psychological processes as well (Lee, 1968). Gynecology as a specialty concerned with the disturbances of the female reproductive system is one of the most active departments in the hospitals of the nation. Difficulties arising in association with menopause constitute one of the most common disorders the gynecologist is called upon to solve.

In the male, often beginning in the early sixties, there may appear enlargement of the prostate gland. While no unanimity of opinion exists concerning a male climacteric, administration of male sex hormones has frequently proven beneficial. Some urologists believe the male problems of this period are mostly psychological, but they admit that they do exist.

Deterioration of the cells of the brain results in various kinds of disturbances in the behavior of older people. Relatively few reports in the literature describe any evidence of nerve cell growth or recovery from trauma. Some important observations were made by Weiss (1956). He showed that the elements of the nervous system are by no means static and immutable fixtures, but are in a dynamic state of constant self-renewal which renders them amenable to progressive changes of biochemical character. This discovery introduces a new dimension into modern concepts of operative and adaptive mechanisms of nervous and mental functions, including learning.

Weiss (1956) notes that nerve cells deprived of excitation atrophy. Conversely, the nucleus and cell body will enlarge in response to excessive functional bombardment. His statement is adverse to the traditional point of view that adult nerve cells cannot divide and reproduce themselves. Body cells exist in a state of perpetual reorganization, and cell size varies throughout life. For Weiss, the measure of aging is an estimate of the kinetics of decline of body vigor and motivation.

Using radioactive isotopes as tracers of the various elements which participate in cell growth, maturation, and decline, a more exact understanding of biological growth may be attained.

Hazards of Medicated Survival

As individuals grow into the later years, the most common afflictions involve the cardio-vascular system, the brain and nervous system, the bones and joints, and the digestive tract. A lesion attracting much scientific attention today is tissue deterioration of the blood vessels. Cholesterol and the triglycerides are much in the scientific news because of their effect on diminishing the caliber and frequently totally occluding an artery, thus shutting off the blood supply to the area beyond the blocked vessel. Narrowing of a coronary artery, through which arterial blood flows to the heart muscle, frequently results in severe chest pain popularly known as angina pectoris. The occlusion of small vessels within the brain is frequently followed by disturbed behavior. If a large vessel is involved, a stroke is the result, with partial or complete paralysis.

A detailed discussion of the physiological mechanisms involved which produce clinical syndromes is, of course, beyond the scope of this presentation. Much progress has occurred in medical management of many of these conditions. Unfortunately, restorative measures may be life-saving, yet sequelae eventuate in a vegetative being.

The current era of organ transplantation poses problems which society must solve. "With death postponable in every age group, we are met with the dilemma of weighing medicated survival against the possible hardships for the person and for the community" (Aring, 1968, p. 158). Mere life extension can well be hazardous. This problem is faced daily by the medical profession in the hospitals of the nation.

Blood and urine assays for sex hormones suggest that in women at the menopause there is a diminution of the hormones and a corresponding increase in the pituitary gonado-tropines. In the male as in the female, though less commonly, substitution therapy has proven beneficial for the alleviation of symptoms.

Studies of the relationship between stress and disease, particularly those of William Raab (1946), Hans Selye (1946), and Lennart Levi (1967) have demonstrated the intimate relationship between the endocrine glands and the central nervous system. These findings have shown measurable changes in endocrine function of neurotic origin which may affect a variety of organs and organ symptoms (especially the heart and blood pressure).

Modern man, according to George Bernard Shaw, is not God's final creation. The techniques of hormonal assays, electro-chemistry, and physiology are producing insights concerning basic body function, disease, and behavior. Progress is occurring so rapidly that statistical data must be constantly subject to review.

What has all this to do with retirement? The health and well-being of older citizens is of first importance. There is no record of any individual having died of old age. The most common killers are breakdown of the blood vessels and cancer. Together they destroy approximately a million citizens each year. Research directed to the basic nature of these disorders has demonstrated that the early lesion, that is, the deposition of lipids within the blood vessels, can be produced experimentally. In the early stages, they can be eliminated. The earlier the cancerous lesions are identified and removed, the higher will be the percentage of cure.

Physical fitness is attainable by a program of conditioning.

Proper diet, adequate vitamins, basic foods and minerals, and generous quantities of fluid daily, with exercise, recreation, and an interesting job enhance well-being. The paradox is that much information is available yet the public ignores it until illness strikes. Studies of Raab (1959) in Russia, Germany, and the United States demonstrate the value of conditioning. The dangers of overweight, tobacco, and alcoholism arise from common indulgences.

Abelson (1968) has referred to the study made in Framingham, Massachusetts, which identified many factors contributing to heart disease. The most sedentary individuals had a mortality rate from coronary artery disease five times that of individuals who were active. Abelson refers to another study in a community of 110,000 men and women. The incidence of rapidly fatal myocardial infarction among sedentary individuals who were smokers was nine times the incidence among physically active non-smokers of similar age (Millis, 1967).

The maturing elite seem to enjoy life to the full with passing time. Granted, many have infirmities of various kinds, some quite major, but their attitude and their engagement in the thrill of living protects them against premature psychic deterioration. Clinical surveys of the lives of these individuals uncover many earlier trials and tribulations during which they showed ability to adjust and make the most of what life had to offer.

Environmental Manipulation

Continued mature competence beyond retirement has been demonstrated by individuals who have seemed to get their second wind and who have shown by their actions and accomplishments that, "Age has it opportunities no less than youth itself," to quote Longfellow. More and more individuals in excellent health are anticipating second careers. For those equipped with experience,

know-how, and stability, there are abundant opportunities, especially in service areas, for interesting employment. With new
industries in the making, there is a drastic shortage of teachers and
personnel in the health service fields. The necessity for a
nationwide educational and training program indicates the advisa-
bility for a new concept of education for a century-long life span.
Elucidation of the various components that tend to modify the
direction of development subsequent to critical points, such as
adolescence, marriage, menopause, and retirement, is the first
requirement in search of more understanding. It is established that
infants born into a deficient environment, lacking in adequate
nutrition and tender care, may carry lifelong stigmata.

The early years of growth and development comprise the period
when training and experience largely determine the life work until
the milestone of retirement is reached. Obviously, the better the
education and the more ubiquitous the experiences, the less likely
the hazards of retirement. Cessation of work should open corridors
to a new and attractive position that, in itself, contributes to the
maturation process. Life can be an ascending experience leading to
new levels of human development. The alternative to this positive,
bouyant program may be dangerous and dehumanizing. At best,
the alternative is existence at the dull level of mediocrity.

Experimental psychologists are now demonstrating that various
drugs can heighten intellectual function in both man and lower
animals. According to one psychologist (Krech, 1967), the time
may come (in ten or fifteen years) when it will be possible to
manipulate behavior and development through environmental and
biochemical influences on the brain. Krech points out that we can
now experiment with drugs, psychological procedures, and environmental conditions that will permit us to raise or lower the I.Q.,
memory ability, and learning capacity of any man. This should be
one of the major areas for study.

FLEXIBLE RETIREMENT

The spectacular changes in all areas of productivity, with labor-saving methods eliminating thousands of jobs, has threatened the earning power and financial security of many in the working force of the nation. Management, labor, and government are searching for ways to maintain incomes of workers who are at top efficiency in ability and capable of staying in good physical condition for additional decades. The retirement age is being reduced from 65 to 60, and in many special fields to 55. In addition, reduction of the work week from 45 to 40 to 36 hours is rapidly being promoted.

Once dismissed from productive employment, the older laboring man is handicapped in obtaining another job because of insurance obstacles that make it inadvisable for another company to employ him. Many of the large industries are now offering advice to employees who are approaching compulsory retirement. For many in the labor force who give no thought to removal from their jobs, the effect may result in retirement shock, well known to physicians. This particular reaction could well be studied on an industry-wide basis. As yet, no reliable statistics are available. Masked suicides are not rare.

To anticipate and neutralize retirement shock, a sliding scale of gradually shorter hours or part-time employment is advised and is in use by many companies. Meanwhile, new fields are opening, for the spectrum of adult human life is increasing. At present, there is a glaring shortage of personnel in practically all areas of medical service. Especially in the metropolitan areas where many individuals need aid, there is a disinclination to join the service force caring for the elderly who need sympathetic, kindly care. This is further confirmation of the traditional point of view that one's active work period should be terminated on a chronological basis.

The fact is, according to Mead, "In a rapidly changing society like ours, we need older people as we have never needed them before" (1967, p. 117). She was speaking in particular for the Olver Wendell Holmes Association, a group that is promoting interest in the "creative and constructive usefulness of retired people of considerable experience and education, attempting to develop for them roles of usefulness in the community and continuing leadership" (ibid, p. 117). Mead goes on to emphasize that we need them far more than we recognize today. It is a ridiculous paradox that this large group of talented, knowledgeable individuals is so often entirely unnoticed, while there is a drastic shortage of leaders and teachers in practically every community of the nation.

Retirement is change from one job to another, or from a life of commitment to a place on the sidelines "watching the world go by." This latter transition can be perilous. Aimless living is sick living, for life has lost its momentum. To avoid this misfortune, Gardner (1967) suggests a mid-career clinic, on the theory that people will change jobs frequently. They may retire several times, moving upward or downward. Post-retirement neurosis is most effectively cured by the interesting activity of a new job. Without incentive to carry on, the individual may in time become a charge on his family.

George Washington retired three times; each time he became depressed and introspective. The first time at the age of 26 while in command of the Virginia Militia in 1758, he decided to retire because of poor health. In a letter to a friend he wrote, "I have not too much reason to apprehend an approaching decay." With the outbreak of the Revolutionary War, he was recalled from retirement and, against his wish, was placed in command of the Continental Army. In 1783, he retired again; his words, "The scene is at length closed. I will move gently down the stream of life until I sleep with my fathers." But again, at 51, he was recalled to serve as the first President of the Constitutional Convention. Two centuries later, the same condition is relived by individuals retired from active duty. Washington might have lived far into the later years, had medical science been as expert in disease control in colonial times as it is today.

/ Retirement as an industrial policy is in a state of rapid change. In regard to "Leisure and Disengagement in Retirement," Kleemeier (1964) noted that Western culture is geared to work. There is no place for leisure in this social matrix. If man was made to work, the ideal prescription for retirement is not to retire, so the reasoning goes. Work in a different setting is the denial of retirement. From a different approach, in today's complex social milieu, the original image of retirement suggests disengagement. Cumming and Henry (1961) contended that with increasing age beyond maturity there is a growing tendency for the individual to withdraw from social relationships, to conserve his energies, and to reduce his life span. This, however, is not consonant with experiments on physical conditioning that prove the body capable of extended vitality. This theory is readily promising for experimental exploration.

In a paper, "From Retirement to the Second Career," Sargent (1961) discussed his experiences with employees of Consolidated Edison of New York who were approaching 65 years of age. He reported that the great majority of men who continue working beyond 65 do so because they need to have an income. Now, this is compounded by inflation, the older citizens' major fear. Seventy-five percent of employees have the ability and interest to continue working. While many are capable, Sargent says that not more than 10% are able to get a job. He reports that mandatory retirement fails to take into account the ability of the worker. He would rather continue in his first job, if permitted by his employer to do so. Sargent describes some of the difficulties encountered by retirees seeking new employment, as, for example,

experienced engineers being denied teaching positions because of
the lack of a degree in education.

Onstott (1960) has outlined the policy of the Bell Telephone
Company in "Mandatory Retirement at Age 65." Their employee
pension plan was set up in 1913. Men with 20 years or more years
of service may retire at age 60, and women at 55. Pensions are not
discounted for early retirement. The associated Bell companies
adopted rules at the inception of their plans, fixing the mandatory
age for retirement at age 70. Onstott reported that, "A fixed
retirement rule has as its basic purpose the maintenance of a vital,
dynamic and effective organization." Conflicting interests or
wishes of individuals affected should be disregarded, so that the
interests of society will be better served by the particular
organization following this practice. The Bell policy is in line with
policies followed by powerful industries that apparently have not
been informed of the newer knowledge regarding the potentials of
living in the higher decades. This is an area which industry and
labor should investigate in depth.

BEYOND RETIREMENT

There are numerous articles in the literature, lay and professional, describing how various individuals met the challenge of
retirement. In "They Retired—and Got Busy," Dutton (1951)
discusses a novel experiment which originated in Wilmington,
Delaware, and was set up by Maurice du Pont Lee, an engineer
who was in rugged health beyond his eightieth milestone. With the
headquarters of the duPont Company and also of the Hercules and
Atlas Chemical Companies in Wilmington, the city claims a certain
uniqueness. It probably has more experienced top-rank technical
specialists to the square mile than any other city, regardless of
size.

As those companies have inflexible retirement rules—out at 65—each year the city has more pensioned retirees who, in most instances, as Dutton quotes Lee,". . . have nothing else to do than fret over the world's ills, their stiffening tendons and worsening golf scores. We're building the biggest graveyard of rusting brains ever assembled in one spot" (p. 81): Lee contends the same situation exists in most industrial communities. Even junked automobiles are salvaged, an advantage cars have over discarded older men. Lee organized Consulting and Advisory Services, Inc., bringing together a vigorous and healthy group of experienced leaders from different fields, including engineers, lawyers, purchasing agents, artists, architects, and other specialty representatives.

With Lee and "Pop" Warner, a real estate expert, the service group quickly found a number of small business concerns that were in difficulty. Guidance by members of the service soon was being sought by people in various unfortunate situations because of unwise management or financing. The story of Mr. Lee's success in activating retired men of long years of experience is an example of what can be accomplished. There is a quickening interest all over the country in the manifold problems facing the 65-year-old. This is a germinal field for research.

A preliminary report of studies on "Individual Response to Enforced Retirement" (McEwan & Sheldon, 1968) offers two theories to explain the tendency of older people to withdraw from social interaction. One group of sociologists interprets withdrawal as a normal by-product of aging, which reduces the demands to cope with the exigencies of the later years. The second group maintains that the older individual does not retire because he wants to, but because he has to. These individuals abandon the society that abandons them. Deprived of the privilege of work in an industrial culture, the retiree becomes a person without social function or position. He feels that "society offers no meaning for a life in which work no longer is a part" (p. 3). McEwan and Sheldon point out that compulsory retirement may act as a challenge to some individuals and a repelling threat to others. This is a key point in assessment and is a promising assignment for critical evaluation.

This report presented findings on the careers of 500 men and women in the Boston area. Morale was the dependent variable. Eighty-five percent of the subjects regarded themselves as healthy; 11% as in "adequate health"; and 4% in poor health. With health as the first independent variable, finances were the second. Curiously, the authors found that subjects with high income and those with low income found retirement to be less of a handicap, whereas those in the middle income range encountered the most difficulty. They point out that: "High income groups tend to insure against later periods of life, while low income groups are inured to poverty by long experience" (p. 4). Personality is the third independent variable. Those with higher educational and occupational status apparently enjoy more activities and have more associations. Self-satisfaction, these investigators state, is of less concern among the highly educated. They also conclude that high intelligence facilitates change in life style. Family support is the final independent variable McEwan and Sheldon identify.

These authors see an emergence of four basic patterns:

1. Withdrawal; disengagement from society to a life devoid of satisfying context.
2. Maintenance; transfer of skills to one's own workshop.
3. Change to an activity with equal satisfaction.
4. Change of content leading to different satisfactions.

Thus, three interrelating components emerge to form a conceptual framework: personality, response pattern, and morale. A number of independent variables affect the relationships between these components. McEwan and Sheldon believe their studies may bring some information for predicting responses to retirement (organic, as well as behavioral). It may then be possible to intervene before the event, in order to influence responses to be of benefit to the individual and advantage to society.

Substantial additions to our knowledge of the health of older individuals indicate it is readily possible to enjoy a satisfactory state of health up to and beyond the hundred-year milestone. The four major threats of life beyond sixty are: deterioration of the heart and arteries (coronary occlusion, stroke, chronic brain syndrome), cancer, arthritis, and mental deficits. For these medical science is in a period of exciting, productive research. It can be predicted with confidence that before the year 2000 these four common maladies will be conquered. This means that a century-long life span will become the rule.

With the age of retirement now being lowered to 60, 55 and even 50 years in industry, there will be an extended number of years from the retirement age until life's curtain falls. The situation requires imaginative study and a reappraisal of the content of living in the most important and potentially promising period, "the last of life for which the first was made," to recall Robert Browning. Planning a life program of ten decades can most directly be outlined by establishing a long-range educational system that will emphasize the nature of the various highlights and critical periods each person will experience at a particular time in his schedule. As a fundamental first principle, emphasis on the positive features should be stressed. Medical science can render a real support and furnish leadership, but at present most medical practice is almost exclusively curative and episodic rather than holistic.

Research for clarification of the various precedents and sequelae of retirement is a matter of immediate need. Therefore, the organization of teams of investigators from the various disciplines concerned is a matter of first importance. The result of their findings should be made a part of the lifetime learning course in all primary and secondary schools and college curricula.

In a key paper on "Culture, Politics and Pedagogy," Bruner (1968) states that "Cognitive mastery in a world that generates stimuli far faster than we can sort them depends on strategies for reducing the complexity and the clutter" (p. 71). In a life involved in an increasingly technical society, education must take up a larger portion of the life span. Indeed, Bruner states, "Education becomes a part of the way of life" (p. 71). A philosophy of effective living in the high years must conceptualize the main issues in our sovereign potential, utilizing all that has gone before. By self-renewal, a challenge for research, these potentials may be more nearly realized.

Creative Leisure

A new life of adventure and exploration is available to the individual who is not willing to resign from creative activity. Webster's dictionary defines "create" as: "To produce; to bring a new form into being." A new environment creates new forms of life. Hoagland (1959), Executive Director of the Worcester Foundation for Experimental Biology, writes that one of the most fundamental factors in behavior is curiosity. This, he states, is a biological characteristic of most mammals, and is particularly observable in monkeys and human beings. It follows that the key to the basic biological drives which motivate behavior includes efforts to learn new things. To continue to live effectively, there needs to be a persistent reaching from within the individual, plus imagination, which Einstein regarded as more important than knowledge, so that continued learning becomes second nature.

Curiosity stimulates motivation, the antecedent of creativity. The waning life force, an accompaniment of long life, can be minimized by stretching muscles and mind. As pointed out early in this discussion, each cell, organ, and body has a cycle of growth, development, and maturation. The healthy, mature person today has an expectancy of 35 to 50 years post-retirement. With this in mind, the problem becomes one of leisure, of the second career, the avocation, which for many people offers a satisfactory way of "passing the time." Fishing, games, Golden Age Clubs are easily available. Yet, the real substance of rich living involves creativity.

This applies at every stage of the life span. Conceptualization of retirement should include and enlarge the opportunities for new experiences and accomplishments. There is need for clearer recognition of peer groups, their responsibilities, and ways to bring them closer to the underprivileged as a social obligation. Gardner (1962) believes that the way to keep our organization alive is to grant freedom to creative people to bring change. For self-renewal, it is paramount to develop skills and habits of mind that will be instruments for continuous change and growth on the part of the individual.

The individual with the capacity for continuous renewal:

1. Is not imprisoned by fixed habits, attitudes, and routines.
2. Never ceases to explore his own potentialities. (Gardner says it is most unfortunate that the majority of people go through life unaware of their abilities. This applies particularly to mature older citizens.)
3. Will risk failure in order to learn. (To continue to learn is to keep on risking failure.)
4. Respects the sources of his own energy and motivation.

A number of reports have appeared concerning the health and behavior of healthy centenarians. Dunbar (1963) has described a syndrome of longevity. Dunbar writes that research scientists can detect potential centenarians by age 50, or even earlier, by an investigation of their previous health and life patterns. Through all of the histories of potential centenarians there is a common denominator. This includes ways to combat anxiety and stress, thereby reducing the risk of a vascular catastrophe (stroke, occlusion). "Whom the gods would destroy, they first make mad." The impatient, the "hurry-hurry" person, invites excessive wear and tear (adrenalin release).

Centenarians, cites Dunbar, are curious and adventurous; they have fun. (One took a bride of 81, but the marriage was abruptly dissolved because, "He married me for my money.") Dunbar summarizes the factors in longevity:

> Men over 95 have a high emotional stability; rarely are they elated or depressed; they are in good health and keep active; they stay well—their dreams are pleasant; mishaps are taken in stride; they keep flexible—they try new things; they enjoy each day, looking forward to tomorrow; they have "a constant cheerfulness"; they place first things first—they have definite ideas about things that count; they have a self-imposed discipline that is natural; healthy centenarians work hard all their lives at something they enjoy (p. 3).

With advancing years, there is always a certain loss of memory. Beard (1968) has carried out a series of investigations on many characteristics of the elderly. In a recent report concerning their memory ability, she concludes that few centenarians are much embarrassed by poor memory, although some regard it as a nuisance. Some try definitely to retain their powers of memory and are gratified with the results. People who exercise their memory retain it longer than those who do not. Individuals who maintain many interests and activities have better memories, for both recent and remote events. One centenarian commented: "Why shouldn't youngsters have better memories? They have nothing to remember."

As emphasized, behavioral development should be seen as a continuing process from birth through one's entire life. This progression includes experiences of varying degrees of importance. Unfortunately, the influence of one particular experience on later behavior is difficult to evaluate. Stimuli come from heredity or the environment. Accumulating data (Krech, 1967) stress the strong influence environment plays in views of the future, for the person approaching retirement.

Why do some workers anticipate retirement eagerly as an opening of new vistas for adventure and a chance to relish more of the zest for life, while others timidly accept the end of employment as an inevitable price one must pay only because he has arrived at the fearful 65 milestone? This key issue lends itself ideally to further study. The need to achieve is an imperative compulsion in the lives of all citizens who hope for a long and active life. McClelland (1966) has discussed the urge to achieve. He is confident that the achievement motive can be identified and stimulated. He compares groups of men, some of whom are more highly motivated than others. This comparison is concerned with groups in the mid-sixties and beyond.

Those individuals who are strongly motivated are likely to be more concerned with personal achievement than with the rewards of success per se. These men have a strong preference in which they can get concrete feedback on how well they are doing; they can review their progress, and estimate their future gain and whether the tempo might beneficially be speeded up. McClelland says these people are habitually thinking about doing things better. Highly motivated persons will extend themselves to secure expert guidance, whereas mildly motivated workers may rely on adjacent friends and neglect to seek further for self-improvement. The urge to achieve is plainly evident among community leaders and artists and experts in other fields. Our next step is to develop this need in low-income groups. As is well known, a favorable environment is a powerful component.

Old Age Clubs, retirement villages, and entertainment merely to pass the time for older citizens fail to emphasize the need for personal achievement. As such, they can depress or totally eliminate progressive, productive achievement. In a closely reasoned article, "Social Science and Purposive Behavior," Kattsoff states: "Whether we like it or not, human behavior indicates direction" (1953, p. 24). This is an important but exceedingly difficult challenge for sociology and the life sciences because it involves emotional valuations. Appreciation of values is a strongly individual quality that is ever shifting in intensity, duration, and focus. Benjamin Franklin was quoted as observing, "The reasonable man is he who finds a reason for everything he wants to do" (Schiller, 1968).

The problem of motivating those beyond the retirement age is an order of biological significance, since it necessitates sufficient exercise of body and mind to reduce the drain on body reserves, which is one consequence of growing older. This deals also with a phenomenon of national vitality, that is, the health and well-being of some twenty million citizens beyond the 65-year-old hurdle. More active and successful modes of behavior are essential to replace outworn practices no longer consonant with the healthy lengthening span of years.

If social science can develop new outlets for our citizens at the summit of their years, more burdens will be eliminated. Schiller (1968) quotes from *The Quiet Crisis* by Secretary of the Interior Udall: "One of the paradoxes of American society is that while our economic standard of living has become the envy of the world our environmental standard has steadily declined" (p. 21).

Our nation's productive proficiency has made it possible for a large percentage of the citizens to have more leisure during the 40 or 50 years of their lives following retirement. Time for travel, and days off at a more leisurely pace, add an increment to the stature of mature citizens that youth can never know. Contemplation, re-thinking, remembering the lights and shadows of one's entire life, can lead to new possibilities for further accomplishment. Creativity is a part of the process. It can be the mending of an individual tiny cell, or the replacement of a damaged heart, or the renewal of a waning spirit.

An old friend and brilliant scientist, Dr. Fred Hammett, once described the human being as "a chemical converter of energy, an intellectual catalyst, an emotional dynamo, a social explorer and, finally, a spiritual wonderer." To savor of the best life has to offer requires the quiet soul and the continued wondering of the mind of a child. This makes for successful living in autumn's harvest years.

Enrichment

One of the most fortunate appointments made by President L. B. Johnson to his Cabinet was the designation of the distinguished American scholar John W. Gardner as Secretary of the Department of Health, Education and Welfare. For the first time, this major post was handed over to a qualified expert, an author of renown, and an accepted leader of first magnitude. His small monographs on *Excellence* (1961) and *Self-Renewal* (1965) are classics and widely read.

Welfare for those requiring assistance has for years been a troublesome, unsolved problem. The term "welfare" has assumed so many different meanings that it has been downgraded as a term. Yet, there are thousands of highly trained workers in the field of public assistance who have devoted their lives, selflessly, to endeavoring to improve conditions for less fortunate citizens.

Income maintenance, housing, health, and employability are the major needs. In addition, however, Gardner added a term that is a ringing challenge to every responsible citizen. We need to aim for enrichment of the lives of our fellow men. Granted, many persons, for various reasons, do not display traits of reliability or constancy. However, enrichment of one's life as he ascends the later heights is an invigorating concept. Enrichment is a tonic word. Possibilities are infinite. Examples of persons who have led the way for their fellowmen to reach higher ground are many. They spring from high and low estate. Some are scholars, while the majority have been self-taught and self-propelled.

Curiously (or not), the majority have been great spiritual leaders: Jesus, Mohammed, Buddha, St. Luke, St. Paul, St. Augustine, and, more recently, Pope John XXIII and Ghandi. The list is endless, but the inspiration abides. Some were young, but many were old. Imagination, great inspiration, striving to be a part, no matter how small, of the infinite wonder of creative nature—this is the goal envisioned in enrichment. The need is emergent in time, the field worldwide; the source for leaders and workers is the over 20 million Americans over 65, beyond retirement. But there must be a distillation of the new knowledge now ready to be applied. Research for goals and methods is essential.

PSYCHO-SOCIAL RESEARCH

A pilot study of the significance of life-goals in aging adjustment reported by the California Department of Mental Hygiene (Simon and Brisette, 1967) summarizes the views of its members on life-goals derived from an analysis of statements by 79 subjects (40 residents and 39 dischargees from a psychiatric facility). They proposed a life-goals study in order to understand the psychopathology of the aging process through the analysis of life histories of both community and hospitalized subjects. They recommended an exploration of the failure to attain the goals. A lack of self-actualization is conducive to depression and illness in the elderly.

The concept of life-goals is a most attractive idea invoked by ego psychologists. It is a useful item in our appraisal of individuals approaching and beyond the retirement age. Life-goals are seen by some as "human longings." "Self-actualization," a term coined by personality psychologists, suggests a state of achievement for the individual struggling toward identity. All healthy animals, especially men, have this drive, a manifestation of the instinct for survival. It can be intensified, redirected, and altered in innumerable ways by currents within the immediate environment. There are chemicals now available to markedly alter and distort the original "élan vital." The image of life-goals varies with age: the child is captured by entertainment, the adolescent by love magic, the newlywed by the stirring of new life within the womb. Ultimately, the well-ordered existence (this is itself a concept—Utopian?) is identified in healthy older citizens who have successfully weathered life's storms. The concept of life-goals contains a wealth of suggestions for research on those approaching the later period of life through the door of retirement.

Crystallization of views may be a strong stimulus for those uncertain of the next step. The long view of the long life can be fostered by group discussions. The infinite range of choices open to the large number of individuals with years of experience is a heritage of science's additions to our understanding of biological progression. Now we have arrived at the stage of psycho-social evolution, a point emphasized by Sir Julian Huxley (1959). He writes that the Atomic Era, by giving us a fuller comprehension of nature as a whole, has brought us to the threshold of a greater and more revolutionary age, the Humanist Era. By exploiting the possibilities of the human mind, the psycho-social phase of human development has been initiated. This phase operates much faster than biological evolution and produces new kinds of results. Our capacity for reason and imagination has been tremendously amplified. Now, being conscious of our new dimensions, we can reach new levels of achievement and creativity. This is the starry dome for man to contemplate in the new years beyond retirement. This exciting new awareness, this new perspective which Pierre Teilhard de Chardin (1959) designated as the process of hominization, the better realization of man's intrinsic possibilities, has hardly begun.

It behooves scholars to survey the huge scene and to lead in charting new courses. By stretching muscle and mind in the pursuit of new goals in the mature years, the recharge mechanism existing in every healthy body and mind is set in motion. Second wind for the second career appears. Illiteracy spawned by indifference and ignorance should be combatted by an energetic school system as the basis for lifetime learning. The real measure of each individual will be maximized by an educational philosophy that will facilitate communication of underdeveloped individuals and groups with attractive centers of learning, the schools. Setting up realizable goals according to individual capacity is a much needed technique that peer groups may emphasize to young and old alike. The science of human possibilities, Huxley writes (1959), will invoke a radical re-thinking of our systems of education, their aims, content, and techniques.

Psycho-social science as a major division in the study of human development is an emergent idea. The approach is positive rather than specific-disease oriented. Investigations of heart disease, cancer, arthritis, and metabolic disorders are episodic, whereas the concept expressed in the study of human development is holistic. The entire group of relevant disciplines, with adequate cross fertilization of ideas, has unique potential for clarifying the identity and destiny of modern man.

REFERENCES

Abelson, P. H. Physical fitness. *Science,* 1968, **161**, 1299.

Allport, G. W. *Personality: A psychological interpretation.* New York: Henry Holt, 1937.

Allport, G. W. *Becoming.* New Haven: Yale University Press, 1955.

Allport, G. W. The open system in personality theory. *Journal of Abnormal and Social Psychology,* 1960, **61**, 301-311.

Allport, G. W. *Pattern and growth in personality.* New York: Holt, Rinehart and Winston, 1961.

Anastasi, A. *Differential psychology.* New York: Macmillan, 1958.

Anderson, J. E. Research problems in aging. In J. E. Anderson (Ed.), *Psychological aspects of aging.* Washington D.C.: American Psychological Association, 1956.

Anderson J. E. Dynamics of development: System in process. In D. Harris (Ed.), *The concept of development.* Minneapolis: University of Minnesota Press, 1957.

Anderson, J. E. Psychological research on changes and transformations during development and aging. In J. E. Birren (Ed.), *Relations of development and aging.* Springfield, Ill.: Charles C. Thomas, 1964.

Ansbacher, H. L. & Ansbacher R. R. (Eds.). *The individual psychology of Alfred Adler.* New York: Basic Books, 1956.

Ardrey, R. *The territorial imperative.* New York: Atheneum Press, 1966.

Arensberg, C. M. *The Irish countryman: An anthropological study.* New York: Macmillan Company, 1937.

Ariés, P. *Centuries of childhood: A social history of family life.* New York: Knopf, 1962.

Aring, C. D. Intimations of mortality. *Annals of Internal Medicine,* 1968, **69**, 148-158.

Arth, M. J. An interdisciplinary view of the aged in Ibo culture. *Journal of Geriatric Psychiatry,* Fall 1968, 2, No. 1, 33-39.

Ash, P. Pre-retirement counselling. *The Gerontologist,* 1966, **6**, 27-127.

Baldwin, A. L. The study of child behavior and development. In P. H. Mussen (Ed.), *Handbook of research methods in child development.* New York: Wiley, 1960.

Baldwin, A. L. *Theories of child development.* New York: Wiley, 1967.

Banham, K. M. Senescence and the emotions: A genetic theory. *Journal of Genetic Psychology,* 1951, **78**, 175-183.

Barron, F. *Creativity and psychological health.* Princeton, New Jersey: D. Van Nostrand, 1963.

Barron, M. L. *The aging American: An introduction to social gerontology and geriatrics.* New York: Crowell, 1961.

Bayley, N. & Olden, M. H. The maintenance of intellectual ability in gifted adults. *Journal of gerontology,* 1955, **10**, 91-107.

Beard, B. B. Some characteristics of recent memory of centenarians. *Journal of Gerontology,* 1968, **23**, 23-30.

Becker, E. *The birth and death of meaning.* Glencoe: Free Press, 1962.

Becker, H. S. & Carper, J. W. The development of identification with an occupation. *American Journal of Sociology,* 1956, **61**, 289-298.

Becker, H. S. & A. Strauss. Careers, personality and adult socialization. *American Journal of Sociology,* 1956, **62**, 253-263.

Belbin, R. M. *Employment of older workers, 2: Training methods.* Paris: Organization for Economic Cooperation and Development, 1965.

Belbin, R. M. *Employment of older workers, 6: The discovery method, an international experiment in retraining.* Paris: Organization for Economic Cooperation and Development, 1969.

Belbin, E. & Waters, P. Organized home study for older retrainees. *Industrial Training International,* 1967, **2**, 196-198.

Benedek, T. Climacterium: A developmental phase. *Psychoanalytic Quarterly,* 1950, **19**, 1-27.

Benedek, T. Parenthood as a developmental phase: A contribution to the libido-theory. *Journal of the American Psychological Association,* 1959, **7**, 389-417.

Benge, E. L. & Copell, D. F. Employee morale survey. *Modern Management,* 1947, **7**, 19-22.

Berezin, M. A. Some intra-psychic aspects of aging. In N. Zinberg (Ed.), *The normal psychology of the aging process.* New York: International Universities Press, 1963. Pp. 93-117.

Berkey, B. R. & Stoebner, J. B. The retirement syndrome: A previously unreported variant. *Military Medicine,* 1968, **133**, No. 1, 5-8.

Bertalanffy, L. V. *Problems of life.* London: Watts, 1952.

Bertalanffy, L. V. General systems theory—a critical review. In W.

Buckley (Ed.) *Modern systems research for the behavioral scientist.* Chicago: Aldine Press, 1968.

Birren, J. E. Behavioral theories of aging. In N. Shock (Ed.), *Aging: Some social and biological aspects.* Washington: American Association for the Advancement of Science, 1960.

Birren, J. E. *Relations of development and aging.* Springfield, Illinois: Thomas, 1964.(a)

Birren, J. E. *The psychology of aging.* Englewood Cliffs: Prentice-Hall, 1964.(b)

Birren, J. E. Increments and decrements in the intellectual status of the aged. Paper presented at a Regional Research Conference on Aging in Modern Society: Psychological and Medical Aspects, at the University of California San Francisco Medical Center, March 1967.

Black, M. Linguistic relativity: The views of Benjamin Lee Whorf. In R. A. Manners & D. Kaplan (Eds.), *Theory in anthropology, a sourcebook.* Chicago: Aldine Press, 1968. Pp. 432-437.

Blake, J. & Davis, K. On norms and values. In R. A. Manners & D. Kaplan (Eds.), *Theory in anthropology, a sourcebook.* Chicago: Aldine Press, 1968. Pp. 465-472.

Blauner, R. Work satisfaction and industrial trends in modern society. In W. Galenson & S. M. Lipset (Eds.), *Labor and trade unionism: An interdisciplinary reader.* New York: Wiley, 1960. Pp. 339-360.

Blauner, R. Dealth and social structure. *Psychiatry,* 1966, **29**, 378-394.

Bloom, B. S. *Stability and change in human characteristics.* New York: Wiley, 1964.

Bortner, R. W. Adult development or idiosyncratic change? A plea for the developmental approach. *The Gerontologist,* 1966, **6**, 159-164.

Bortner, R. W. Personality and social psychology in the study of aging. *The Gerontologist,* 1967, 7, 23-36.

Bortner, R. W. Descriptive theories of adult development. Memorandum on File at the Pennsylvania State University, 1968.

Bortz, E. L. *Diabetes control.* Philadelphia: Lea & Feberger, 1951.

Bortz, E. L. *Creative aging.* New York: Macmillan, 1963. Pp. 162-170.

Bortz, E. L. *Man in transition.* In press.

Botwinick, J. *Cognitive processes in maturity and old age.* New York: Springer, 1967.

Breen, L. Z. Retirement—norms, behavior, and functional aspects of normative behavior. In R. H. Williams (Ed.), *Processes of aging,* Vol. II. New York: Atherton Press, 1963.

Breuer, J. & Freud, S. On the psychical mechanism of hysterical phenomena: Preliminary communication (1893). In *Studies on hysteria* in *The standard edition of the complete psychological works of sigmund Freud,* Vol. II. London: Hogarth Press, 1955. Pp. 1-17.

Bridges, K. M. B. A genetic theory of emotions. *Journal of Genetic Psychology,* 1930, **37**, 514-527.

Britton, J. H. Dimensions of adjustment of older adults. *Journal of Gerontology,* 1963, **18**, 60-65.

Broadhurst, P. L. Emotionality and the Yerkes-Dodson law. *Journal of Experimental Psychology,* 1957, **54**, 345-352.

Bromley, D. B. *The psychology of human aging.* Baltimore: Penguin Books, 1966.

Bronfenbrenner, U. Developmental theory in transition. In H. W. Stevenson (Ed.), *Child psychology.* Chicago: National Society for the Study of Education, 1963.

Brotman, H. B. Income of families and unrelated individuals. *Useful Facts #1.* Washington, D.C.: Administration on Aging, revised September 1967.

Brotman, H. B. A profile of the older American. Address before the Conference on Consumer Problems of Older People, New York City, October 16, 1967. AOA No. 228, May 1968. Pp. 1-15.(a)

Brotman, H. B. Who are the aged: A demographic view. In *Occasional papers in gerontology.* Ann Arbor, Michigan: Institute of Gerontology, University of Michigan-Wayne State University, November 1968.(b)

Bruner, E. M. The psychological approach in anthropology. In S. Tax (Ed.), *Horizons of anthropology.* Chicago: Aldine Press, 1964. Pp. 71-80.

Bruner, J. Culture, politics and pedagogy. *Saturday Review,* May 18, 1968, 71-73.

Buhler, C. Theoretical observations about life's basic tendencies. *American Journal of Psychotherapy,* 1959, **13**, 561-581.

Buhler, C. Meaningful living in the mature years. In R. W. Kleemeier (Ed.), *Aging and leisure.* New York: Oxford University Press, 1961.

Buhler, C., *et al.* Old age as a phase of human life. *Human Development,* 1968, **11**, 53-63.

Burgess, E. Personal and social adjustment in old age. In M. Derber (Ed.), *The aged and society.* Champaign, Illinois: Industrial Relations Research Association, 1950. Pp. 138-156.

Burgess, E. Family living in the later decades. *The Annals of the*

American Academy of Political and Social Science, 1952, **279**, 106-114.

Burgess, E. Family structure and relationships. In E. Burgess (Ed.), *Aging in western societies.* Chicago: University of Chicago Press, 1960. Pp. 271-298.

Busse, E. W. Changes in thinking and behavior in the elderly: An interdisciplinary study. Paper presented at the annual meeting of the American Psychiatric Association, Detroit, Michigan, May 1967.

Butler, R. N. The life review: An interpretation of reminiscence in the aged. *Psychiatry,* 1963, **26**, 65-75.

Butler, R. N. The destiny of creativity in later life: Studies of creative people and the creative process. In S. Levin & R. J. Kahana (Eds.), *Psychodynamic studies on aging: Creativity, reminiscing and dying.* New York: International Universities Press, 1967. Pp. 20-63.

Butler, R. N. Patterns of psychological health and illness in retirement. In F. Carp (Ed.), *The retirement process.* Public Health Service Publication No. 1778. Washington D.C.: Government Printing Office, 1968. Pp. 27-41.(a)

Butler, R. N. Toward a psychiatry of the life cycle: Implications of sociopsychological studies of the aging process for policy in and practice of psychotherapy. In A. Simon & L. J. Epstein (Eds.), *Aging in modern society.* Washington D.C.: American Psychiatric Association. Psychiatric Report No. 23, February 1968. Pp. 233-248.(b)

Caldwell, B. The usefulness of the critical period hypothesis in the study of filiative behavior. *Merrill-Palmer Quarterly,* 1962, **8**, 229-242.

Canestrari, R. E., Jr. Paced and self-paced learning in young and elderly adults. *Journal of Gerontology,* 1963, **18**, 165-168.

Caplan, G. *Principles of preventive psychiatry.* New York: Basic Books, 1964.

Carp, F. M. *A future for the aged: Victoria Plaza and its residents.* Austin, Texas: University of Texas Press, 1966.

Carp, F. M. The impact of environment on old people. *The Gerontologist,* 1967, **7**, 106-109.

Carp, F. M. Background and statement of purpose. In F. M. Carp (Ed.), *The retirement process.* Public Health Service Publication No. 1778. Washington, D.C.: Government Printing Office, 1968. Pp. 1-26.(a)

Carp, F. M. Summary and prospect. In F. M. Carp (Ed.), *The retirement process.* Public Health Service Publication No 1778.

Washington, D.C.: Government Printing Office, 1968. Pp. 151-160.(b)

Carp, F. M. (Ed.) *The retirement process.* Public Health Service Publication No. 1778. Washington, D.C.: Government Printing Office, 1968.(c)

Carroll, J. B. (Ed.) *Language, thought, and reality: Selected writings of Benjamin Lee Whorf.* New York: Wiley, 1956.

Cattell, R. B. Personality theory from quantitative research. In S. Koch (Ed.), *Psychology: A study of a Science, Vol. III.* New York: McGraw-Hill, 1959.

Cavan, R. S., Burgess, E. W., Havighurst, R. J., & Goldhamer, H. *Personal adjustment in old age.* Chicago: Science Research Associates, 1949.

Chodoff, P. Late effects of the concentration camp syndrome. *Archives of General Psychiatry,* April 1963, 8, 323-333.

Clark, M. *Health in the Mexican-American culture.* Berkeley, California: University of California Press, 1959.

Clark, M. The anthropology of aging, a new area for studies of culture and personality. *The Gerontologist,* 1967, 7, 55-64.

Clark, M. & Anderson, B. G. *Culture and aging.* Springfield, Illinois: Thomas, 1967.

Clark, M. & Mendelson, M. Mexican-American aged in San Francisco: A case description. *The Gerontologist,* 1969, 9, 90-95.

Clément, F. The relative development of several psycho-physiological and psychometric variables with different occupations and intellectual levels. In H. T. Blumenthal (Ed.), *Interdisciplinary topics in gerontology,* Vol. 4. Basel and New York: Karger, 1969.

Comfort, A. *The biology of senescence.* New York: Rinehart, 1956. Pp. 59-113.

Condorcet de, J. A. N. C. The advantages of the American revolution which are relative to the perfectability of the human race. In Justice Buchler et al. (Eds.), (trans. S. J. Gendzier) *Introduction to contemporary civilization in the West.* (3rd ed.) Vol. I. New York: Columbia University Press. 1960. Pp. 1334-1342.

Cowdry, E. V. (Ed.) *Problems of aging: Biological and medical aspects.* (2nd ed.) Baltimore, Maryland: Williams and Wilkins, 1942.

Cowdry, E. V. The broader implications of aging. *Journal of Gerontology,* 1947, 2, 277-282.

Crespi, I. Some observations on the dimensions of satisfaction in the U.S. and other countries around the world. *Public Opinion Quarterly,* 1966, **30**, 438.

Cumming, E. & Henry, W. E. *Growing old: The process of disengagement.* New York: Basic Books, 1961.

Cumming, E. New thoughts on the theory of disengagement. In R. Kastenbaum (Ed.), *New thoughts on old age.* New York: Springer Publishing Company, 1964. Pp. 3-18.

Davidson, W. R. & Kunze, K. R. Psychological, social, and economic meanings of work in modern society: Their effects on the worker facing retirement. *The Gerontologist,* 1965, **5**, 129-133.

De Chardin, P. T. *The phenomenon of man.* New York: Harper, 1959.

Denenberg, V. H. An attempt to isolate critical periods of development in the rat. *Journal of Comparative and Physiological Psychology,* 1962, **55**, 813-815.

Denenberg, V. H. Critical periods, stimulus input, and emotional reactivity: A theory of infantile stimulation. In N. S. Endler, L. R. Boulter, & H. Osser (Eds.), *Contemporary issues in developmental psychology.* New York: Holt, Rinehart, and Winston, 1968.

Denenberg, V. H. & Kline N. J. Stimulus intensity versus critical periods: A test of two hypotheses concerning infantile stimulation. *Canadian Journal of Psychology,* 1964, **18**, 1-5.

Deutscher, M. Adult work and developmental models. *American Journal of Orthopsychiatry,* 1968, **38**, 882-891.

Diaz-Guerrero, R. The active and the passive syndromes. *Revista Interamericana de Psicologia,* 1967, **1**, 265-272.

Donahue, W. Psychological aspects. In E. V. Cowdry (Ed.), *The care of the geriatric patient.* (3rd ed.) St. Louis: Mosby, 1968.

Donahue, W., Orbach, H. L. & Pollak, O. Retirement: The emerging social pattern. In C. Tibbitts (Ed.), *Handbook of social gerontology.* Chicago: University of Chicago Press, 1960. Pp. 330-397.

Dubin, R. Industrial workers' worlds: A study of the central life interest of industrial workers. *Social Problems,* 1963, **3**, 131-142.

Dunbar, F. What are the secrets of long life? *Executive Health,* 1963, **1**, 1-3.

Duncan, L. E. Forward. In F. M. Carp (Ed.), *The retirement process.* Public Health Service Publication No. 1778. Washington D.C.: Government Printing Office, 1968. P. ix.

Dutton, W. S. They retired—and got busy. *The Saturday Evening Post,* June 16, 1951, 36-37, 75, 78, 80-81.

Ehinger, G. Declin des aptitudes avec l'age. *Archives de Psychologie,* 1931, **23**, 67-73.

Eisdorfer, C. Discussion. In F. M. Carp (Ed.), *The retirement process.* Public Health Service Publication No. 1778. Washington D.C.: Government Printing Office, 1968. Pp. 97-104.

Eisdorfer, C., Axelrod, S., & Wilkie, F. Stimulus exposure time as a factor in serial learning in an aged population. *Journal of Abnormal and Social Psychology,* 1963, **67**, 594-600.

Eissler, K. R. *The psychiatrist and the dying patient.* New York: International Universities Press, 1955.

Ellison, D. L. Work, retirement, and the sick role. *The Gerontologist,* 1968, **8**, No. 3, 189-192.

Emmerick, W. Personality development and concepts of structure. *Child Development,* 1968, **39**, 671-690.

Erikson, E. *Identity and the life cycle.* New York: International Universities Press, 1959.(a)

Erikson, E. The healthy personality. In *Psychological Issues,* Vol. I, No. 1. New York: International University Press, 1959. Pp. 50-100.(b)

Erikson, E. The problem of ego identity. In M. Stein, A. J. Vidich, and D. M. White (Eds.), *Identity and anxiety.* Glencoe: Free Press, 1960.

Erikson, E. *Childhood and society.* (2nd ed.) New York: W. W. Norton, 1963.

Escalona, S. The influence of topological and vector psychology upon current research in child development: An addendum. In L. Carmichael (Ed.), *Manual of child psychology.* (2nd ed.) New York: Wiley, 1954.

Eysenck, H. J. *The structure of human personality.* London: Methuen, 1953.

Fenichel, O. *The psychoanalytic theory of neurosis.* New York: Norton, 1945.

Ferenczi, S. (trans. H. A. Bunker) *Thalassa. A theory of genitality.* Albany, New York: Psychoanalytic Quarterly, Inc., 1938.

Festinger, L. Cognitive dissonance. *Scientific American,* 1962, **207**, No. 4, 93-102.

Fiske, D. W. & Maddi, S. R. *Functions of varied experience.* Homewood, Illinois: Dorsey Press, 1961.

Fiske, M. *Book selection and censorship.* Berkeley and Los Angeles: University of California Press, 1959, revised 1968.

Fox, H. & Kerpen, M. C. *Corporate retirement policies, National Industrial Conference Board studies on personnel policy No. 190.* New York: National Industrial Conference Board, 1964.

Freud, S. *Civilization and its discontents.* London: Hogarth, 1930.

Freud, S. The theory of instincts. In C. Thompson (Ed.), *An outline of psychoanalysis.* (Rev. ed.) New York: Random House, 1955.

Freud, S. Three essays on the theory of sexuality (1905). *The standard edition of the complete psychological work of Sigmund Freud,* Vol. VII. London: Hogarth Press, 1956, Pp. 125-245.

Friedman, E. A. & Havighurst, R. J. *The meaning of work and retirement.* Chicago: University of Chicago Press, 1954.

Fromm, E. *Escape from freedom.* New York: Rinehart, 1941.

Gardner, D. B. *Development in early childhood: The preschool years.* New York: Harper and Row, 1964.

Gardner, J. W. *Excellence. Can we be equal and excellent too?* New York: Harper and Row, 1961.

Gardner, J. W. You can tell a creative company by the people it keeps. *Think Magazine,* November-December 1962.

Gardner, J. W. *Self-renewal. The individual and the innovative society.* New York: Harper and Row, 1965.

Gardner, J. W. What self-renewal can do for retirement. *Think Magazine,* 1967, **33**, 3-6.(a)

Gardner, J W. Testimony given before the Subcommittee on Retirement and the Individual. Special Committee on Aging, *Retirement and the individual.* Washington: The Committee, 1967.(b)

Gill, R. Topography and systems in psychoanalytic theory. *Psychological issues,* Vol. III, No. 2. New York: International Universities Press, 1963.

Ginzburg, R. The negative attitude toward the elderly. *Geriatrics,* 1952, **7**, 297-302.

Goffman, E. *Stigma.* Englewood Cliffs, New Jersey: Prentice Hall, 1963.

Goldfarb, A. I. Psychodynamics and the third generation family. In E. Shanas and G. F. Streib (Eds.), *Social structure and the family: Generational relations.* Englewood Cliffs, New Jersey: Prentice Hall, 1965. Pp. 10-45.

Goldstein, K. *Human nature in the light of psychopathology.* New York: Schocken Books, 1963.

Goldstein, K. Autobiography. In E. G. Boring and G. Lindzey (Eds.), *A history of psychology in autobiography,* Vol. V. New York: Appleton-Century-Crofts, 1967.

Gruen, W. Adult personality: An empirical study of Erikson's theory of ego development. In B. L. Neugarten (Ed.), *Personality in middle and late life.* New York: Atherton Press, 1964.

Guthrie, E. R. *The psychology of learning.* New York: Harper, 1935.

Guthrie, E. R. *The psychology of learning.* (Rev. ed.) New York: Harper, 1952.

Gutmann, D. L. An exploration of ego configurations in middle and later life. In B. L. Neugarten et al. (Eds.), *Personality in middle and late life.* New York: Atherton Press, 1964. Pp. 114-148.

Gutmann, D. L. Aging among the Highland Maya: A comparative study. *Journal of Personality and Social Psychology,* 1967, 7, 28-35.(a)

Gutmann, D. L. Ego psychological and developmental approaches to the 'retirement crisis' in men. Paper presented at the National Institute of Child Health and Human Development Conference, Washington, D.C., April 3-5, 1967.(b)

Hall, E. T. Proxemics: The study of man's spatial relations. In I. Galdston (Ed.), *Man's image in medicine and anthropology.* New York: International Universities Press, 1963. Pp. 422-445.

Hall, G. S. *Senescence: The last half of life.* New York: Appleton-Century-Crofts, 1923.

Hall, O. The stages in a medical career. *American Journal of Sociology,* 1948, 53, 327-336.

Hallowell, A. I. *Culture and experience.* Philadelphia: University of Pennsylvania Press, 1955.

Halperin, S. Markov models for human development: Statistical testing and estimation. *Education Abstracts,* 1966.

Hanson, D. A. & Hill, R. Families under stress. In H. T. Christensen (Ed.), *Handbook of marriage and the family.* Chicago: Rand-McNally, 1964.

Harris, D. B. *The concept of development.* Minneapolis: University of Minnesota Press, 1957.

Harris, D. B. The concept of developmental stages. Talk presented before the American Education Research Association, New York City, February, 1967.

Hartman, H. *Ego psychology and the problem of adaption.* New York: International Universities Press, 1958.

Hartmann, H. *Essays on ego psychology. Selected problems in psychoanalytic theory.* New York: International Universities Press, 1964.

Haug, M. & Sussman, M. B. The second career—variant of a

sociological concept. *Journal of Gerontology*, 1967, **22**, Part 1, 439-444.

Havighurst, R. J. *Human development and education.* New York: Longmans, Green, 1953.

Havighurst, R. J. The nature and values of meaningful free-time activity. In R. W. Kleemeier (Ed.), *Aging and leisure.* New York: Oxford University Press, 1961. Pp. 309-344.

Havighurst, R. J. Personality and patterns of aging. *The Gerontologist*, 1968, **8**, 20-23.(a)

Havighurst, R. J. A social-psychological perspective on aging. *The Gerontologist*, 1968, 8, 67-71.(b)

Havighurst, R. J. & Albrecht, R. *Older people.* New York: Longmans, Green and Company, 1953.

Havighurst, R. J., Neugarten, B. L., & Tobin, S. S. Disengagement, personality, and life satisfaction in the later years. In P. F. Hansen (Ed.), *Age with a future: Proceedings of the Sixth International Congress of Gerontology, Copenhagen 1963.* Copenhagen, Denmark: Munksgaard, 1964. Pp. 419-425.

Hays, W. Age and sex differences in the rorschach experience balance. *Journal of Abnormal and Social Psychology*, 1952, **47**, 390-393.

Heard, G. *The five ages of man.* New York: Julian Press, 1963.

Hemmendinger, L. A genetic study of structural aspects of perception as reflected in rorschach responses. Unpublished doctoral dissertation, Clark University, 1951.

Heron, A. & Chown, S. *Age and function.* London: Churchill, 1967.

Herskovitz, M. J. *Man and his works.* New York: Alfred A. Knopf, 1948.

Hess, E. H. Imprinting in birds. *Science*, 1964, **146**, 1128-1139.

Hilgard, E. R. & Marquis, D. G. *Conditioning and learning.* (2nd ed., by F. A. Kimble.) New York: Appleton-Century-Crofts, 1961.

Hoagland, H. Some reflections on science and society. *Bulletin of the Atomic Scientists*, 1959, **XV**, 284-287.

Holmberg, A. R. Age in the Andes. In R. W. Kleemeier (Ed.), *Aging and leisure.* New York: Oxford University Press, 1961. Pp. 86-90.

Hsu, F. L. K. *Psychological anthropology, approaches to culture and personality.* Homewood, Illinois: Dorsey, 1961.

Hughes, C. C. The concept and use of time in the middle years: The St. Lawrence Island Eskimos. In R. W. Kleemeier (Ed.), *Aging and leisure.* New York: Oxford University Press, 1961. Pp. 91-95.

Hummel, A. The Eastern view of aging. A paper presented at the meeting of the Forum for Professionals and Executives, Washington, D.C., November 28, 1967.

Huxley, J. The future of man. *Bulletin of the Atomic Scientists,* 1959, **XV**, 402-405.

Hyman, H. Reflections on reference groups. *Public Opinion Quarterly,* 1960, **24**, 383-396.

Inhelder, B. & Matalon, B. The study of problem solving and thinking. In P. H. Mussen (Ed.), *Handbook of research methods in child development.* New York: Wiley, 1960.

Jackson, J. K. The adjustment of the family to alcoholism. *Marriage and Family Living,* 1956, **81**, 361-369.

Janis, I. L. *Psychological stress, psychoanalytic and behavioral studies of surgical patients.* New York: Wiley, 1958.

Jacques, E. Death and the mid-life crisis. *The International Journal of Psycho-Analysis,* 1965, **46**, 502-514.

Johnson, D. E. A depressive retirement syndrome. *Geriatrics,* 1958, **13**, 314-319.

Jones, H. E. Trends in mental abilities. Unpublished paper (summarized by author), in Intelligence and problem-solving. In J. E. Birren (Ed.), *Handbook of aging and the individual.* Chicago: University of Chicago Press, 1959, Pp. 700-733.

Jung, C. G. The stages of life. In *Modern man in search of a soul.* New York: Harvest, 1933. Pp. 95-114.

Jung, C. G. *The undiscovered self.* Boston: Atlantic-Little, Brown, 1958.

Kagan, J. & Moss, H. A. The stability of passive and dependent behavior from childhood through adulthood. *Child Development,* 1960, **31**, 313-321.

Kaplan, B. Personality and social structure. In R. A. Manners and D. Kaplan (Eds.), *Theory in anthropology, a sourcebook.* Chicago: Aldine Press, 1968. Pp. 318-342.

Kaplan, O. *Mental disorders in later life.* (2nd ed.) Stanford: Stanford University Press, 1956.

Kastenbaum, R. Is old age the end of development? In R. Kastenbaum (Ed.), *New thoughts on old age.* New York: Springer, 1964.

Kastenbaum, R. Engrossment and perspective in later life: a developmental-field approach. In R. Kastenbaum (Ed.), *Contributions to the psychobiology of aging.* New York: Springer, 1965. Pp. 3-18.

Kastenbaum, R. Developmental-field theory and the aged person's inner experience. *The Gerontologist,* 1966, **6**, 10-13.

Kastenbaum, R. What happens to the man who is inside the aging body? An inquiry into the developmental psychology of later life. Speech prepared for the Duke University Seminars in Gerontology, 1967.

Kastenbaum, R. & Cameron, P. Cognitive and emotional dependency in later life. In R. A. Kalish (Ed.), *The dependencies of older people.* Occasional Papers in Gerontology No. 6, Institute of Gerontology, University of Michigan—Wayne State University, August 1969. Pp. 39-57.

Katona, G. & Morgan, J. N. Retirement in retrospect and prospect. In *Retirement and the individual.* Hearings before the Subcommittee on Retirement and the Individual of the Special Committee on Aging, United States Senate, 90th Congress, July 26, 1967. Washington, D.C.: U.S. Government Printing Office, 1967. Pp. 587-598.

Kaufmann, W. *Existentialism from Dostoevsky to Sartre.* New York: Meridian, 1956.

Kent, D. Aging: Fact and fancy. *The Gerontologist,* 1965, **5**, No. 2, 51-56.

Kessen, W. Research design in the study of developmental problems. In P. H. Mussen (Ed.), *Handbook of research methods in child development.* New York: Wiley, 1960.

Kessen, W. 'Stage' and 'Structure' in the study of children. *Monographs of the Society for Research in Child Development,* 1962, **27**, 65-81.

Kleemeier, R. W. Leisure and disengagement in retirement. *The Gerontologist,* 1964, **4**, 180-184.

Klein, D. C. & Lindemann, E. Preventive Intervention in Individual and family crisis situations. In G. Caplan (Ed.), *Prevention of mental disorders in children: Initial exploration.* New York: Basic Books, 1961. Pp. 283-306.

Kluckhohn, C. Values and value-orientations in the theory of action: An exploration in definition and classification. In T. Parsons and E. A. Shils (Eds.), *Toward a general theory of action.* Cambridge: Harvard University Press, 1962. Pp. 388-433.

Kluckhohn, F. R. Dominant and substitute profiles of cultural orientations: Their significance for the analysis of social stratification. *Social Forces,* 1950, **28**, 376-394.

Kluckhohn, F. R. & Strodtbeck, F. L. *Variations in value orientations.* Evanston, Illinois: Row, Peterson, 1961. Pp. 1-49.

Koch, S. *Psychology: A study of a science.* New York: McGraw-Hill, 1959.

Kogan, N. Attitudes toward old people in an older sample. *Journal of Abnormal Social Psychology,* 1961, **62**, 616-622.

Korenchevsky, V. *Physiology and pathology of aging.* New York: Hasner, 1961.

Kornhauser, A. *Mental health of the industrial worker: A Detroit study.* New York: Wiley, 1965.

Kramer, M., Taube, C. & Starr, S. Patterns of use of psychiatric facilities by the aged: Trends and implications. *Psychiatric Research Report 23*, American Psychiatric Association, February 1968, 89-150.

Krech, D. Psycho-chemical manipulation and social policy. *Annals of Internal Medicine,* 1967, **67**, Supplement 7, 19-24.

Kreps, J. M. (Ed.) *The employment, income and retirement problems of the aged.* Durham: Duke University Press, 1963.

Kreps, J. M. The allocation of leisure to retirement. In F. Carp (Ed.), *The retirement process.* Washington, D.C.: Government Printing Office, 1966. Pp. 137-144.(a)

Kreps, J. M.(Ed.) *Technology, manpower and retirement policy.* Cleveland: World, 1966.(b)

Kreps, J. M. *Lifetime allocation of work and leisure.* Research Report #22. Social Security Administration, Office of Research and Statistics. Washington, D.C.: Government Printing Office, 1968.

Kreps, J. M. & Ferguson, C. E. *Principles of economics.* New York: Holt, Rinehart & Winston, 1962, revised 1965.

Kreps, J. M., Ferguson, C. E., & Folsom, I. M. Employment of older workers, labor force requirements and labor supply, 1970 and 1975. In J. M. Kreps (Ed.), *The Employment, income and retirement problems of the aged.* Durham: Duke University Press, 1963. Pp. 51-108.

Kreps, J. M. & Spengler, J. J. The leisure component of economic growth. In *The employment impact of technological change,* Appendix, Vol. II. National Commission on Technology, Automation, and Economic Progress. Washington, D.C.: Government Printing Office, 1966. Pp. 353-397.

Kroeber, A. L. *Anthropology.* New York: Harcourt, Brace, 1948.

Kuo, Z-Y. *The dynamics of behavior development: An epigenetic view.* New York: Random House, 1967.

Langer, T. S. & Michael, S. T. *Life stress and mental health: The Midtown Manhattan study.* London: Collier-Macmillan, 1963.

Lasswell, H. D. *Psychopathology and politics.* Chicago: University of Chicago Press, 1930.

Lawton, M. P. The problem of functional assessment. Paper presented at the annual meeting of the Gerontological Society, Denver, Colorado, 1968.

Lazarus, R. S., Opton, E. M., Jr., & Averill, J. R. The management of stressful experiences. Paper presented at the Foundations' Fund for Research in Psychiatry Conference on Adaptation to Change, Dorado Beach, Puerto Rico, June 22-27, 1968.

Lee, D. Lineal and non-lineal codifications of reality. *Psychosomatic Medicine,* May 1959, **12**, 30-45.

Lee, R. V. The nature, course and calibration of aging. *The Pharos,* 1968, **31**, 14-16.

Le Gros Clark, F. *Work, age and leisure.* London: Michael Joseph, 1966.

Le Gros Clark, F. The status in modern society of retired persons, Unpublished paper, 1968.

Le Play, F. *Les ouvriers Europiéns.* Paris, 1855.

Levi, L. Sympatho-adrenomedullary responses to emotional stimuli: Methodologic, physiologic and pathologic considerations. In E. Bajusz and S. Karger (Eds.), *An introduction to clinical neuroendocrinology.* New York: Basel, 1967. Pp. 78-105.

Levy, S. J. *The meanings of work.* Chicago: Center for the Study of Liberal Education for Adults, 1963.

Lewin, K. Field theory and experiment in social psychology: Concepts and methods. *American Journal of Sociology,* 1939, **44**, 868-896.

Lewin, K. Behavior and development as a function of the total situation. In L. Carmichael (Ed.), *Manual of child psychology.* (2nd ed.) New York: Wiley, 1954.

Linden, M. E. & Courtney, A. B. The human life cycle and its interruptions: A psychologic hypothesis. *American Journal of Psychiatry,* 1953, **109**, 906-915.

Locascio, R. Delayed and impaired vocational development: A neglected aspect of vocational development theory. *Personnel and Guidance Journal,* 1964, **42**, 885-887.

Lohnes, P. R. Markov models for human development research. *Journal of Counseling Psychology,* 1965, **12**, 322-327.

Lowenstein, A. Work incentives in the age of automation. *American Journal of Orthopsychiatry,* 1968, **38**, 893-899.

Lowenthal, M. F. *Lives in distress: The paths of the elderly to the psychiatric ward.* New York: Basic Books, 1964.

Lowenthal, M. F. Antecedents of isolation and mental illness in old age. *Archives of General Psychiatry,* 1965, **12**, 245-254.

Lowenthal, M. F. Notes on a developmental model for the study of retirement. Paper presented at Retirement Conference, College Park, Pennsylvania, May 15-17, 1967.

Lowenthal, M. F. Intentionality: Toward a framework for the study of adaptation in adulthood, *Aging and Human Development,* in press.

Lowenthal, M. F. Berkman, P. L. & Associates. *Aging and mental disorder in San Francisco: A social psychiatric study.* San Francisco: Jossey-Bass, 1967.

Lowenthal, M. F. Spence, D., & Thurnher, M. Transitions, goals, and adaptation in the course of the life cycle. Paper presented at the Foundations' Fund for Research in Psychiatry Conference on Adaptation to Change, Dorado Beach, Puerto Rico, June 22-27, 1968. (Publication pending,)

Maddox, G. L. Disengagement theory: A critical evaluation. *The Gerontologist,* 1964, **4**, 80-83.

Maddox, G. L. Retirement as a social event in the United States. In T. C. McKinney and F. T. de Vyver (Eds.), *Aging and social policy.* New York: Appleton-Century-Crofts, 1966.

Maddox, G. L. Retirement as a social event. In B. L. Neugarten (Ed.), *Middle age and aging: A reader in social psychology.* Chicago and London: University of Chicago Press, 1968. Pp. 357-365.

Mandelbaum, D. G. (Ed.) *Selected writings of Edward Sapir in language, culture and personality.* Berkeley and Los Angeles: University of California Press, 1949.

Manpower Report of the President. Washington, D.C.: U.S. Government Printing Office, 1968.

Martin, J. & Doran, A. Perception of retirement: Time and season. Pilkington Research Project on Retirement, University of Liverpool, 1967. (Unpublished paper.)

Maslow, A. H. *Motivation and personality.* New York: Harper and Row, 1954.

Maslow, A. H. *Towards a psychology of being.* Princeton, New Jersey: Van Nostrand, 1962.

Mathiason, G. (Ed.) *Criteria for retirement.* New York: Putman, 1953.

McClelland, D. C. That urge to achieve. *Think Magazine,* November-December 1966, 19-23.

McEwan, J. M. & Sheldon, A. P. Individual response to enforced retirement. *Geriatric Focus,* 1968, **7**, 1-4.

McLuhan, M. *Understanding media: The extensions of man.* New York: McGraw-Hill, 1964.

Mead, M. In testimony before the Subcommittee on Aging of the United States Senate, S. J. Resolution 117. *Congressional Record,* October 18, 1967, 117-120.

Meerloo, J. Transference and resistance in geriatric psychotherapy. *Psychoanalytic Review,* 1955, **42**, 72-82.

Merton, R. K. Fiske, M., & Curtis, A. *Mass persuasion.* New York: Harpers, 1946.

Merton, R. K. Fiske, M., & Kendall, P. *The focused interview.* New York: Free Press, 1948.

Meyerhoff, H. *Time in literature.* Berkeley: University of California Press, 1955.

Miller, G., Galanter, E., & Pribram, K. H. *Plans and the structure of behavior.* New York: Holt, Rinehart and Winston, 1960.

Miller, S. J. The social dilemma of the aging leisure participant. In B. L. Neugarten (Ed.), *Middle age and aging: A reader in social psychology.* Chicago and London: University of Chicago Press, 1968. Pp. 366-374.

Millis, J. T. Lecture delivered at the Annual Clinical Session of the American Medical Association, Houston, Texas, November 30, 1967.

Mitchell, W. L. *Social Security in the United States.* New York: McKay, 1964.

Mitchell, W. L. Report on preparation for retirement. Washington, D.C.: American Association of Retired Persons, 1967. Appendix IIB and IIIB.

Mitchell, W. L *Preparation for retirement.* Washington, D.C.: American Association of Retired Persons, 1968.

Moberg, D. O. Religiosity in old age. *The Gerontologist,* 1965, **5**, 78-89.

Moore, W. E. *Man, time and society.* New York: Wiley, 1963.

Moran, J. & Doran, A. Evidence concerning the relationship between health and retirement. *The Sociological Review,* 1966, **14**, 329-343.

Morris, R. & Binstock, R. H. *Feasible planning for social change.* New York: Columbia University Press, 1966.

Murphy, G. *Human potentialities.* New York: Basic Books, 1961.

Murray, H. A. Preparations for the scaffold of a comprehensive system. In S. Koch (Ed.), *Psychology: A study of a science.* Vol. III. *Formulations of the person and the social context.* New York: McGraw-Hill, 1959.

Murray, H. A. Toward a classification of interactions. In T. Parsons and E. Shils (Eds.), *Toward a general theory of action.* Cambridge: Harvard University Press, 1962. Pp. 434-464.

Neisser, U. Cultural and cognitive discontinuity. In R. A. Manners and D. Kaplan (Eds.), *Theory in anthropology, a sourcebook.* Chicago: Aldine Press, 1968. Pp. 354-364.

Neugarten, B. L. Review of aging and personality. *Contemporary Psychology,* 1963, **8**, 276-277.

Neugarten, B. L. (Ed.), *Personality in middle and late life.* New York: Atherton Press, 1964.

Neugarten, B. L. Adult personality: A developmental view. *Human Development,* 1966, **9**, 61-73.

Neugarten, B. L. The awareness of middle age. In R. Owen (Ed.), *Middle age.* London: British Broadcasting Corp., 1967.

Neugarten, B. L. Adaptation and the life cycle. Paper presented at the Foundations' Fund for Research in Psychiatry Conference on Adaptation to Change, Dorado Beach, Puerto Rico, June 22-27, 1968.

Neugarten, B. L. and Associates. *Personality in middle and late life.* New York: Atherton Press, 1964.

Neugarten, B. L. & Garron, D. The attitudes of middle-aged persons toward growing older. *Geriatrics,* 1959, **14**, 21-24.

Neugarten, B. L. & Gutmann, D. Age-sex role and personality in middle age: A thematic appreception study. *Psychological Monographs,* 1958, **72**, 470.

Neugarten, B. L, Havighurst, R., & Tobin, S. The measurement of life satisfaction. *Journal of Gerontology,* 1961, **16**, 134-143.

Nosow, S. F. & Form, W. H. *Man, work and society.* New York: Basic Books, 1962.

Odell, G. The case of early retirement. *Industrial Relations,* 1965, **4**, 15-28.

Oetting, E. R. Developmental definition of counseling psychology. *Journal of Counseling Psychology,* 1967, **14**, 382-385.

Olds, J. Comments on Professor Maslow's paper. In M. R. Jones (Ed.), *Nebraska symposium on maturation.* Lincoln: University of Nebraska Press, 1955.

Onstott, H. K. Mandatory retirement at age 65. Paper presented at the Conference on Personnel Directors at the Meeting of the National Committee on Aging, 1960.

Orbach, H. L. & Shaw, D. M. Social participation and the role of the aging. *Geriatrics,* 1957, **12**, 241-246.

Ostfeld, A. Frequency and nature of health problems of retired persons. In F. M. Carp (Ed.), *The retirement process.* Washington, D.C.: U.S. Government Printing Office, Public Health Service Publication No. 1778, 1968, Pp. 83-96.

Owens, W. A. Age and mental abilities: A longitudinal study. *Genetic Psychology Monographs,* 1953, **48**, 3-54.

Palmore, E. Retirement patterns among men: Findings of the 1963 survey of the aged. *Social Security Bulletin,* 1964, **27**, 3-10.

Pearce, J. & Newton, S. *The conditions of human growth.* New York: The Citadel Press, 1963.

Pearl, R. & Pearl, R. De W. Studies on human longevity. *Human Biology,* 1934, **6**, 98-222.

Peck, R. F. Psychological developments in the second half of life. In J. E. Anderson (Ed.), *Psychological aspects of aging.* Washington, D.C.: American Psychological Association, 1956.

Peck, R. F. & Berkowitz, H. Personality and adjustment in middle age. In B. L. Neugarten (Ed.), *Personality in middle and late life.* New York: Atherton Press, 1964.

Piaget, J. *The moral judgment of the child.* New York: Free Press of Glencoe, 1948.

Piaget, J. (trans. M. Cook) *The origins of intelligence in children.* New York: International Universities Press, 1952.

Piaget, J. (trans. M. Cook) *The construction of reality in the child.* New York: Basic Books, 1954.

Piaget, J. *The psychology of intelligence.* New York: Littlefield, 1960.

Pressey, S. L. Tests 'indigenous' to the adult and older years. *Journal of Counseling Psychology,* 1957, **4**, 144-148.

Pressey, S. L. Not all decline. *The Gerontologist,* 1966, **6**, 125.

Pressey, S. L. & Pressey, A. Two insiders' searching for best life in old age. *The Gerontologist,* 1966, **6**, 14-16.

Proceedings of Ontario Conference. Aging is everyone's concern. Proceedings of the First Ontario Conference on Aging, University Extension, University of Toronto, May 31-June 30, 1957. Pp. 1-206.

Raab, W. Degenerative heart disease from lack of exercise (neurohormonal pathogenic mechanisms). *Exercise and fitness.* Urbana: University of Illinois Press, 1959. Pp. 10-19.

Rapaport, D. On the psychoanalytic theory of motivation. In M. Jones (Ed.), *Nebraska Symposium on motivation.* Lincoln: University of Nebraska Press, 1960. Pp. 173-247.

Raven, J. C. The comparative assessment of intellectual ability. *British Journal of Psychology,* 1948, 12-19.

Reichard, S., Livson, F., & Petersen, P. G. *Aging and personality: A study of eighty-seven older men.* New York: Wiley, 1962.

Reif, F. & Strauss, A. The impact of rapid discovery upon the scientist's career. *Social Problems,* 1965, **7**, 297-311.

Retirement and the individual. Hearings before the Subcommittee on Retirement and the Individual of the Special Committee on Aging, United States Senate, 90th Congress, July 26, 1967. Washington, D.C.: U.S. Government Printing Office, 1967.

Riegel, K. F. Personality theory and aging. In J. E. Birren (Ed.), *Handbook of aging and the individual.* Chicago: University of Chicago Press, 1959.

Riesman, D. *The lonely crowd.* New Haven: Yale University Press, 1950.

Riesman, D. Some clinical and cultural aspects of aging. *American Journal of Sociology,* 1954, **59**, 379-383.

Riesman, D. Some clinical and cultural aspects of the aging process. In D. Riesman, *Individualism reconsidered.* Glencoe, Illinois: The Free Press, 1954. Pp. 484-491.

Riesman, D. & Roseborough, H. Careers and consumer behavior. In L. H. Clark (Ed.), *Consumer behavior.* Vol. II. *The life cycle and consumer behavior.* New York: New York University Press, 1955.

Rogers, C. R. Actualizing tendency in relation to 'motives' and to consciousness. In M. R. Jones (Ed.), *Nebraska Symposium on maturation.* Lincoln: University of Nebraska Press, 1963.

Roman, P. & Taietz, P. Organizational structure and disengagement: The emeritus professor. *The Gerontologist,* 1967, **7**, 147-152.

Rosen, J. Neugarten, B. Ego functions in the middle and later years. *Journal of Gerontology,* 1960, **15**, No. 1, 62-67.

Rosow, I. Old age: One moral dilemma of an affluent society. *The Gerontologist,* 1962, **2**, 189-191.

Rosow, I. Adjustment of the normal aged. In R. H. Williams, C. Tibbitts, and W. Donahue (Eds.), *Processes of aging.* Vol. II. New York: Atherton Press, 1963, Pp. 195-223.

Rosow, I. *Social integration of the aged.* New York: The Free Press, 1967.

Rosow, I. Socialization to old age. Paper prepared for a Conference on Adult Socialization and Retirement. Sponsored by the National Institute of Child Health and Human Development, San Francisco, California, February 29-March 2, 1968.

Rowe, W. L. The middle and later years in Indian society. In R. W. Kleemeier (Ed.), *Aging and leisure.* New York: Oxford University Press, 1961. Pp. 104-109.

Rubin, I. *Sexual life after sixty.* New York: Basic Books, 1965.

Rustom, C. The later years of life and the use of time among the Burmans. In R. W. Kleemeier (Ed.), *Aging and leisure.* New York: Oxford University Press, 1961. Pp. 100-103.

Ryser, C. & Sheldon, A. Retirement and health. *Journal of the American Geriatrics Society,* 1969, **17**, No. 2, 180-190.

Sargent, D. S. From retirement to the second career. Paper presented at the 18th Annual Meeting of the American Geriatrics Society, New York, June 23, 1961.

Schachtel, E. G. *Metamorphosis.* New York: Basic Books, 1959. Pp. 5-15.

Schaie, K. W. A general model for the study of developmental problems. *Psychological Bulletin,* 1965, **64**, 92-107.

Schaw, L. & Henry W. E. A method for the comparison of

groups: A study in thematic apperception. *Genetic Psychology Monographs,* 1956, **54,** 207-253.

Schiller, H. I. Social control and individual freedom. *Bulletin of the Atomic Scientists,* May 1968, 21-23.

Schoeppe, A. & Havighurst, R. J. A validation of development and adjustment hypotheses of adolescence. *Journal of Educational Psychology,* 1952, **43,** 339-353.

Scott, J. P. Critical periods in behavioral development. *Science,* 1962, **38,** 949-958.

Secord, P. R. & Backman, C. W. Personality theory and the problem of stability and change in individual behavior: An interpersonal approach. *Psychological Review,* 1961, **68,** 21-32.

Seyle, H. The general adaptation syndrome and the diseases of adaptation. *Think Magazine,* 1961, **27,** 20-22.

Shanas, E. *The health of older people, a social survey.* Cambridge: Harvard University Press, 1962.

Shanas, E. & Madge, J. H. (Eds.) *Interdisciplinary topics in gerontology.* Vol. II. *Methodogical problems in cross-national studies in aging.* Switzerland: Karger, 1968.

Shanas, E. & Streib G. F. (Eds.) *Social structure and the family: Generational relations.* Englewood Cliffs, New Jersey: Prentice-Hall, 1965.

Shanas, E., Townsend P., Wedderburn, D., Friis, H., Milhj, P., & Stehouwer, J. (Eds.), *Old people in three industrial societies.* New York: Atherton Press, 1968.

Sherif, M., Harvey, O. J. White, J. B., Hood, W. R., and Sherif, C. W. *Intergroup conflict and cooperation.* Norman: University of Oklahoma, 1961.

Shukin, A. & Neugarten, B. Personality and social interaction. In B. Neugarten (Ed.), *Personality in middle and later life.* New York: Atherton, 1964. Pp. 149-157.

Simmel, G. (trans. A. W. Small) The sociology of conflict. *American Journal of Sociology,* 1903-4, **9,** 672-798.

Simmons, L. W. *Role of the aged in primitive society.* New Haven, Connecticut: Yale University Press, 1945.

Simon, A. & Brisette, G. Y. *Research Monograph No. 9.* California Department of Mental Hygiene, 1967, 2-7.

Simon, A., Lowenthal, M. F. & Epstein, L. J. *Crisis and intervention: The fate of the elderly mental patient.* San Francisco: Jossey-Bass, 1970.

Simpson, I. H. Back, K. W. & McKinney, J. C. Work and retirement. In I. H. Simpson and J. C. McKinney (Eds.), *Social aspects of aging.* Durham: Duke University Press, 1966. Pp. 45-46.

Slater, P. Prolegomena to a psychoanalytic theory of aging and death. In R. Kastenbaum (Ed.), *New thoughts on old age*. New York: Springer, 1964. Pp. 19-40.

Slavick, F. & Wolfbein, S. L. The evolving work life pattern. In C. Tibbitts (Ed.), *Handbook of gerontology, societal aspects of aging*. Chicago: University of Chicago Press, 1960.

Smith, J. Culture differences and the concept of time. In R. W. Kleemeier (Ed.), *Aging and leisure*. New York: Oxford University Press, 1961. Pp. 109-111.

Smith, K. U., & Smith, M. F. *Cybernetic principles of learning and educational design*. New York: Holt, Rinehart & Winston, 1965.

Snygg, D. & Combs, A. W. *Individual behavior*. (Rev. ed.) New York: Harper, 1959.

Sorokin, P. A. *Explorations in altruistic love and behavior*. Boston: Beacon Press, 1950.

Special Committee on Aging. United States Senate. *Developments in aging 1967*. Report No. 1098. Washington, D.C.: Government Printing Office, 1968.

Spiker, C. C. The concept of development: Relevant and irrelevant issues. In H. W. Stevenson (Ed.), The concepts of development. *Monographs of the Society for Research in Child Development*, 1966, **31**, No. 107, 40-54.

Spiro, M. E. Culture and personality: The natural history of a false dichotomy. *Psychiatry*, 1951, **14**, 18-46.

Stagner, R. *Psychology of personality*. (3rd ed.) New York: McGraw-Hill, 1961.

Stein, R. L. & Travis, J. Labor force and employment in 1960. *Monthly Labor Review*, 1961, **84**, 344-354.

Stephenson, W. *The study of behavior*. Chicago: University of Chicago Press, 1953.

Strehler, B. L. Dynamics theories of aging. In N. W. Shock (Ed.), *Aging: Some social and biological aspects*. Washington, D.C.: American Association for the Advancement of Science, 1960.

Strehler, B. L. *Time, cells, and aging*. New York: Academic Press, 1962.

Strehler, B. L. (Ed.) *The biology of aging*. Washington, D.C.: American Institute of Biological Sciences, 1960.

Streib, G. F. Morale of the retired. *Social Problems*, 1956, **2**, 270-276.

Streib, G. F. & Orbach, H. L. Aging. In P. F. Lazarsfeld, W. H. Sewell, and H. L. Wilensky (Eds.), *The uses of sociology*. New York: Basic Books, 1967.

Streib, G. F. & Thompson, W. E. (Eds.), Adjustment to Retirement. *The Journal of Social Issues,* 1958, **14**, (Whole No. 2).

Suchman, E., Streib, G., & Phillips, B. An analysis of the validity of health questionnaires. *Social Forces,* 1958, **36**, 223-232.

Sullivan, H. S. *The interpersonal theory of psychiatry.* New York: W. W. Norton, 1953.

Sussman, M. B. *Community structure and analysis.* New York: Crowell, 1959.

Sussman, M. B. (Ed.) *Sociology and rehabilitation.* American Sociological Association in cooperation with the Vocational Rehabilitation Administration of the United States Department of Health, Education and Welfare, 1966.

Sussman, M. B. Adaptive, directive, and integrative behavior of today's family. *Family Process,* 1968, **7**, 239-250.(a)

Sussman, M. B. (Ed.) *Sourcebook in marriage and the family.* (3rd ed.) Boston: Houghton Mifflin, 1968.(b)

Sussman, M. B. & Haug, M. R. New sources for workers in the blindness system. Workshop Conference on Rehabilitation and Visual Impairment, New York City, December 1967.

Sussman, M. B., Cates, J. N., & Smith, D. T. *The family and inheritance.* Russel Sage Foundation, 1970.

Svancara, J. Child study and applied gerontology: A comment. *The Gerontologist,* 1966, **6**, 90.

Swados, H. The myth of the happy worker. In M. Stein, A. J. Vidich, and D. M. White (Eds.), *Identity and anxiety.* Glencoe: Free Press, 1960. Pp. 198-204.

Szewczuk, W. Rehabilitation of the aged by means of new forms of activity. *The Gerontologist,* 1966, **6**, 93-94.

Tanner, J. *Education and physical growth: Implications of the study of children for educational theory and practice.* London: University of London, 1961.

Taylor, L. *Occupational psychology.* New York: Oxford University Press, 1968.

Thompson, W. E. & Streib, G. F. Situational determinants: Health and economic deprivation in retirement. *Journal of Social Issues,* 1958, **14**, No. 2, 18-34.

Thompson, W. E., Streib, G. F., & Kosa, J. The effect of retirement on personal adjustment: A panel analysis. *Journal of Gerontology,* 1960, **14**, 165-169.

Thoreau, H. D. *Walden.* (Dolphin Ed.) Garden City, New York: Doubleday, 1960.

Tinbergen, N. *Social behavior in animals.* New York: Wiley, 1953.

Tobin, S. S. & Neugarten, B. L. Life satisfaction and social interaction in the aging. *Journal of Gerontology,* 1961, **16**, 34-46.

Toynbee, A. Man at work in the light of history. In G. Demille (Ed.) *Man at work in God's world.* New York: Longmans, Green & Co., 1938.

Tuckman, J. & Lorge, I. Attitudes toward old people. *Journal of Social Psychology,* 1953, **37**, 249-260.

Tuddenham, R. D. Constancy of personality ratings over two decades. *Genetic Psychology Monographs,* 1959, **60**, 3-29.

Von Mering, O. & Weniger, F. L. Social-cultural background of the aging individual. In J. E. Birren (Ed.), *Handbook of aging and the individual.* Chicago: University of Chicago Press, 1959.

Wallace, A. F. C. *Culture and personality.* New York: Random House, 1961.

Wallach, M. A. & Kogan, N. Aspects of judgment and decision making: Interrelationship and changes with age. *Behavioral Science,* 1961, **6**, 23-26.

Watson, R. I. *Psychology of the child.* New York: Wiley, 1959.

Welford, A. T. *Aging and human skill.* London: Oxford University Press, 1958.

Welford, A. T. Changes with age in the speed of performance. *Ergonomics,* 1962, **5**, 139-145.

Werner, H. *Comparative psychology of human development.* (Rev. Ed.) Chicago: Follet, 1948.

Werner, H. The concept of development from a comparative and organismic point of view. In D. Harris (Ed.), *The concept of development: An issue in the study of human behavior.* Minneapolis: University of Minnesota Press, 1957.

Westley, W. A. & Epstein, N. B. *The silent majority: Families of emotionally healthy college students.* San Francisco: Jossey-Bass, 1969.

Wheeler, R. H. *The laws of human nature.* New York: Appleton, 1932.

White, L. A. The individual and the culture process. In *Centennial, American Association for the Advancement of Science,* New York, 1948, Pp. 74-81.

White, L. A. *The science of culture.* New York: Farrar, Straus & Co., 1949.

White, R. W. Motivation reconsidered: The concept of competence. In D. W. Fiske and S. R. Maddi (Eds.), *Function of varied experience.* Homewood, Illinois: Dorsey Press, 1961. Pp. 278-325.

Wilensky, H. L. Orderly careers and social participation. *American Sociological Review,* 1961, **26**, 521-539.

Williams, R. H. & Wirths, C. G. *Lives through the years: Styles of life and successful aging.* New York: Atherton Press, 1965.

Wolbein, S. L. *Changing patterns of working life.* U.S. Department of Labor. Washington, D.C.: Government Printing Office, 1963. Pp. 10.

Wood, V. & Bultena, G. The American retirement community: Bane or blessing? *Journal of Gerontology*, **24**, No. 2, 209-217.

Worchel, P. & Byrne, D. (Eds.) *Personality change.* New York: Wiley, 1964.

Wright, B. A. *Physical disability—a psychological approach.* New York: Harper, 1960.

Zaccaria, J. S. Developmental tasks: Implications for the goals of guidance. *Personnel and Guidance Journal,* 1965, **44**, 372-375.

Zetzel, E. R. Metapsychology of aging. In M. A. Berezin and S. H. Cath (Eds.), *Geriatric psychiatry.* New York: International Universities Press, 1965.

Zigler, E. Metatheoretical issues in developmental psychology. In M. H. Marx (Ed.), *Theories in contemporary psychology.* New York: Macmillan, 1963.

Zinberg, N. & Kaufman, I. Cultural and personality factors associated with aging: An introduction. In N. Zinberg (Ed.), *Normal psychology of the aging process.* New York: International Universities Press, 1963. Pp. 17-71.

Zinker, J. C. & Fink, S. L. The possibility for psychological growth in a dying person. *Journal of General Psychology,* 1966, **74**, 185-199.

Zola, I. Feelings about age among older people. *Journal of Gerontology,* 1962, **17**, 65-68.

Zubeck, J. P. & Solberg, P. A. *Human development.* New York: McGraw-Hill, 1954.

AUTHOR INDEX

SUBJECT INDEX

141050